The African Exchange

Toward a Biological History

of Black People

Kenneth F. Kiple, editor

Duke University Press

Durham and London   1987

Portions of this book originally appeared in
Social Science History, volume 10, number 4.

© 1988 Duke University Press
All rights reserved
Printed in the United States of America
on acid-free paper ∞

Library of Congress Cataloging-in-Publication Data
The African exchange.

Includes bibliographies and index.
1. Blacks—Diseases—America—History. 2. Slavery—
America—Condition of slaves—History. 3. Health and
race—America—History. I. Kiple, Kenneth F.,
1939–
RA442.A37 1988 614.4′273′08996073 87–30333
ISBN 0-8223-0731-6

Contents

FOR PHILIP D. CURTIN

Acknowledgments

THIS VOLUME is the product of a remarkable growth. Its kernel lay in a session on "Biology and Black History" that took place at the 1985 Social Science History Association meeting in Chicago. Presented there were earlier drafts of the three essays included in this work by Philip D. Curtin, Jerome S. Handler (and coauthors Arthur C. Aufderheide, Robert S. Corruccini, Elizabeth M. Brandon, and Lorentz E. Whittmers, Jr.), and Richard H. Steckel.

A special issue of *Social Science History* (10, no. 4 [1986]) devoted to "The Biological Past of the Black" represents the next stage of growth. Joining the articles by the authors mentioned above are the contributions by Donald B. Cooper and Thomas W. Wilson, along with two efforts of my own.

The third stage of growth is contained in this work, with the addition of two more splendid studies, one by Dauril Alden and Joseph C. Miller and the other by Robert Dirks, and an expanded article of mine. The whole of the work is representative of the very finest work being done on the biohistory of the black in both Africa and the Western Hemisphere.

The personal debts of the authors are acknowledged in their respective articles. Here, however, I would like to acknowledge some collective debts of considerable magnitude. One of them is to James Q. Graham, Jr., managing editor of *Social Science History,* who suggested the need for a collection of work on the biological past of the black in the first place and subsequently encouraged and nurtured the effort at every stage of its development.

Another immense debt we have incurred is owed to Rachael Rockwell Graham, executive editor of *Social Science History*. For it was Rachael who gave freely of her keen judgment for historical writing as well as countless hours of labor in gently pointing up errors of reasoning, problems of organization, and grammatical infelicities as she brought stylistic order to the volume. Rachael is, very simply, the finest editor with whom I have ever worked.

A final debt is owed by all of us in slavery studies and African studies, as well as black biological history, to Philip D. Curtin who led and is still leading the way in these fields. It is, therefore, particularly appropriate that this volume be dedicated to him.

KENNETH F. KIPLE

A Survey of Recent Literature on the Biological Past of the Black

KENNETH F. KIPLE

IT WAS EVIDENT from the very beginning of the colonization of the Americas that the West African had experienced a biological past that differed in significant ways from that of other peoples. For in that beginning, dead Indians began accumulating "in heaps, like bedbugs" as they succumbed to diseases that accompanied the Spanish conquistadores and their animals from Iberia.[1] But the black slaves who also accompanied them did not die, or rather, the Spaniards temporized, "if we did not hang a Negro, he would never die."[2] In addition to this immunologic hardiness, the black was physically sturdier. Common wisdom had it that he could do the work of four Indians.[3]

The holocaust of disease that sooner or later brought demographic disaster to Indian populations throughout the hemisphere did it sooner in the West Indies than anywhere else so that very early in the sixteenth century the Spaniards were confronted with a rapidly diminishing Indian labor force, and because black slaves born in Iberia (*ladinos*) were too few in number to replace the dying Indians, a clamor arose for the importation of slaves directly from Africa (*bozales*). The clamor was heard and yielded to by

Kenneth F. Kiple is professor in the department of history at Bowling Green State University, Bowling Green, OH 43403.
The author wishes to express his gratitude to the American Council of Learned Societies for a grant-in-aid in 1985 and to the Faculty Research Committee of Bowling Green State University for the Major Research Grant awarded for the years 1985 and 1986 that made research for this and other projects possible.

the Spanish crown, and the transatlantic slave trade was under way.[4]

A transatlantic flow of African pathogens was also under way, for as the Europeans before them, the West Africans also carried their diseases to the New World. Foremost among these were those two great tropical killers, falciparum malaria and yellow fever, which fell on the Europeans with the same ferocity that European diseases had fallen on the Indians. Yet, once again the black proved resistant. Thus it is small wonder that the conviction that the black was peculiarly suited for hard work in hot places was quickly born in the white mind. It is also small wonder that Africa, the homeland of those fevers beginning to sweep the West Indies, Brazil, and North America, swiftly became infamous in that same mind, which came to view the regions south of the Sahara as the "white man's grave."[5]

In a more tender age this ethnocentric whimpering would also have acknowledged that much of the Americas had become the "black man's grave." For despite the West African's immunological and physical sturdiness, the demographics of a slave trade that delivered far more men than women to the New World, the rigors of sugar slavery, poor nutrition for the slaves, and their own disease susceptibilities all combined to ensure a continuing demand for Africans in the Americas and, therefore, a slave trade of perpetual motion.

Many of the disease susceptibilities evidenced by the slaves became the subject of morbid fascination for the white physicians who treated them. Some, such as leprosy and yaws, were hideously disfiguring. Others, such as a propensity for consuming earth, were merely disgusting, but the whole was bundled together under the rubric of "Negro diseases" and scrutinized through the distorting lens of a burgeoning scientific racism. Not surprisingly, under the spur of the Enlightenment, which prescribed equality for all men, the judgment that emerged from this scrutiny was that blacks were not men, or at least not a species of man sufficiently advanced to benefit from egalitarianism.

It can be said then, with little fear of exaggeration, that black-related disease immunities played a crucial role in the wholesale enslavement of the West African, while black disease susceptibilities played a similarly crucial role in rationalizing that enslavement.

Yet, in what seems a remarkable commentary on the historiography of the African in the Americas, these crucial roles played by disease in shaping the black past went unrecognized or ignored by most social scientists even as science and medicine were establishing beyond all cavil the importance of the blacks' biological distinctiveness (Lewis, 1942; Allison, 1954a; 1954b; Motulsky and Campbell-Kraut, 1961; Williams, 1965; Shiloh and Selvan, 1974; Miller et al., 1976). In retrospect it is easy to see that the social scientists, in their revulsion to the racism of Hitler's Germany in particular, and to the kind of scientific racism that had characterized Western thought for so long in general, as well as in their determination to correct the pages of black history, were in no mood to brook any notion, no matter how scientifically respectable, that smacked of white/black biological differences—differences that they held to constitute a myth in the first place (Stampp, 1956; Jordan, 1968; Rout, 1976). In maintaining this well-meaning stance, they cheerfully committed what David Hackett Fischer (1970: 235) has termed "the counterfallacy of anti-racism."

The scholar who was instrumental in gently but firmly pulling a generation of scholars out of this obscurantism was Philip Curtin, to whom we are doubly indebted both for his courage in so doing and for his scholarship, which revealed the vital importance of bio-studies to a holistic understanding of the African in the Americas as well as in his ancestral homeland. This demonstration began with his studies of British perceptions of Africa during the late eighteenth century and the first half of the nineteenth century in which he discovered that many of those perceptions had been shaped by a disease environment alive with fevers—but fevers that seemed to attack European newcomers with extraordinary virulence while all but ignoring the native population (Curtin, 1961; 1964).

Curtin correctly identified the fevers in question as yellow fever and malaria and then, in his seminal look at epidemiology within the context of the slave trade, bridged Africa and the Americas by revealing the enormously different rates of mortality inflicted by these diseases on white and black on both sides of the Atlantic (Curtin, 1967). For Professor Curtin the tremendous mortality suffered by the Europeans in the face of these great tropical killers seemed an important reason for the long delay in the European effort to colonize Africa on the one hand and for the selection of the black for slavery in tropical America on the other.

Then, shifting from epidemiology to "macro" demography, Curtin took up the question of the reliability of extant estimates of the volume of the slave trade to the Americas over the course of almost four centuries, with the result a landmark effort to provide scholars with a reliable measurement of that volume (Curtin, 1969). However, if the study represented a huge stride in resolving quantitative questions of how many slaves were imported to the hemisphere, it raised a perhaps even more important set of questions revolving around the problem of why some slaveholding regions of the hemisphere such as the Caribbean Islands or Brazil had relied on a heavy volume of imports to maintain the size of their labor force while, by contrast, the slave population of North America had grown by natural means.

Curtin framed the problem deftly and dramatically by contrasting the number of slaves imported to each of the major slaveholding regions of the Americas with the percentage of the hemisphere's black population that those regions contained at the midpoint of this century. Thus North America, for example, which had imported fewer than 5% of the hemisphere's slaves, contained about one-third of the hemisphere's Afro-American population. Yet, the Caribbean Islands, which together had imported more than 40% of the slaves, could account for only 20% of the hemisphere's Afro-American population.[6]

By the beginning of the 1970s, then, Curtin had not only sensitized scholars to the possibility of a significantly different black/white experience with disease, but he had also presented them with a complex problem in comparative history that would require a new and complex set of tools to unravel.

The unraveling process began slowly. Curtin's demonstration of a dramatically different white/black experience with "fevers" in Africa was scrutinized by Feinberg (1974) and Davies (1975). While Feinberg found a somewhat less devastating experience for the Dutch on the Gold Coast than Davies (and Curtin) had discovered for the English in Sierra Leone and elsewhere on Africa's West Coast, Curtin's initial findings remained to remind us of, among other things, the manner in which Africa's diseases had long protected her inhabitants from serious European incursions into the region and, consequently, of the heretofore unrecognized part that disease and disease immunities have played in African history.[7]

Meanwhile, in a seminal epidemiological study of the West Indies, Francisco Guerra (1966) had revealed the tremendous impact of yellow fever and malaria on the seventeenth- and eighteenth-century military history of the region by deciding battles, shaping policy, and in the end stimulating the employment of black troops by the British in their struggle for Caribbean supremacy because of the troops' superior resistance to these tropical killers.

Historians of slavery in the United States were first exposed to this new "bio" orientation by Peter Wood (1974) who explored the extent to which malaria (and yellow fever) resistance may have been an important rationale for the enslavement of the black to till the mosquito-infested low-lying areas of South Carolina. Equally important, Wood was among the first since Curtin to discuss the probable genetic mechanisms that conferred this protection. Darrett B. Rutman and Anita H. Rutman (1976) followed the lead of Curtin and Wood in stressing the historical importance of malaria immunities in the enslavement of Africans in the Chesapeake region and in the process expanded the explanation of black genetic protection. Moreover, they very shrewdly speculated on the ways in which the planters' lack of resistance to malaria may have shaped his social, economic, and even intellectual behavior. Kiple and Kiple (1977c) continued the scrutiny of the ability of blacks to resist disease with a study of differential black/white yellow fever mortality in nineteenth-century United States, while Gary Puckrein (1979) broadened the focus to demonstrate how tropical disease had, by discouraging white labor, encouraged the employment of black labor in much of English America.

Another major leap forward came out of the controversy triggered by the depiction by Robert Fogel and Stanley Engerman of the North American slaves' *Time on the Cross* (1974). This study has had the effect of dramatically advancing our knowledge of slavery in many areas, but nowhere has the advance been swifter than in fostering progress in our understanding of the biological past of the black.

Fogel and Engerman very clearly understood the implications contained in the work of Curtin for the demographic well-being of slaves in the American South, and a major thrust of *Time on the Cross* was an attempt to shed light on why this had been the case. One effort in this attempt was an examination of slave nutrition and health that suggested a level of physical well-being for slaves quite similar to that of whites. Quite obviously it also suggested an important reason for the vastly better demographic performance of the North American slave population than that of other slave populations of the hemisphere.

The initial reaction to the nutritional findings of Fogel and Engerman, while largely negative, nonetheless constituted a positive methodological step forward as social scientists were forced to grapple with new concepts while they set out in a distinctly novel direction. Richard Sutch (1975; 1976) was first to pick a quarrel with Fogel and Engerman by reworking their data on the kinds and quantities of foods consumed by the slaves on the one hand and by pointing to diseases that seemed to have been the result of nutritional deficiencies on the other. Leslie Howard Owens (1976) also discovered a slave experience with diet and disease that was distinctly at odds with the Fogel and Engerman portrait, while Kiple and Kiple (1977a; 1977b; 1980a; 1980b; Kiple and King, 1981) found the slave diet to have been perilously unbalanced. However, their disagreement with Fogel and Engerman over the issue of slave nutrition centered not so much on the nutriments and nutrients available to slaves, as on the ability of persons of West African descent to utilize properly the nutrients in question. A major difficulty with calculating the slaves' nutritional intake has been the question of the extent to which the slaves supplemented the plantation food allotment by foraging on their own. Studies by Genovese (1974) and Gibbs, Cargill, Lieberman, and Reitz (1980) make strong cases that this supplementation was considerable.

Simultaneously with the debate over slave nutrition,[8] and the kinds of nutritional diseases poor nutrition might have provoked, there arose an interest in other black disease susceptibilities. The first effort since that of Postell (1951; 1952; 1953; 1954; 1967) to survey systematically disease among the slaves of North America[9] was made by Todd L. Savitt (1975). He started by looking at the phenomenon of slave infants supposedly "smothered" by mothers who had "overlain" them during the night and pointing out the remarkable similarities between the sudden deaths of these infants and the modern concept of the Sudden Infant Death Syndrome (SIDS) or "crib death." Savitt followed this with an examination of filariasis in the United States (1977) and then with his *Medicine and Slavery* (1978) which concentrated on, as the subtitle states, *The Diseases and Health Care of Blacks in Antebellum Virginia.* In this work Savitt carefully examined both black disease immunities and susceptibilities with an eye on the extent to which the black disease experience differed from that of whites during the same period.

Kiple and King (1981) covered some of the same ground as Savitt while attempting to link both the disease susceptibilities of blacks with their genetic heritage and biochemical makeup derived from Africa and the growth of scientific racism in the United States. In addition, by expanding their earlier work on slave nutrition and black-related diseases, Kiple and King tried to show how the nutrients available to slaves would have rendered infants and children particularly subject to the ravages of malnutrition and, consequently, to a much higher death rate than their white counterparts.

In the late 1970s Richard Steckel (1979a; 1979b; 1982; 1986a; 1986b) began a series of what can only be called breathtakingly innovative studies that have pursued the interrelationship of slave nutrition, disease, and fertility. His work tends to corroborate suspicions that very high death rates did indeed prevail among the slave young. Other recent investigations of the slaves' biological past in the United States include the Lee and Lee (1977) study of the health of blacks as slaves and freemen in Savannah, David Whitten's (1977) comparison of slave health in Louisiana with that of the South Carolina low country, Kulikoff's (1977, 1986) examinations of the demographic forces at work among eighteenth-century slaves on the Chesapeake, the Cardell and Hopkins (1978) study of the phenomenon of lactose intolerance among the slaves, Johnson's (1981) continuation of the search for an explanation for the smothered slave infant, Angel's and Kelley's (1983) look at the health of colonial ironworker slaves, John Campbell's (1984) important insights into the continuing and vexing questions of slave infant mortality, and Jill Dubish's (1985) reminder of the importance of malaria in shaping slavery in South Carolina.

Exciting contributions are coming as well from anthropologists whose findings, derived from analyzing plantation artifacts and slave skeletal remains, are shedding important new light on questions of slave morbidity, mortality, and nutrition. The most dramatic results, thus far, have been achieved in Barbados, where Handler and associates (Handler and Lange, 1978; Handler and Corruccini, 1983; Corruccini, Handler, Mutaw, and Lange, 1982; Corruccini, Handler, and Jacobi, 1985; and Handler et al., this volume) have led the way in this area of investigation and whose studies will be discussed shortly.

A summary of the work done in the United States to 1984 may be found in Fairbanks (1984), who also discusses his own pioneering findings since the 1960s regarding the slave diet. Since then, Angel and Kelley (in press) have examined slave skeletal remains in Maryland, Virginia, and North Carolina and discovered signs of significant nutritional deprivation including widespread anemia. Rathbun, in a very sophisticated study (in press), has also discovered anemia to have been a severe problem of health for slaves on a South Carolina plantation and, in addition, has found evidence of a serious crisis of health among the very young in the form of linear enamel hypoplasia—a crisis apparently triggered by protein calorie malnutrition.[10] Singleton (1985) contains thirteen quite technical chapters dealing with slave life, diet, and problems of health.

After slavery, it would seem that most of these health problems continued among blacks. An investigation of Afro-American remains in Arkansas by Martin, Magennis, and Rose (in press) revealed a high incidence of iron deficiency anemia and protein calorie malnutrition, as well as rickets.

Others have also begun to scrutinize questions of the Afro-American's biological past after slavery and thereby have begun to deal with illnesses that were apparently not particularly serious on the plantations. Examples of these studies are Marion Torchia's (1977) depiction of the magnitude of the problem of tuberculosis among the black population of the United States from 1830 to 1950, Joseph McFalls's (1973) evaluation of the impact of venereal disease on black fertility, and the Cutright and Shorter (1979) treatment of black health problems (including VD) and black fertility. In addition, ailments that plagued blacks during slavery and have continued to do so have been considered by John Hunter in his magnificent studies of lactose intolerance (1971), pica usage (1973), and lead poisoning (1977; 1978) among blacks; by Jerry

Weaver's (1977) look at the problem of the continuing high levels of black infant mortality after slavery; and by Savitt's (1981) discussion of the tragedy of sickle cell anemia. In addition Rousey (1985) has demonstrated the relationship between the presence of yellow fever in Memphis and the employment of black policemen, Cooke (1983) has investigated the health of blacks in the District of Columbia during the Civil War years and (1983) the health of blacks during reconstruction, while McBride (1981) has moved north to look at the health of blacks in Philadelphia during much of this century.

The scandal-ridden story of the infamous Tuskegee experiment that involved the deliberate withholding of treatment for black people stricken with syphilis has been eloquently told by James Jones (1981) in what is surely a landmark study in medical ethics. Finally, Thomas Wilson (1986) has, by correlating a lack of adequate salt supplies in much of ancient West Africa with black hypertension today, demonstrated the relevance of bio-historical work on blacks for modern medical science, while Leslie Sue Lieberman (unpublished a and b) has led the way in pursuing the "thrifty gene" hypothesis to explain black susceptibility to hypertension and diabetes.

Much work concerned with the biological past of the black has also been done in the field of Caribbean slavery. For Jamaica, a central focus of concentration has been on the fact that, despite their relative resistance to some tropical ailments, slaves in Jamaica suffered a considerable excess of deaths over births. Early studies such as those by Roberts (1951; 1957) and Patterson (1967) calling attention to the demographic plight of the slaves on the island have served as building blocks for later works such as those by Michael Craton, who from the beginning of the 1970s (1971; 1975; 1976; 1978; Craton and Walvin, 1970) has probed the causes of mortality among those Jamaican slaves who resided on Worthy Park Plantation. Craton has also examined birth records and the amounts of food available to the slaves, and from these "case studies" there emerged a demographic profile of Worthy Park slaves that indicated high mortality rates for adults, and especially for infants and children, as well as low fertility.

Barry Higman (1976) produced a major quantitative effort that incorporated previous work on Jamaican slaves with much rich data from plantation records. He made a detailed presentation of the major causes of slave deaths and also provided a comprehensive treatment of slave fertility, which he estimated to be quite low even after allowing for incomplete slave registration records.

A similarly dismal demographic profile for slaves was drawn for other slaveholding islands of the Caribbean. For Barbados a major early study, which indicated that slaves had fared poorly demographically for most of their stay on the island, came from the pen of Harry Bennett (1958). These findings were amplified in a study by Handler and Lange (1978), who pioneered in the employment of slave archeological artifacts to buttress evidence derived from more traditional literary sources. They too left little doubt that slaves in Barbados had experienced an extremely high level of mortality and one that fell with special weight on the very young.

Manuel Moreno Fraginals (1977) has also reported a high rate of infant and child mortality for Cuban slaves and in addition has indicated that in Cuba, as elsewhere in the Caribbean, a low rate of slave fertility seems to have exacerbated the problem of population growth. In suggesting the latter, Moreno Fraginals was implicitly quarreling with Jack Eblen (1974), who had estimated Cuban slave fertility to be rather high.

• Yet lower fertility rates for Caribbean slaves have seemed to many to be a plausible explanation for the lack of population growth. The focus became truly comparative when Herbert Klein and Stanley Engerman (1978) advanced a provocative explanation to account for the net natural decrease experienced by slaves in the West Indies on the one hand and the net natural increase enjoyed by slaves in the United States on the other. The explanation revolved around West African cultural attitudes toward breast feeding. They argued the practice would have been kept alive through the conduit of the slave trade from Africa to the Caribbean but would have withered without this reinforcement in the United States where the slave trade had slowed dramatically by the last quarter of the eighteenth century and ceased altogether shortly after the turn of the nineteenth century.

West African custom prescribed both prolonged lactation (which up to a point can prevent pregnancies) and a taboo against sexual relations with a woman while she was lactating. The result, Klein and Engerman hypothesized, would have been significantly greater child spacing in the West Indies than in North America and thus, of course, significantly reduced fertility. Then, for good measure, Klein and Engerman also suggested that the reputedly poor nutritional status of Caribbean slave women would quite possibly have hastened menopause and delayed the age of menarche, with the result of even less fertility.

Klein and Engerman had been drawn to the importance of the age of menarche by the ingenious work of Trussel and Steckel (1978), which had revealed a method of estimating that age by studying the heights of girls and young slave women so as to discover the time of the adolescent growth spurt. For the United States, Trussel and Steckel found the age of menarche to be fairly low, a finding consistent with most estimates that found fertility to have been high for the slave women of North America.

The appearance of studies containing data on slave heights for the United States by Steckel (1979b), Margo and Steckel (1982), and Fogel, Engerman, and Floud (1983), and for the Caribbean by Moreno Fraginals (1977), Higman (1979), Eltis (1982), and Friedman (1982) has opened a fascinating chapter in the biological history of transplanted Africans for a number of reasons besides that of helping to determine the age of menarche of the women. For one, it would appear that despite the low quality of the Caribbean slave diet (as suggested by Debien in 1964), this diet was nonetheless better, or at least more protein-laden, than that consumed by West Africans in their homeland because the height data portray clearly that slaves born in the Caribbean were significantly taller than the newly arriving Africans.

For another, it seems that United States slaves were substantially better fed than Caribbean counterparts because they in turn were significantly taller. For still another, it appears that height variations across the Caribbean pinpoint sugar slaves as shorter than slaves engaged in other occupations, suggesting that their diet contained less protein or that they expended more energy or both.

Suspicions were sharpened that the Caribbean slave diet was far from satisfactory for even marginal health and was greatly inferior to the diet of slaves in the United States (despite the continuing debate over the quality of that diet) with the appearance of studies toward the end of the 1970s by Robert Dirks (1978) and Kiple and Kiple (1980b). Both inquiries discovered evidence of widespread deficiency diseases such as pellagra and beriberi among the slaves, and Kiple and Kiple suggested that such widespread deficiency diseases implied a terrible slaughter of the very young.

Confirmation that this may well have been the case, at least for Barbados, came in the form of still another novel and intriguing, as well as crucially important, method of exploring the biological past of the black. Studies by Corruccini, Handler, Mutaw, and Lange (1982), Corruccini, Handler, and Jacobi (1985), and Handler and Corruccini (1983; 1986) reported on their analysis of slave skeletal remains excavated from a slave plantation cemetery. Included among their many exciting findings were growth arrest lines (enamel hypoplasias) in excavated teeth, indicating a severe nutritional crisis for slave youngsters shortly after weaning.

Poor nutrition, of course, cannot have been the sole reason for the poor demographic performance of Caribbean slaves, and indeed its relative importance has become a matter of some debate. Barry Higman (1984) in his superb latest work on slave populations in the British Caribbean would seem to rank the rigors of sugar slavery and the slaves' disease environment above the nutritional factor as the most important detriment to slave survival, while Richard Sheridan (1985), building on a long and enormously fruitful career of examining the economic, demographic, medical, and biological aspects of Caribbean slavery (1975; 1976; 1982), appears to give labor, disease, and nutrition equal weight. Kiple (1984) and Dirks (1986), however, find nutrition (through causing much infant and child mortality) to be the single most important factor in the inability of Caribbean slaves to reproduce their numbers. Interestingly, a study by Lamur (1981) that compared two Caribbean slave populations implies that poor slave nutrition may also have had the effect of depressing fertility.

In addition to studies linking slave nutrition with disease, there have been a fair number of epidemiological and mortality studies that speak to questions of black history in the region. Enormously useful is the series of articles done by K. H. Uttley (1959; 1960a; 1960b; 1960c; 1960d; 1960e; 1960f; 1960g) on differential disease mortality by race over a century-long period on the island of Antigua, while more recently Koplan (1983) has provided an excellent statistical analysis of the causes of slave deaths in Grenada. A splendid history of helminth and protozoal infection in the West Indies has been done by M. T. Ashcroft (1965), while many pathologies have been discovered as a result of the examination of slave dentition by Corruccini et al. (1982) and Handler and Corruccini (1986). Kiple (1985) has considered the carnage wrought by cholera among Caribbean blacks; Hunter and DeKleine (1984) have investigated pica usage among the Black Caribs; Goodyear (1978) has advanced some intriguing thoughts on the possibility of a connection between sugar cultivation and yellow fever outbreaks; Buckley (1979) has shown in much detail the epidemiological, as well as the political and military, variables that led to slaves donning red coats as part of the British West India regiments; and Geggus (1982) has studied the importance of disease in the emergence of Haiti as an independent nation.

For the Mother Continent, the literature on the diet and diseases of Africans is so vast that only a sampling can be provided in this brief survey. Gelfand (1971), Lewicki (1974), and Curtin (1983) all deal with the African diet within the context of African history, while Kiple and King (1981) and Kiple (1984) have examined the genetic and biochemical characteristics produced by the West African nutritional and disease environments.

The study of African diseases has, until quite recently, been the nearly exclusive property of medical scientists. There are, however, exceptions. The spread of disease in Africa has been considered by Good (1972) and Hartwig (1975). Modern problems have been considered in superb fashion by Hunter (1966), Hughes and Hunter (1970), Hunter and Thomas (1984), and Domergue (1981), while Ransford (1984) has recently produced a full-scale monograph on the history of disease in Africa south of the Sahara. Patterson (1975; 1975a) has considered the impact of disease on the Gabon Coast, and an enormously useful volume on *Disease in African History* has been edited by Hartwig and Patterson (1978) that reveals something of the enormous diversity of the disease ecology of that massive continent. Indeed, the ecological conditions in all their complexity of those regions that supplied most of the slaves to the Americas have become the focus of intense interest for scholars who are attempting to understand the biological consequences of the slave trade from its beginnings deep in Africa through the middle passage to the ordeal of seasoning in the New World.

Thus famine in West Central Africa has come under the scrutiny of Jill Dias (1981) and Joseph Miller (1982), who have shown that as famine bred disease the two operated in tandem to stimulate slave sales to America. Miller, moreover, has just completed a forthcoming work that examines in great detail the connection between nutritional and disease conditions in Angola and the volume of the slave trade—a work that holds important implications for West as well as for West Central Africa. Stewart (1985) has examined the influence of smallpox on British slave trading policies, while Eltis in turn (1984) has pointed out the connection between blacks sold to slavers during times of famine and increased mortality during the middle passage.

Among the many other studies of mortality during the middle passage, some, including Klein (1978), Palmer (1981), Rawley (1981), Miller (1980; forthcoming), Eltis (1983; 1984), Steckel and Jensen (1986), and Alden and Miller (this volume), have also connected African nutritional and epidemiological conditions with mortality in the middle passage and during seasoning in the Americas, thereby linking the disease environments of both continents, as R. Hoeppli (1969) had done earlier in his pioneering documentation of the transmission of parasitic disease to the New World via the slave trade.

Returning to the Americas, a major problem for comparative historical studies of the Afro-American's biological past throughout the Western Hemisphere is that, after leaving the historiography of North America and the West Indies, one discovers that very little groundwork has been laid. Indeed, save for David Chandler's (1981) examination of the health conditions of slaves in New Granada and the work done by Carroll and colleagues (1979) on Jalapa in Mexico, which revealed how disease among the Indians led to their replacement by black slaves, almost all of the efforts outside of the United States and the Caribbean have concentrated on Brazil.

It has been a long time since Gilberto Freyre (1933; 1936) and Coutinho (1934) opened the question of the importance of slave diseases and nutrition in the history of Brazilian slavery by portraying the slave population, in the sugar-growing northeast at least, as relatively healthy and certainly well nourished, although much of the latter was accomplished by individual effort. Similarly, Stanley Stein (1957) found the diet of slaves in Brazil's coffee-growing region (specifically the municipio of Vassouras in the Parahyba Valley) to be adequate if somewhat limited. Yet, at the same time it also appeared to Stein that the slaves he was studying had suffered a fairly high level of mortality, especially the young. Mattoso (1974), by working with slave inventory lists, was able to estimate that roughly (and only) 15% of the slave force of working age in Bahia were in poor health.

However, this relatively benign portrait of the material conditions of Brazilian slavery has not withstood close scrutiny, at least not for Rio. Mary Karasch (1987), in what is by far the most biologically oriented of the studies on Brazilian slavery, reports a much more somber situation in which the slaves residing in and around that city were seriously malnourished and experienced a tremendous rate of mortality from countless ailments. Indeed, her exhaustive examination of slave illnesses and nutrition leaves little doubt that slaves in Rio faced dismal odds against survival from birth onward.

In another biologically oriented work, Sam Adamo (1983) extended the study of blacks in Rio to the first half-century after slavery. Like Karasch, he probed extensively into nutritional and mortality data, and, like Karasch, he discovered them to have been a malnourished and disease-ridden people with tuberculosis by far their major killer.

Save for the work done on Rio, however, the study of the blacks' biological past in Brazil remains very much in its infancy. Stuart Schwartz (1978) has demonstrated how disease that reduced the Indian population helped to create the institution of black slavery, and in sorting through the conditions that provoked slave revolts in northeastern Brazil (1970), has implicitly taken issue with Freyre's glowing depiction of the slave diet in that region by his own judgment that it was "especially poor." In addition, in a very recent study (1985), Schwartz has presented evidence of nearly incredible levels of slave mortality on some of the fazendas of Bahia. Demographic overviews of slavery that are suggestive of the bleak chances of a long life for the slaves have been done by Slenes (1976) and Carvalho de Mello (1983). In addition, Russell-Wood (1968) in studying the Santa Casa da Misericordia of Bahia has also touched on matters of slave health and medical care, and Conrad (1983) has recently published a marvelous collection of documents on Brazilian slavery positively crammed with materials that bear on the question of the blacks' biological history in that country.

Since the publication by Octavio de Freitas (1935) of a study of diseases brought to Brazil by the slave trade, little has been done on the subject. Important exceptions are the work by Alden and Miller (this volume) on the deadly career of smallpox as it traveled this conduit, and Donald Cooper's (1975) meticulous examination of the course of yellow fever in Brazil. Another valuable contribution has been made by James Goodyear (1982), who has studied the impact of tropical diseases on both colonial Brazil and the colonial medical mind.

It seems appropriate to close this survey with two questions. The first concerns exactly what it is that we have learned about the biological past of the black over the last two decades that we did not know before, while the second has to do with the extent to which scholars involved in the study of that past have responded to Curtin's challenge to explain the vast demographic differences that existed in the different slave societies of the Americas.

The first question is a pleasure to deal with, for we have learned an enormous amount. We now know, for example, the crucial historical importance of the black's relative (to whites) ability to resist the ravages of malaria and yellow fever. On the one hand, these diseases long helped to forestall a European colonization of West Africa, which in fact required modern tropical medicine to make possible. On the other hand, these same diseases virtually guaranteed that the black, by the deadly process of elimination, was to be the chief European instrument for colonizing the vastness of Plantation America.

We know too that Mother Africa, by protecting her sons and daughters from outside illnesses, left them especially susceptible to such diseases as tuberculosis, pneumonia, and syphilis, while at the same time cursing them with a variety of other ailments that the European found especially offensive such as leprosy and yaws. If we cannot measure the extent to which these diseases (suffered by blacks to a much greater degree than by whites in the New World) set the black apart in the white mind as a biologically different type of man, we nonetheless know that they did and thus made an important contribution to the growth of scientific racism.

We also know, albeit in a still vague sort of way, that African ancestry has affected the nutritional status of Afro-Americans in many ways. Lactose intolerance and different bodily mechanisms than those of European ancestry for handling sodium, iron, calcium, magnesium, even some of the vitamins, doubtless evolved, at least in part, because of millennia of nutritional hardship—hardship that at times seems to have facilitated the sale of slaves to the Americas and that rendered those slaves significantly shorter than American-born counterparts.

Yet within the Americas, slave heights varied from slave society to slave society, suggesting a considerable qualitative difference in nutritional intakes. Because we know that poor nutrition takes its heaviest toll on the very young, both by impairing the mother's ability to bear and nourish healthy infants and by rigorously pruning youngsters after weaning, it has been relatively easy to pinpoint nutrition as an important factor in the very high infant and child mortality rates that seem to have characterized almost all slave societies in the hemisphere.

Much less is known, however, about slave fertility, let alone the place that nutrition was assigned in the fertility equation, and thus the subject promises much debate for some time to come.

The question concerning responses to Curtin's challenge is more difficult. Superficially, it would seem that the outlines of a response to Curtin's challenge have taken shape. Yet those outlines are very blurred, in no small part because of the uneven nature of research efforts across the hemisphere. For studies of the United States, scholars are most blessed with source materials; here most of the work on slave demography and black-related disease immunities and susceptibilities has been done. Nonetheless, scholars are bogged down in untangling questions of slave fertility from those having to do with infant and child mortality. In the Caribbean, where much more remains to be done, such questions are still for the most part being attacked with speculations only, while in Brazil, where practically everything remains to be done, such questions have yet to be raised. Obviously, full-scale comparative studies that could sharpen the outlines are a considerable distance in the future.

Yet there is cause for optimism, for anyone who glances at the publication dates of the literature cited in this survey cannot fail to be impressed with the enormous amount accomplished in the past decade alone. Nor can anyone who reads the articles that follow fail to be impressed with the enormous degree of sophistication that studies of the biological past of the black have achieved.

NOTES

1 Quoted by Crosby (1972: 52).
2 Las Casas (1951: 3: 275–276).
3 Rout (1976: 23). For the destruction of the American Indian by European disease see Ashburn (1947), Crosby (1972), Borah (1976), and Kiple (1984).
4 Unless otherwise indicated the following is based on Kiple (1984).
5 For the first time the term apparently appeared in print see Rankin (1836). Evidence that the region was indeed a "white man's grave" prior to the advent of modern medicine may be found in the work of Curtin (1961) and (1967), Kiple and King (1981), Kiple (1984), Davies (1975), and Cohen (1983).
6 Among other things this had the salubrious effect of throwing cold water on the then on-going debate over where the slave was "better off," with many leaning toward the Latin Americas. For the fascinating details of what seems in retrospect to have been a fairly silly argument that managed to advance our knowledge of slavery by stimulating the need for a hemispheric perspective in spite (or perhaps because) of its silliness see Genovese's (1968) attempt to bring some semantical order to the debate.
7 Findings by Shick (1971), however, that seem to indicate that Africans returning to Africa from the Americas were losing their ability to resist yellow fever and malaria have yet to be completely explained.
8 Other studies that have considered the slave diet are Hilliard (1972) and Taylor (1982).
9 The reader is reminded that the subject at hand is that of *recent* work on the biological past of the black. It should be noted, however, that many older studies have served as building blocks of sorts for recent work, among them Ashburn (1947) whose work on diseases reaching the Americas from Africa and Europe has become a classic. Phillips (1918; 1929) meticulously probed many aspects of slave life, including diet and disease, while numerous inquiries from the 1930s onward examined slave health and the medical establishment. Noteworthy are Shryock (1930), Swados (1941), Mitchell (1944), Jordan (1950), Wall (1950), Postell (1951; 1952; 1953; 1954; 1967), Duffy (1959), Fisher (1968), and Sikes (1968).
10 For other investigations of plantations and skeletal remains, see also Rathbun and Scurry (1983), Harris and Rathbun (unpublished), Reitz, Gibbs, and Rathbun (1985) and Cleavenger, Ousley, and Orser (in press). For the "Stresses of First Freedom" in nineteenth-century Philadelphia see Angel and Kelley (in press).

REFERENCES

Adamo, S. (1983) "The Broken Promise: Race, Health, and Justice in Rio de Janeiro, 1890–1940," Ph.D. dissertation, University of New Mexico.

Alden, D. and J. C. Miller (this volume) "Unwanted Cargoes: The Origins and Dissemination of Smallpox via the Slave Trade from Africa to Brazil."

Allison, A. C. (1954a) "Protection Afforded by Sickle-Cell Trait Against Subtertian Malarial Infection." British Medical Journal 1: 290–294.

—— (1954b) "The Distribution of the Sickle Cell Trait in East Africa and Elsewhere, and Its Apparent Relationship to the Incidence of Subtertian Malaria." Transactions of the Royal Society of Tropical Medicine and Hygiene 48: 312–318.

Angel, J. and J. Kelley (1983) "Health Status of Colonial Iron-Worker Slaves." Journal of Physical Anthropology 60: 170–171. ·

—— (in press) "Stresses of First Freedom: 19th Century Philadelphia." American Journal of Physical Anthropology. ·

Ashburn, P. (1947) The Ranks of Death: A Medical History of the Conquest of America. New York.

Ashcroft, M. T. (1965) "A History and General Survey of the Helminth and Protozoal Infections of the West Indies." Annals of Tropical Medicine and Parasitology 59: 479–493.

Bennett, J. H. (1958) Bondsmen and Bishops: Slavery and Apprenticeship on the Codrington Plantations of Barbados, 1710–1838. Berkeley.

Borah, W. (1976) "Renaissance Europe and the Population of America." Revista de Historia 53: 47–61.

Buckley, R. N. (1979) Slaves in Red Coats: The British West Indies Regiments, 1795–1815. New Haven, CT.

Campbell, John (1984) "Work, Pregnancy and Infant Mortality Among Southern Slaves." Journal of Interdisciplinary History 14: 793–812. ·

Cardell, N. S. and M. M. Hopkins (1978) "The Effect of Milk Intolerance on the Consumption of Milk by Slaves in 1860." Journal of Interdisciplinary History 8: 507–513. ·

Carroll, P., C. Palmer, A. Palerm et al. (1979) "Black Laborers and Their Experience in Colonial Jalapa," in El Trabajo y Los Trabajadores en La Historia de Mexico. Mexico City.

Carvalho de Mello, P. (1983) "Estimativa da longevidade de escravos no Brasil na segunda metade do seculo XIX." Estudos Economicos 13: 151–181.

Chandler, D. L. (1981) Health and Slavery in Colonial Colombia. New York.

Cleavenger, G. L., D. W. Ousley and C. E. Orser (in press) "Demography and Pathologies of Skeletons from New Orleans' First Cemetery." American Journal of Physical Anthropology. ·

Cohen, William B. (1983) "Malaria and French Imperialism." Journal of African History 24: 23–36. ·

Conrad, R. E. [ed.] (1983) Children of God's Fire: A Documentary History of Black Slavery in Brazil. Princeton.

Cooke, M. (1983) "The Health of Blacks during Reconstruction, 1862–1870," Ph.D. dissertation, University of Maryland.

—— (1984) "The Health of Blacks in the District of Columbia, 1860–65." Proceedings of the South Carolina Historical Association: 6–14. ·

26   KENNETH F. KIPLE

Cooper, D. B. (1975) "Brazil's Long Fight Against Epidemic Diseases, 1849–1917, with Special Emphasis on Yellow Fever." Bulletin of the New York Academy of Medicine 51: 672–96.

Corruccini, R., J. Handler, R. Mutaw, and F. Lange (1982) "Osteology of a Slave Population from Barbados, West Indies." American Journal of Physical Anthropology 59: 443–459.

Corruccini, R., J. Handler, and K. Jacobi (1985) "Chronological Distribution of Enamel Hypoplasias and Weaning in a Caribbean Slave Population." Human Biology 57: 699–711.

Coutinho, R. (1934) "Alimentação e estado nutricional do escravo no Brasil," in Estudos Afro-Brasileiros (1° Congresso Afro-Brasileiro) Recife.

Craton, M. (1971) "Jamaican Slave Mortality: Fresh Light From Worthy Park, Longville and the Tharp Estates." Journal of Caribbean History 3: 1–27.

——— (1975) "Jamaican Slavery," in S. L. Engerman and E. D. Genovese (eds.) Race and Slavery in the Western Hemisphere: Quantitative Studies. Princeton.

——— (1976) "Death, Disease and Medicine on Jamaican Slave Plantations: The Example of Worthy Park, 1767–1838." Histoire Sociale-Social History 18: 237–255.

——— (1978) "Hobbesian or Panglossian? The Two Extremes of Slave Conditions in the British Caribbean, 1783–1845." William and Mary Quarterly 35: 324–356.

Craton, M. and J. Walvin (1970) A Jamaican Plantation: The History of Worthy Park, 1670–1970. Toronto.

Crosby, A. W. (1972) The Columbian Exchange: Biological and Cultural Consequences of 1492. Westport, CT.

Curtin, P. D. (1961) "The White Man's Grave: Image and Reality, 1780–1850." Journal of British Studies 1: 94–101.

——— (1964) The Image of Africa: British Ideas and Action, 1750–1850. Madison.

——— (1967) "Epidemiology and the Slave Trade." Political Science Quarterly 83: 190–216.

——— (1969) The Atlantic Slave Trade: A Census. Madison, WI.

——— (1983) "Nutrition in African History." Journal of Interdisciplinary History 14: 371–82.

Cutright, P. and E. Shorter (1979) "The Effects of Health on the Completed Fertility of Nonwhite and White U.S. Women Born Between 1867 and 1935." Journal of Social History 13: 191–217.

Davies, K. G. (1975) "The Living and the Dead: White Mortality in West Africa, 1684–1732," in S. L. Engerman and E. D. Genovese (eds.) Race and Slavery in the Western Hemisphere: Quantitative Studies. Princeton.

Debien, G. (1964) "La nourriture des esclaves sur les plantations des Antilles Françaises aux XVIIe et XVIIIe siecles." Caribbean Studies 4: 3–27.

Dias, J. R. (1981) "Famine and Disease in the History of Angola, 1830–1930." Journal of African History 22: 349–378.

Dirks, R. (1978) "Resource Fluctuations and Competitive Transformations in West Indian Slave Societies," in Laughlin, C. and I. Brady (eds.) Extinction and Survival in Human Populations. New York.

――― (1986) Black Saturnalia. Gainesville, FL.

Domergue, D. (1981) "Le Lutte Contre la Trypanosomiase en Cote d'Ivoire, 1900–1945." Journal of African History 22: 63–72.

Dubish, J. (1985) "Low Country Fevers: Cultural Adaptations to Malaria in Antebellum South Carolina." Social Science and Medicine 21: 641–649.

Duffy, J. (1959) "Medical Practice in the Antebellum South." Journal of Southern History 25: 53–72.

Eblen, J. E. (1974) "On the Natural Increase of Slave Populations: The Example of the Cuban Slave Population, 1775–1900," in S. Engerman and E. Genovese (eds.) Slavery and Race in the Western Hemisphere: Quantitative Studies. Princeton.

Eltis, D. (1982) "Nutritional Trends in Africa and the Americas: Heights of Africans 1819–1839." Journal of Interdisciplinary History 12: 453–475.

――― (1983) "Free and Coerced Transatlantic Migrations: Some Comparisons." American Historical Review 88: 251–280.

――― (1984) "Mortality and Voyage Length in the Middle Passage: New Evidence from the Nineteenth Century." Journal of Economic History 44: 301–308.

――― (1987) Economic Growth and the Ending of the Trans-Atlantic Slave Trade. New York.

Fairbanks, C. H. (1984) "The Plantation Archeology of the Southeastern Coast." Historical Archeology 18: 1–14.

Feinberg, H. M. (1974) "New Data on European Mortality in West Africa: The Dutch on the Gold Coast, 1719–1760." Journal of African History 15: 357–371.

Fischer, D. H. (1970) Historians' Fallacies. New York.

Fisher, W. (1968) "Physicians and Slavery in the Antebellum Southern Medical Journals." Journal of the History of Medicine and Allied Sciences 23: 36–49.

Fogel, R. W. and S. L. Engerman (1974) Time on the Cross: The Economics of American Negro Slavery, 2 vols. Boston.

――― and R. Floud (1983) "Secular Changes in American and British Stature and Nutrition." Journal of Interdisciplinary History 14: 445–481.

Freitas, O. de (1935) Doenças Africanas no Brasil. São Paulo.

Freyre, G. (1933) Casa-Grande e Senzala, Formação da familia Brasileira sob o regimen de economia patriarchal. Rio de Janeiro.

――― (1936) Sobrados e Mucambos: Decadencia do Patriarchado rural no Brasil. São Paulo.

Friedman, G. (1982) "The Heights of Slaves in Trinidad." Social Science History 6: 482–515.

Geggus, D. (1982) "The British Army and the Slave Revolt: Saint Domingue in the 1790s." History Today 32: 35–39.

Gelfand, M. (1971) Diet and Tradition in African Culture. Edinburgh.

Genovese, E. D. (1968) "Materialism and Idealism in the History of the Negro Slave in the Americas." Journal of Southern History 1: 371–394.

——— (1974) Roll Jordan Roll. New York.

Gibbs, T., K. Cargill, L. Lieberman, and E. Reitz (1980) "Nutrition in a Slave Population: An Anthropological Perspective." Medical Anthropology 4: 175–262. ▸

Good, C. M. (1972) "Salt, Trade and Disease: Aspects of Development in Africa's Northern Great Lakes District." International Journal of African History 5: 543–586.

Goodyear, J. D. (1978) "The Sugar Connection: A New Perspective on the History of Yellow Fever." Bulletin of the History of Medicine 52: 5–21.

——— (1982) "Agents of Empire: Portuguese Doctors in Colonial Brazil and the Idea of Tropical Disease," Ph.D. dissertation, Johns Hopkins University.

Guerra, F. (1966) "The Influence of Disease on Race, Logistics and Colonization in the Antilles." Journal of Tropical Medicine and Hygiene 69: 23–35. ◟

Handler, J. and R. Corruccini (1983) "Plantation Life in Barbados: A Physical Anthropological Analysis." Journal of Interdisciplinary History 14: 65–90. ▸

——— (1986) "Weaning among West Indian Slaves: Historical and Bioanthropological Evidence from Barbados." William and Mary Quarterly, 3d ser. 43: 111–117.

Handler, J. S. and F. W. Lange (1978) Plantation Slavery in Barbados. Cambridge, MA.

Hartwig, G. W. (1975) "Economic Consequences of Long Distance Trade in East Africa: The Disease Factor." African Studies Review 18: 63–77.

——— and K. D. Patterson [eds.] (1978) Disease in African History. Durham, NC.

Harris, E. and T. Rathbun (unpublished) "Small Tooth Sizes in a 19th Century South Carolina Plantation Slave Series."

Higman, B. W. (1976) Slave Population and Economy in Jamaica, 1807–1834. Cambridge, England.

——— (1979) "Growth in Afro-American Slave Populations." American Journal of Physical Anthropology 50: 373–385. ◟

——— (1984) Slave Populations of the British Caribbean, 1807–34. Baltimore.

Hilliard, S. B. (1972) Hog Meat and Hoecake: Food Supply in the Old South, 1840–1860. Carbondale, IL. ▸

Hoeppli, R. (1969) Diseases in Africa and the Western Hemisphere: Early Documentation and Transmission by the Slave Trade. Basel.

Hughes, C. and J. Hunter (1970) "Diseases and Development in Africa." Social Science and Medicine 3: 443–493. ◟

Hunter, J. M. (1966) River Blindness in Nangodi, Northern Ghana: A Hypothesis of Clinical Advance and Retreat." The Geographical Review 56: 398–416.

———— (1971) "Geography, Genetics and Cultural History: The Case of Lactose Intolerance." Geographical Review 61: 605–608. ✓

———— (1973) "Geophagy in Africa and the United States: A Culture-Nutrition Hypothesis." Geographical Review 63: 170–195.

———— (1977) "The Summer Disease: An Integrative Model of the Seasonality Aspects of Childhood Lead Poisoning." Social Science and Medicine 1: 691–703. ●

———— (1978) "The Summer Disease: Some Field Evidence on Seasonality in Childhood Lead Poisoning." Social Science and Medicine 12: 85–94. ✓

———— and M. Thomas (1984) "Hypothesis of Leprosy, Tuberculosis and Urbanization in Africa." Social Science and Medicine 19: 27–57. ●

———— and R. DeKleine (1984) "Geophagy in Central America." The Geographical Review 74: 157–169.

Johnson, M. (1981) "Smothered Slave Infants: Were Slave Mothers at Fault?" Journal of Southern History 47: 492–520. ●

Jones, J. H. (1981) Bad Blood: The Tuskegee Syphilis Experiment. New York.

Jordan, W. (1950) "Plantation Medicine in the Old South." Alabama Review 3: 83–107.

Jordan, W. D. (1968) White Over Black. Chapel Hill, NC.

Karasch, M. (1987) Slave Life and Culture in Rio de Janeiro. Princeton.

Kiple, K. F. (1984) The Caribbean Slave: A Biological History. New York.

———— (1985) "Cholera and Race in the Caribbean." Journal of Latin American Studies 17: 157–177.

Kiple, K. F. and V. H. King (1981) Another Dimension to the Black Diaspora: Diet, Disease, and Racism. New York.

Kiple, K. F. and V. H. Kiple (1977a) "Slave Child Mortality: Some Nutritional Answers to a Perennial Puzzle." Journal of Social History 10: 284–309. ●

———— (1977b) "Black Tongue and Black Men: Pellagra in the Antebellum South." Journal of Southern History 63: 411–428. ●

———— (1977c) "Black Yellow Fever Immunities, Innate and Acquired, as Revealed in the American South." Social Science History 1: 419–436.

———— (1980a) "The African Connection: Slavery, Disease and Racism." Phylon 41: 211–222. ✓

———— (1980b) "Slave Nutrition, Disease and Infant Mortality in the Caribbean." Journal of Interdisciplinary History 11: 197–215.

Klein, H. S. (1978) The Middle Passage: Comparative Studies in the Atlantic Slave Trade. Princeton.

———— and S. L. Engerman (1978) "Fertility Differentials Between Slaves in the United States and the British West Indies: A Note on Lactation Practices and Their Possible Implications." William and Mary Quarterly 32: 357–374. ●

Koplan, J. P. (1983) "Slave Mortality in Nineteenth Century Grenada." Social Science History 7: 311–320.

Kulikoff, A. (1977) "A 'Prolifick' People: Black Population Growth in the Chesapeake Colonies, 1700–1790." Southern Studies 16: 396–424. ✓

———— (1986) Tobacco and Slaves: The Development of Southern Cultures in the Chesapeake, 1680–1800. Chapel Hill.

Lamur, H. (1981) "Demographic Performance of Two Slave Populations in the Dutch Speaking Caribbean." Boletin de Estudios Latinoamericanos y del Caribe 30: 87–102.

Las Casas, B. de (1951) Historia de las Indias, 3 vols. Mexico.

Lee, A. S. and E. S. Lee (1977) "The Health of Slaves and the Health of Freedmen: A Savannah Study." Phylon 38: 170–180. •

Lewicki, T. (1974) West African Food in the Middle Ages: According to Arabic Sources. London. •

Lewis, J. H. (1942) The Biology of the Negro. Chicago.

Lieberman, L. S. (unpublished a) "Genetic and Lifestyle Aspects of Diabetes in American Blacks: A Redefined 'Thrifty Gene' Hypothesis."

———— (unpublished b) "Dietary Changes and Disease Consequences among Afro-Americans."

Margo, R. and R. Steckel (1982) "The Heights of American Slaves: New Evidence on Slave Nutrition and Health." Social Science History 6: 516–538.

Martin, D. L., A. L. Magennis, and J. C. Rose (in press) "Cortical Bone Maintenance in an Historic Black Cemetery Sample from Cedar Grove, Arkansas." American Journal of Physical Anthropology. •

Mattoso, K. M. de Q. (1974) "Os escravos na Bahia no alvorecer do seculo xix (estudo de um grupo social)." Revista de Historia 47: 109–135.

McBride, D. (1981) "Black Health Care Labor and the Philadelphia Medical Establishment 1910–1965," Ph.D. dissertation, Columbia University.

McFalls, J. A. (1973) "Impact of VD on the Fertility of the U.S. Black Population, 1880–1950." Social Biology 20: 2–19. •

Miller, J. C. (1980) "Mortality in the Atlantic Slave Trade: Statistical Evidence on Causality." Journal of Interdisciplinary History 11: 385–423.

———— (1982) "The Significance of Drought, Disease and Famine in the Agriculturally Marginal Zones of West-Central Africa." Journal of African History 23: 17–61.

———— (forthcoming) Way of Death: Merchant Capitalism and the Angolan Slave Trade, 1730–1830.

Miller, L. H. et al. (1976) "The Resistance Factor to *Plasmodium vivax* in Blacks: the Duffy-Blood-Group-Genotype, *FyFy*." New England Journal of Medicine 295: 302–304. •

Mitchell, M. (1944) "Health and the Medical Profession in the Lower South, 1845–1860." Journal of Southern History 10: 424–446. •

Moreno Fraginals, M. (1977) "Africa in Cuba: A Quantitative Analysis of the African Population in the Island of Cuba," in V. Rubin and A. Tuden (eds.) Comparative Perspectives on Slavery in New World Plantation Societies. New York Academy of Science, Annals, 292: 187–204.

Motulsky, A. G. and J. M. Campbell-Kraut (1961) "Population Genetics of Glucose-6-Phosphate Dehydrogenase Deficiency of the Red Cell," in B. S. Blumberg (ed.) Proceedings of the Conference on Genetic Polymorphisms and Geographic Variation in Disease. New York.

Owens, L. H. (1976) This Species of Property: Slave Life and Culture in the Old South. New York.

Palmer, C. (1981) Human Cargoes: The British Slave Trade to Spanish America, 1700–1739. Urbana, IL.

Patterson, K. D. (1975) "The Vanishing Mpongue: European Contact and Demographic Change in the Gabon River." Journal of African History 16: 217–238.

——— (1975a) The Northern Gabon Coast to 1875. Oxford.

Patterson, O. (1967) The Sociology of Slavery: An Analysis of the Origins, Development and Structure of Negro Slave Society in Jamaica. London.

Phillips, U. B. (1918) American Negro Slavery. New York.

——— (1929) Life and Labor in the Old South. Boston.

Postell, W. D. (1951) The Health of Slaves on Southern Plantations. Baton Rouge.

——— (1952) "A Review of Slave Care on Southern Plantations." Virginia Medical Monthly 79: 101–105. •

——— (1953) "Mental Health among the Slave Populations on Southern Plantations." American Journal of Psychiatry 110: 52–54. •

——— (1954) "Survey on the Chronic Illnesses and Physical Impairments among the Slave Populations in the Antebellum South." Bulletin of the Medical Library Association 42: 158–162. •

——— (1967) "Slaves and Their Life Expectancy." Bulletin of the Tulane Medical Faculty 26: 7–11. •

Puckrein, G. (1979) "Climate, Health and Black Labor in the English Americas." American Studies 13: 179–193.

Rankin, F. H. (1836) The White Man's Grave: A Visit to Sierra Leone, in 1834. London.

Ransford, O. (1984) "Bid the Sickness Cease": Disease in the History of Black Africa. London.

Rathbun, T. A. (in press) "Health and Disease at a South Carolina Plantation: 1840–1870." American Journal of Physical Anthropology. •

——— and J. D. Scurry (1983) "Status and Health in Colonial South Carolina: Belleview Plantation 1837–1856." American Journal of Physical Anthropology 60: 242. •

Rawley, J. (1981) The Transatlantic Slave Trade: A History. New York.

Reitz, E. J., T. Gibbs, and T. A. Rathbun (1985) "Archaeological Evidence for Subsistence on Coastal Plantations," in T. A. Singleton (ed.) Archaeological Studies of the Plantation System. New York.

Roberts, G. W. (1951) "A Life Table for a West Indian Slave Population." Population Studies 5: 238–242.

——— (1957) The Population of Jamaica. Cambridge, England.

Rousey, D. C. (1985) "Yellow Fever and Black Policemen in Memphis: A Post-Reconstruction Anomaly." The Journal of Southern History 51: 357–374.

Rout, L. B. (1976) The African Experience in Spanish America. Cambridge, England.

Russell-Wood, A. J. R. (1968) Fidalgos and Philanthropists: The Santa Casa da Misericordia of Bahia, 1550–1755. London.

Rutman, D. B. and A. H. Rutman (1976) "Of Agues and Fevers: Malaria in the Early Chesapeake." William and Mary Quarterly 33: 31–60. •

Savitt, T. L. (1975) "Smothering and Overlaying of Virginia Slave Children: A Suggested Explanation." Bulletin of the History of Medicine 49: 400–404. •

——— (1977) "Filariasis in the United States." Journal of the History of Medicine 32: 140–150. •

——— (1978) Medicine and Slavery: The Diseases and Health Care of Blacks in Antebellum Virginia. Urbana, IL.

——— (1981) "The Invisible Malady: Sickle Cell Anemia in America, 1910–1970. Journal of the National Medical Association 8: 739–746. •

Schwartz, S. (1970) "The Mocambo: Slave Resistance in Colonial Bahia." Journal of Social History 3: 313–333.

——— (1978) "Indian Labor and New World Plantations: European Demands and Indian Responses in Northeastern Brazil." The American Historical Review 83: 43–79.

——— (1985) Sugar Plantations in the Formation of Brazilian Society. Cambridge, England.

Sheridan, R. B. (1975) "Mortality and the Medical Treatment of Slaves in the British West Indies," in S. L. Engerman and E. D. Genovese (eds.) Race and Slavery in the Western Hemisphere: Quantitative Studies. Princeton.

——— (1976) The Crisis of Slave Subsistence in the British West Indies during and after the American Revolution." William and Mary Quarterly 33: 615–641.

——— (1982) "The Guinea Surgeons on the Middle Passage: The Provision of Medical Services in the British Slave Trade." International Journal of African Historical Studies 14: 601–625.

——— (1985) Doctors and Slaves: A Medical and Demographic History of Slavery in the British West Indies, 1680–1834. New York. •

Shick, T. W. (1971) "A Quantitative Analysis of Liberian Colonization from 1820 to 1843 with Special Reference to Mortality." Journal of African History 12: 45–59.

Shiloh, A. and I. C. Selvan (1974) Ethnic Groups of America: Their Morbidity, Mortality and Behavior Disorders: Vol. II–The Blacks. Springfield, IL.

Shryock, R. (1930) "Medical Practice in the Old South." South Atlantic Quarterly 29: 160–178.

Sikes, L. (1968) "Medical Care for Slaves: A Preview of the Welfare State." Georgia Historical Quarterly 52: 405–413.

Singleton, T. A. [ed.] (1985) The Archaelogy of Slavery and Plantation Life. Orlando, FL.

Slenes, R. (1976) "The Demography and Economy of Brazilian Slavery," Ph.D. dissertation, Stanford University.

Stampp, K. M. (1956) The Peculiar Institution. New York.

Steckel, R. H. (1979a) "Slave Mortality: Analysis of Evidence from Plantation Records." Social Science History 3: 86–114. •

—— (1979b) "Slave Height Profiles from Coastwise Manifests." Explorations in Economic History 16: 363–380. •

—— (1982) "The Fertility of American Slaves." Research in Economic History 7: 239–286. •

—— (1986a) "Birth Weights and Infant Mortality among American Slaves." Explorations in Economic History 23: 173–198.

—— (1986b) "A Peculiar Population: The Nutrition, Health, and Mortality of American Slaves from Childhood to Maturity." Journal of Economic History 46: 721–741. •

—— and R. A. Jensen (1986) "Determinants of Slave and Crew Mortality in the Atlantic Slave Trade." Journal of Economic History 46: 57–77. •

Stein, S. (1957) Vassouras: A Brazilian Coffee County, 1850–1900. Cambridge, MA.

Stewart, Larry (1985) "The Edge of Utility: Slaves and Smallpox in the Early Eighteenth Century." Medical History 29: 54–70.

Sutch, R. (1975) "The Treatment Received by American Slaves: A Critical Review of the Evidence Presented in Time on the Cross." Explorations in Economic History 12: 355–438.

—— (1976) "The Care and Feeding of Slaves," in Paul A. David et al. (eds.) Reckoning with Slavery. New York.

Swados, F. (1941) "Negro Health on the Ante Bellum Plantations." Bulletin of the History of Medicine 19: 460–472.

Taylor, J. G. (1982) Eating, Drinking, and Visiting in the South: An Informal History. Baton Rouge.

Torchia, M. M. (1977) "Tuberculosis Among American Negroes: Medical Research on a Racial Disease, 1830–1950." Journal of the History of Medicine 32: 252–259. •

Trussel, J. and R. Steckel (1978) "The Age of Slaves at Menarche and Their First Birth." Journal of Interdisciplinary History 8: 477–505.

Uttley, K. H. (1959) "The Epidemiology of Tetanus in the Negro Race over the Last Hundred Years in Antigua, The West Indies." West Indian Medical Journal 8: 41–49.

—— (1960a) "The Birth, Stillbirth, Death, and Fertility Rates of the Coloured Population of Antigua, West Indies from 1857 to 1956." Transactions of the Royal Society of Tropical Medicine and Hygiene 55: 69–78.

—— (1960b) "Infant and Early Childhood Death Rates over the Last Hundred Years in the Negro Population of Antigua, British West Indies." British Journal of Preventive and Social Medicine 14: 185–189.

—— (1960c) "The Mortality and Epidemiology of Diphtheria Since 1857 in the Negro Population of Antigua, British West Indies." West Indian Medical Journal 9: 156–163.

—— (1960d) "The Mortality from Leprosy in the Negro Population of Antigua, West Indies from 1857 to 1956." Leprosy Review 31: 193–199.

—— (1960e) "The Mortality and Epidemiology of Typhoid Fever in the Coloured Inhabitants of Antigua, West Indies Over the Last Hundred Years." West Indian Medical Journal 9: 114–123.

———— (1960f) "The Epidemiology and Mortality of Whooping Cough in the Negro Over the Last Hundred Years in Antigua, British West Indies." West Indian Medical Journal 9: 77–95.

———— (1960g) "The Mortality of Yellow Fever in Antigua, West Indies, Since 1857." West Indian Medical Journal 9: 185–188.

Wall, B. (1950) "Medical Care of Ebenezer Pettigrew's Slaves." Mississippi Valley Historical Review 37: 451–470.

Weaver, J. L. (1977) "The Case of Black Infant Mortality." Journal of Health Policy 1: 433–443.

Whitten, D. O. (1977) "Medical Care of Slaves: Louisiana Sugar Region and South Carolina Rice District." Southern Studies 16: 153–180.

Williams, R. A. [ed.] (1965) Textbook of Black-Related Diseases. New York.

Wilson, T. (1986) "History of Salt Supplies in West Africa and Blood Pressures Today." Lancet i: 784–786. •

Wood, P. (1974) Black Majority: Negroes in Colonial South Carolina From 1670 Through the Stono Rebellion. New York.

Unwanted Cargoes: The Origins and Dissemination of Smallpox via the Slave Trade from Africa to Brazil, c. 1560–1830

DAURIL ALDEN AND JOSEPH C. MILLER

In those slave ships came more than human cruelty and suffering; there came, too, the seeds of terrible epidemics and pandemics.—Ashburn (1947: 29)

Whether the Europeans and Africans came to the native Americans in war or peace, they always brought death with them.—Crosby (1976: 299)

As WE HAVE learned more about the contours of diseases and climate in Africa, it has become clear that drought and smallpox in that region contributed much via the slave trade to the timing and location of epidemics in Portuguese Brazil. Indeed, the epidemi-

Joseph Miller gratefully wishes to acknowledge support from several sources that, over several years, has permitted collection of many of the data informing the present study: the Joint Committee on Africa of the Social Science Research Council and the American Council of Learned Societies (1977), the National Endowment for the Humanities (Summer Stipend) (1977), the Wilson Gee Institute of the University of Virginia (1978), the National Endowment for the Humanities (Fellowship for Independent Study and Research (1978–79), the Center for Advanced Studies of the University of Virginia (Sesquicentennial Associateship) (1978–79), the Calouste Gulbenkian Foundation (Lisbon, Portugal), and in particular the National Library of Medicine (Grant no. LM03003-01) (1978–80). He assumes full responsibility for the conclusions he has contributed to this study, as well as for omissions from it. He is also grateful to John Kneebone for research assistance, to Lenard Berlanstein for guidance to literature on European social and medical history, and to Marion Johnson for permission to cite unpublished works.

Dauril Alden remains grateful for several fellowships that provided opological experience of both continents between the mid-sixteenth and early nineteenth centuries suggests the hypothesis that African reservoirs of endemic smallpox periodically overflowed when droughts left populations in a state of extreme undernourishment. The result, for many, was enslavement, which sent thousands of starving and sick captives to New World shores. The general epidemiological model seems to be one in which slaves were gathered into African trading towns, then moved along slaving paths to be crowded successively into the barracoons on the coast, the holds of slaving ships, and the guinea yards of American ports, with every stage, as well as the whole of the experience, offering almost ideal conditions for transmission of smallpox and other diseases. The model further suggests that newly arrived, infected slaves communicated their contagions to the inhabitants of American seaports and that from there the diseases moved inland.

The resulting well-known epidemics of smallpox, measles, and other contagious diseases, which reduced the native populations of the New World from the sixteenth century onward, seem to represent a tragic constant of colonial American history. Smallpox flared among the slaves of the lowland plantations and the Indians of the backlands; yellow fever spread with particular virulence among European populations of the towns; and measles, coupled with these plagues and with other afflictions as well, repeatedly swept away thousands of Amerindians, especially in the highlands

---

portunities for research incorporated in this essay, particularly the Calouste Gulbenkian Foundation, the National Endowment for the Humanities (for a grant at the Newberry Library, Chicago), and the John Simon Guggenheim Foundation. He thanks Drs. Francis A. Dutra, Michael T. Hamerly, and Dorothy Welker for supplying materials cited in this essay, the last named for her critical comments on an early draft of his portion of this joint project, and Mrs. Dorothy Hanks, the National Library of Medicine, for her very efficient service.

Joint thanks for comments on preliminary drafts of the paper go to Ellen Brickwedde, George Brooks, Ann Carmichael, Marc Dawson, Henry F. Dobyns, David Eltis, Ann McDougall, David Patterson, William B. Taylor, and H. Leroy Vail. We acknowledge stimulation and encouragement received from members of the panel and audience to whom we first presented this paper at the 1982 annual meeting of the American Historical Association (Washington, D.C.). The substance of the argument of this paper appeared in the Journal of Interdisciplinary History 18, no. 1 (1987), and we are grateful, finally, to the editors of that journal for permission to develop the case here at greater length.

of South America. Diseases wiped out Caribs and diminished the ranks of Aztecs, Tupis, and Iroquois, increasing the demand for black labor from Africa[1] and contributing fundamentally to both the difficulties and the opportunities awaiting incoming European conquerers and colonizers.

The ravages of disease in the history of the Americas, a theme of undisputed importance, have usually been attributed to structural implications of intensified contact between previously isolated gene pools, in which human populations long out of touch with one another each possessed distinctive immunities that enabled them to live in reasonable harmony with endemic local pathogens but that failed completely to protect them from alien diseases transferred across the Atlantic in the "Age of Exploration."[2] Left in this static form, the conventional explanation for American epidemiological—and by extension also demographic, economic, and sometimes political—history has little precise historical content. Diseases seem to have swept through the Americas randomly, or in mechanically regular cycles, without sources securely anchored in changing circumstances. We have no fully historical explanation for why Americans of all backgrounds sometimes went for decades without suffering serious outbreaks of disease but at other times endured repeated onslaughts for years at a stretch.

Recent research on African droughts and diseases, coupled with a new survey of the history of epidemics in Brazil, amplifies in detail the connection, long assumed in general terms by Brazilian medical historians (e.g., Freitas, 1935), between slaving and one epidemic malady, smallpox. Africa, they asserted, had been the original source of many diseases endemic to Brazil by the nineteenth century, and Africans arriving on the slave ships common in Brazilian ports down to the termination of legal slaving in 1830 had occasionally introduced massive doses of viruses that erupted in epidemics among the resident populations.[3] They were correct, though more on the basis of imprecise European stereotypes about the general unhealthfulness of Africa than on an accurate understanding of the interplay in the epidemiological transmission. Underlying African malnutrition (Kiple, 1985: 57–75), periodic drought,[4] and demographic pressures produced refugees from famine when prolonged aridity shrank arable and pastoral lands, and many of the displaced people fell into slavery. Those famished slaves were extremely vulnerable to disease, particularly smallpox, when brought into close and continuing contact with one another, and they took their afflictions with them aboard slave ships heading to Brazil.

The devastating effects of drought in the semiarid regions of Africa from the sixteenth through the eighteenth centuries, both in West Africa and in central Africa, or Angola, from where most Brazilian slaves came, conform also to a growing rejection of conventional (though undocumented) assertions that Africa was then generally "underpopulated" (Fage, 1975; Anstey, 1975: 81–82; and particularly Inikori, 1980).[5] Although slaving wars in Africa surely also caused local famines, drought-caused food shortages more generally provoked conflicts in this tropical version of the conundrum linking hunger and hostilities. Ecological limitations on the health and numbers of African farmers and herders contributed to wars, kidnapping, child-selling, and self-sacrifice that directly and indirectly fed the slave trade.[6]

Smallpox (*variola major*) and other contagious diseases could hardly fail to erupt in epidemic form among starving Africans subjected to such climatic instability. Variola was a member of a group of pox viruses that includes cowpox, monkeypox, rabbitpox, and mousepox.[7] Infection proceeded from droplets of human expectorants transferred through close contact to the mucous membranes of the upper respiratory tract. After an incubation period of ten to twelve days, during which the virus multiplied and entered particular cells of the liver, lymph nodes, spleen, bone marrow, and probably the lungs, the victim experienced a high fever. The virus also produced degenerative changes in the epidermis cells, causing homogeneous lesions, especially in the face, hands, and feet, and sometimes leaving in its wake disfiguring scarring, a consequence either of the destruction of sebaceous glands or of secondary bacterial infection. In its severest, haemorrhagic form— the one which particularly afflicted the Amerindians—smallpox brought agonizing death to great numbers. That death generally resulted from dehydration and damage to the internal organs. In Andean America 30% to 50% of those exposed to smallpox during the sixteenth and seventeenth centuries succumbed, and the same may well have been true in coeval Brazil.[8]

MOVEMENTS OF POX AND SLAVES

Smallpox is thought to have originated about 12,000 years ago in India, China, and possibly northeastern Africa. It was reported active in the Near East in the sixth century A.D. and was first introduced to southern Europe in the course of the eighth-century Muslim invasions north of the Mediterranean. Christian crusaders returning from the Holy Lands later spread the infection to more northerly parts of the continent, and by 1426–1427 smallpox had reached Russia (Hopkins, 1983).[9]

The earliest specific report of smallpox in sub-Saharan Africa dates from Angola in the 1620s (Cadornega, 1940–1942: 1: 140–143), but it is thought to have been active in West Africa several centuries earlier.[10] In fact, epidemiologists now believe an apparently separate African strain of the virus—of sufficient antiquity as to be effectively indigenous by the nineteenth century—shifted from endemic to lethally epidemic forms largely in response to drought and famine conditions. The indigenous strain, though normally mild in its effects, was, like all other forms of smallpox, spread only through close contact. Because humidity shortened the survival of the virus outside the human host, it spread more easily in arid surroundings (Joralemon, 1982: 119, citing Dixon, 1962: 304). Africans usually dampened outbreaks of the disease by scattering or by isolating the afflicted sufferer (e.g., Wheeler, 1964: 357, 358), but the disease could assume epidemic proportions when normally dispersed populations flocked into relatively dense settlements around the limited remaining water sources. There intensified contacts among formerly isolated victims and nonimmunes communicated the disease, and 10% to 70% of an exposed population could perish in the course of an outbreak (Dawson, 1983). Attendant malnutrition, while not in itself raising the vulnerability of drought refugees to the infection, contributed indirectly to highly lethal epidemics. Increased trade in foodstuffs at such times of hunger animated the movements of merchants, who spread the disease between teeming towns and marketplaces where they congregated. This epidemiology, well documented for both east and west Africa in the late nineteenth century, may safely be assumed to have also characterized most of the continent during the earlier eras of the slave trade (Dawson, 1979: 245–250).[11]

Growing slaving at such periods of aridity tended to sustain the outbreaks of disease. Extreme hardships and nutritional deprivation on the "path" leading down to the coast[12] raised death rates among the slaves and infected populations concentrated there and in the commercial towns. The slaves had begun to exchange smallpox and other pathogens among themselves by the time traders crowded them still more tightly into the barracoons and castle "trunks" of the coast to await embarkation. No official health inspections in African ports barred afflicted slaves from boarding, and captains seem not to have refused to take them on. Even more cramped conditions on the middle passage, in which the captives sometimes lacked sufficient space even to roll over, made it likely that a single infected slave would spread the pox widely among the three or four hundred persons crammed below decks.[13] Three or four cycles of transmission during the usual thirty- to fifty-day passage would land infective sufferers in Brazil.[14] The release of pox-ridden slaves into the teeming dockside districts of the colonial port towns, retarded only occasionally by quarantine procedures before the end of the eighteenth century—and usually only after the contagion had already reached the city—set the disease loose in America (Goodyear, 1982).

The epidemiology established for African smallpox (and hinted at in the medical literature on comparably tropical India) also explains how infected slaves landed in Brazilian ports could trigger epidemics throughout much of Portuguese America. Allowing for mild indigenous American endemic forms of the disease (*variola minor*) in rural Brazil, colonial towns would still have functioned as reservoirs of virulent imported Eurasian and African strains of the *variola major* virus. Whether the arriving slaves carried the Eurasian or the African strain, they represented one of the most mobile elements in Brazilian society. New slaves moved as rapidly as their owners could advance them past the docks, through the guinea yards of the towns, and along trails and waterways leading to interior settlements, mines, and plantations. If the disease behaved in colonial Brazil as it did in both contemporaneous Europe and modern Africa, the slaves would have spread the alien strains of the virus to stable interior populations otherwise relatively isolated from the urban areas along the coast and hence vulnerable to infection. According to this model, the arrival of greater numbers of infected slaves at a seaport, and their subsequent movement outward from it, would touch off epidemics among nonimmune populations throughout the commercial hinterland. The forced concentration of Brazilian laboring populations in plantation barracks, on mining camps, around missions, and in Indian villages virtually assured widespread communication of the imported virus.

The available historical record does not yet illuminate other variables relevant to the American epidemiological context. It is possible, for example, that autonomous American epidemics might have resulted from the mutation of virulent strains from the endemic local virus. Further reconstruction of Brazil's climate history might reveal how droughts there, like their African and Indian counterparts, turned endemic morbidity into epidemic mortality. Nor can the possibility of transmissions of epidemic smallpox from one American port to another yet be fully accounted for. One ought to take note also of the inherent local periodicity of epidemic smallpox, since endemic morbidity and even epidemics of relatively nonfatal local strains of the virus would have left surviving populations largely immune for a time to new introductions of a closely related alien virus. On the other hand, a cycle of lethal epidemics, once established, whether or not in the wake of drought, would reduce the labor force, thus compelling the Portuguese to replace the lost hands with new populations of nonimmune slaves or to concentrate highly vulnerable Indians, among whom the next wave of infected arriving slaves would spread the pathogen. Lethal epidemics themselves, then, in part repeatedly reset the stage for the entrance of their successors.

The broad patterns of slaving that brought captive Africans to Brazil took shape in the late sixteenth century and changed only in detail thereafter. Portuguese and Brazilian slavers had their strongest positions along the southwestern coasts of Africa, roughly the regions known as "Angola" between 4° and 18° south of the equator. Over the years, shippers supplying Rio de Janeiro tended to become the dominant buyers there. Traders from northeastern Brazil, particularly Bahia, concentrated increasingly in the eighteenth and early nineteenth centuries on the "Mina" coast of what is today Togo, Benin, and southwestern Nigeria. Smaller Portuguese centers in Upper Guinea, Cacheu and Bissau, also supplied slaves to the northeast and later on to the northern Brazilian captaincies of Maranhão and Pará. By the end of the eighteenth century, more and more traders from Rio sailed around the Cape of Good Hope to tap southeastern African sources of labor along the coast of what is today Mozambique.

The partial regional specificity of the African sources for slave labor in each part of Brazil may have thus produced closer epidemiological links between Angola and central/southern Brazil than with the north, and smallpox and drought in West Africa would have been communicated more frequently to northern Brazil than to Rio de Janeiro. The presence of non-Portuguese buyers in the same African supply areas, of course, might be expected to have carried the same pathogens to the Caribbean and, secondarily, to mainland North America and to the slave-buying parts of Spanish America. French, Dutch, and English competitors severely limited the activities of the Portuguese and Brazilians both in Upper Guinea and along the Mina coast from the mid-seventeenth century onward. The same three rivals held similarly commanding positions in central Africa north of the mouth of the Zaire River, and the French briefly posed a major challenge to Portuguese control of the southern parts of the Angola coast between about 1770 and 1790. We have not here attempted the daunting task of casting our net systematically beyond the confines of the Portuguese colony.

SMALLPOX IN THE NEW WORLD: SIXTEENTH CENTURY

In the Americas smallpox generally entered a region within a generation after European conquest. The disease announced its American arrival first in Hispaniola in 1518, coming from Spain at a time before slaves reached the Spanish Indies directly from Africa. It became epidemic in the towns in which the Spaniards were concentrating the Arawaks of the island and massively attacked the entire population in December 1518 (Henige, 1986). The contagion reached the mainland at Veracruz, probably in 1520, allegedly introduced by Francisco de Eguía, the African slave of Pánfilo de Narváez.[15] The epidemic then quickly spread from that mainland beachhead to the central Mexican highlands, where it killed an estimated 3.5 million Aztecs during Cortes's classic conquest. A year or so later it raged throughout Central America, and by the mid-1520s it had jumped south to the Inca Empire in Peru, where its widespread destruction facilitated the Pizarrist conquest (Polo, 1913: 51–53; Dobyns, 1963: 494–496). By 1558–1560 *variola major* of unknown provenience had reached the Río de la Plata, where the geographer Juan Lopez de Velasco tells us that it accounted for the deaths of more than 100,000 non-Europeans (Geografia, 1894: 532). The Brazilian Indians were its next victims.

The Brazilian experience with smallpox, still from European rather than African sources, began during the years 1562–1565. The pandemic of those years was preceded in the central coastal captaincy of Espírito Santo, and perhaps elsewhere as well, by debilitating attacks of pleurisy and bloody flux, that is, bacillary dysentery, which killed hundreds of slaves and weakened the survivors.[16] The onslaught of smallpox began in the captaincy of Bahia in January 1562, following the arrival of a disease-laden ship from Lisbon.[17] Initially the virus plagued nascent Jesuit missions around All Saints Bay, wiping out an estimated 30,000 Indians within three or four months. It then leapfrogged up and down the littoral, attacking the indigenous population wherever there were Portuguese settlements and mission stations, from Pernambuco in the north to São Vicente in the south. From the seacoast of the latter it ascended the plateau to the recently erected Jesuit mission of Piratininga adjacent to the fledgling town of São Paulo.

The outbreak of the 1560s was a classic virgin-soil epidemic that attacked only the indigenous population, usually causing death within three or four days, especially among young children. As has been the case with many other epidemics, pestilence was followed by famine, reflecting the inability of the survivors to harvest sufficient food to sustain themselves.[18]

Although no evidence connects Brazil's first experience with epidemic smallpox to African sources, drought during the early 1560s in Angola provided propitious conditions of the sort that later would provoke outbreaks of the pox on both sides of the Atlantic. The first small numbers of African slaves began to reach Portuguese America at that very time.[19] Trade at São Tomé, the equatorial African island that served as staging post for the early slave trade to Brazil, was reported suffering from shortages of ships, merchandise for the trade, and *"moniçõis"* in 1558, the last perhaps a reference to lack of food supplies. These uncertain hints of famine at São Tomé take on added significance when combined with clear allusions to contemporaneous anxiety among mainland Africans near the Kwanza River origins of many of the slaves passing through São Tomé. Failed rains had provoked hunger there in 1561 and 1563. A Jesuit reaching São Tomé in 1560 expressed dismay at the extremely high mortality he encountered on the island, though he, like all other known sixteenth-century reporters of African diseases, failed to specify the presence of smallpox (Brásio, 1951–1985: 2: 457, 458, 502, 508–509, 510, 511; 4: 631; G. S. Dias, 1934: 238).[20]

Brazil was spared additional major epidemics for the next several decades, although at least three outbreaks of local consequence appeared during the remainder of the sixteenth century. In 1585, for example, an eruption of what appears to have been smallpox occurred in Ilhéus not far south of Salvador, though details are lacking.[21] A dozen years later in 1597, when Portuguese forces were poised to occupy the coast of Rio Grande do Norte, northeasternmost Brazil, an outbreak of smallpox was killing ten to twelve Indians a day and obliged the commander to halt his campaign. Since that coast was frequented by French ships seeking to barter for brazilwood, and since a French vessel that had earlier raided the Portuguese factory at Arguin island off the Saharan far west coast arrived in Bahia the same year bearing smallpox, it is possible that the report from Rio Grande do Norte indicates the first poxian sickness of West African origin in Brazil (Salvador, 1954: 292; Jaboatão, 1858–1862: 1: 167–168).[22] Droughts had struck the Cape Verde Islands, Portugal's commercial bases just off the West African mainland, in 1580–1582 and again in 1594 (Carreira, 1966).[23] In Angola the entire period from 1574 to 1587 had produced repeated allusions to failed rains, famine, and sickness, especially in 1583–1584 (J. C. Miller, 1982: 35–39).

In 1599 a Spanish hulk bound from Spain to Buenos Aires stopped in Rio de Janeiro, where she introduced "a disease . . . like the meazels, but as bad as the plague," which killed "above three thousand Indians and Portugals" within the space of three months ([Knivet], 1906: 237). Since contemporaries were often unable to distinguish the symptoms of smallpox from those of measles and several other eruptive maladies, it is conceivable that this was Brazil's last smallpox outbreak of primarily Iberian origin. Africa would thereafter become the principal launching pad for *variola* strikes against Brazil.

Brazil's relative freedom from the pox during the remainder of the sixteenth century may appear puzzling if one accepts the common assumption that smallpox was long endemic in Africa, in view of the intensification of the slave trade direct to Brazilian ports at that time (especially from the early 1570s when the cane sugar industry began its rapid expansion) (Schwartz, 1986: 65–72) and in view of reports of famine and unspecified sickness in the 1570s and the 1590s in both the West African and the Angolan regions from which most of the workers came (Brásio, 1951–1985: 3: 129–142, 305; 4: 359, 482, 548, 555; G. S. Dias, 1934: 160). The explanation may be that smallpox, which no African source mentions specifically at that time, had not yet reached coastal Africa. However, it seems as likely that the American pandemic of the 1560s had wiped out most of the susceptibles in Brazil. In the latter case, it would require another generation before nonimmune Amerindian children would reach the critical percentage of the population necessary to support new epidemics (Cook, 1981: 62, 64, citing May, 1958).

THE SEVENTEENTH CENTURY

The pace of known (or reported) epidemics increased during the seventeenth century in Brazil, as in other parts of the Americas, and the African connection becomes clearer in the historical record.[24] Smallpox, though joined by measles and later by yellow fever, continued to be the prime infectious killer. Two to four epidemics afflicted the colony during seven of the decades of that century. The first occurred in 1613, when Indians and slaves on Rio de Janeiro's sugar plantations in southern Brazil absorbed extensive losses (Coaracy, 1965: 38).[25] Three years later, what was termed *sarampo e bexigas,* that is, measles and smallpox, the usual designation for haemorrhagic smallpox, attacked the Northeast. Its source was also attributed explicitly to slaves from Kongo in central Africa and from Allada on the Lower Guinea coast. The victims included not only Indians and Guinea slaves but also second-generation whites and mixed bloods (*mamelucos*) (Brandão, 1956: 124–125).[26] Two further outbreaks came at the beginning of the 1620s. The first was a renewed exposure of the north coast to smallpox. In 1621 a ship originating in Pernambuco introduced the scourge to São Luis do Maranhão, where many Indians perished within the space of three days (Berredo, 1905: 1: 292, para. 487). The same epidemic swept through Pernambuco and three other northeastern captaincies between 1621 and 1623. Although the extent of the casualties is unknown, they were severe enough to provoke municipal authorities in Pernambuco to implement the first recorded quarantine for slaves arriving in Brazil (Andrade, 1956: 13; Duarte, 1956: 70–71).[27]

The simultaneous reappearance of smallpox in both northern and southern Brazil in the 1610s coincided with drought in Angola and *sahelian* West Africa (the regions on the edge of the desert) (J. C. Miller, 1982: 17, fn. 3). Although the usually populous southern margins of the Sahara Desert seem to have enjoyed generally high amounts of rainfall in the fifteenth and sixteenth centuries, this moist period gave way to more arid conditions and to a series of droughts that increased in length and frequency throughout the seventeenth and eighteenth centuries, roughly the same period in which European slaving spread along West African coasts. Conceivably, though as yet without direct documentation, the wet years of the sixteenth century had allowed population levels along the margins of the desert to grow beyond the limits that increasing aridity imposed in later decades (Brooks, 1985: 197ff).

Northern Brazil, Maranhão and Pará, depended primarily upon Indian slaves before the middle of the eighteenth century. Its imported Africans came from Portugal's West African slaving stations at Bissau and Cacheu in Upper Guinea rather than from the Angolan sources supplying central and southern Brazilian slaves. These northern ports drew on African trade routes that reached deeply into the sahelian zones most sensitive to these long-term climatic trends (Curtin, 1975; Mettas, 1975). Drought may have appeared in that region in 1617, when it was reported in at least the populous interior delta and along the great bend of the Niger River (Curtin, 1975: 2: 7, citing Cissoko, 1968). Famine and sickness in the Cape Verde islands in 1620, and perhaps earlier, confirm the severity of this drought on the mainland (Senna Barcelos, n.d.: 1: 11; Carreira, 1966: 41–42). Simultaneously, the rains failed widely in Angola from 1614 to 1619, provoking a period of almost universal violence, in which Portuguese conquerors and slavers eagerly joined, among exhausted populations there who had had less than a generation to recover from the previous period of severe aridity between 1572 and 1595 (Cadornega, 1940–1942: 1: 83, 89–90, 93; Heintze, 1981: 206, 208). In that decade a Brazilian source specifically ascribed smallpox to slaves arriving from West and central African coasts for the first time (Brandão, 1956: 62). These droughts in both Angola and the

West African *sahel* and the smallpox then reported on both ocean tracks first associate aridity in Africa with smallpox epidemics both there and in Brazil.

A great smallpox epidemic in Angola, exacerbated by still another recurrence of drought, swept away farmers, foot soldiers, and African royalty from 1625 to 1628 (Cadornega, 1940–1942: 1: 140–141, 143). The monarchs of both Kongo and Ndongo (or Angola), the two major African kingdoms between the Zaire and the Kwanza rivers, perished in the contagion. Armies disbanded, and ships changed course to avoid the infection. Nonetheless, the annual totals of slaves loaded at Luanda rose as rains failed and then fell back with the return of good harvests in a pattern that suggested the power of famine in Africa to generate refugees, whom European buyers sent to America as slaves (Heintze, 1981: table 1, 206). Those who exploited the distress in Africa paid for their callousness with extraordinarily high losses to mortality at sea, and slaving vessels from Angola still landed slaves bearing smallpox in Brazil.[28] However, the diseases reaching Brazilian shores during the 1620s failed to spread among American populations. Temporarily renewed immunities to smallpox among the long-suffering slaves and Indians of Brazil left by the repeated epidemics of the preceding decade may again in this case account for their lack of susceptibility.[29]

The colony appears to have escaped major contagion from 1623 to 1641, despite intense fighting, population dislocations, and accelerated importation of African slaves during the famous Dutch occupations of northeastern Brazil.[30] In 1641 the Dutch finally occupied Maranhão, the seventh and last of the Brazilian captaincies they held. But 1641 was a year of excessively heavy rains in the northeast and also of a virulent pandemic of haemorrhagic smallpox throughout Dutch Brazil and beyond. In a single captaincy, Paraíba, an estimated 1,100 blacks became its victims (Barleu[s], 1940: 236–237; Nieuhof, 1942: 81). Three years later, another smallpox eruption caused extensive losses among Indian villagers of Maranhão (Kiemen, 1954: 54; Studart, 1904–1921: 3: 122–137).

The Brazilian epidemics of the early 1640s again coincided with simultaneous reversions to aridity in both western and central Africa. The pace of droughts in the *sahel* quickened with a four-year failure of the rains from 1639 to 1643. By 1641 Portuguese traders at Cacheu reported devastating famine in the vicinity (Mauro, 1956: 28; Curtin, 1975: 2: 3; Nicholson, 1979: 44–45). The Dutch West Indies Company reported epidemic smallpox in "Guinea" in 1642–1643, and mortality aboard its Brazil-bound ships rose in 1642 and again in 1644–1645 (Boogaart and Emmer, 1979: 367). The persistent central African drought reappeared yet again in 1639 from the Zaire south beyond the Kwanza to the new (since 1617), small Portuguese outpost at Benguela (Cadornega, 1940–1942: 1: 332–333; Delgado, 1945: 138–141). The rains failed continuously until about 1644 or 1645 in Angola, and, though Dutch reports from central Africa in the 1640s, dominated by wars against both the Portuguese and the Africans, made no explicit reference to sickness there, they mentioned every circumstance ordinarily associated with epidemics: a drop in the price of slaves, a sharp increase in the supply of slaves—mostly children and women, and one lot described specifically as "young and weak"—in 1643–1644, food shortages at Luanda, and high mortality at sea (mainly in 1643) (Boogaart and Emmer, 1979: 364, 367–368, 370).

A period of better rains lasting fifteen years followed in Angola, during which swarms of locusts, typically active during moist periods following severe drought (Hielkema et al., 1986) and in this case undoubtedly products of the preceding full century of monotonously recurring failures of the rains, plagued the more northerly parts of the central African coast (Cavazzi de Montecuccolo, 1965: 1: 243; 2: 34; Thornton, 1979: 35–38; J. C. Miller, 1982: 43). No further epidemic disease struck Brazil during those years.

A new wave of epidemics hit the American colony only in the early and mid-1660s. It began with a "pestilential catarrh" (i.e., influenza or tuberculosis) that swept Maranhão in 1660 (Hemming, 1978: 338). Two years later, first the captaincy of Maranhão and then the adjacent northern territory of Pará were struck by a lethal attack of smallpox, whose effects were vividly described by João Felippe Betendorf, a Jesuit father who ministered to the sick Indians. "Maranhão," he wrote, "was burning with a plague of smallpox. The missionary fathers often dug graves with their own hands to inter the dead, for there were villages (*aldeias*) where there were not two Indians upright. Parents abandoned their children and fled into the forests to avoid such a pestilential evil." Stricken Indians were so seriously afflicted that their skin became black, their bodies becoming so fever-ridden that "pieces of their

flesh fell off." The epidemic passed from the seacoast to the interior, at least as far as the Tocantins River, where Betendorf tended
dying natives whose bodies "seemed to me like the smell of white
bread when it is removed from the oven. To confess them I was
forced to put my mouth close to their ears, which were full of nau-
seating matter from the pox, with which they were entirely covered" (Betendorf, 1901: 4: chs. 11–12).[31]

No casualty figures are available for these Maranhão epidemics,
nor for the second Brazilian smallpox pandemic in 1664–1666,
which raced through the entire State of Brazil, especially the sugar-
producing zone extending from Pernambuco to Bahia where most
of the incoming slaves reaching Brazil at that time landed. In Bahia, where famine again followed the pox, some planters lost their
entire labor force to the disease.[32] Thereafter, however, Brazil enjoyed a reprieve of nearly a decade and a half before she was again
visited by mass-killing diseases.

African sources of this pestilence may appear in the historical
record from Angola. By the mid-1650s a sickness of an unspecified
identity had broken out among the Kongo near the Zaire River. In
1655 Angolan slaves were again ordered (unsuccessfully) quarantined at Bahia. Drought drove other Africans to invade the Portu-
guese-held river valleys along the coast near Benguela in 1656,
and harvest failures and a disease described as *inchação* (swell-
ing) dispersed the populations and caused terrible mortality in
even the most fertile parts of the interior east of Luanda by 1660–
1663 (Cavazzi de Montecuccolo, 1965: 1: 24, 243; 2: 34, 213,
256; Goodyear, 1981: 2). While no source specified the presence of
smallpox in Africa, malnutrition surely weakened slaves reaching
Brazil and may have supported the pandemic of the three years
following.[33]

The 1680s and 1690s were the most infectious years of the century for Brazil. They began with a smallpox epidemic in Bahia in
1680 that appears to have endured for the next four years, during
which the captaincy suffered from famine, in part no doubt a consequence of the disease but also the result of a two-year drought
(Salvador [Bahia], c. 1950: 3: 7–8). In 1682 smallpox also broke
out in the captaincy of Pernambuco, its most significant fruit being
publication of the first medical treatise by a Portuguese resident in
Brazil who was familiar with the manifestations of smallpox and
measles (Romão Mõsia Reinhipo in Morão, Rosa e Pimenta, 1956:

73–125).[34] Smallpox in this case was followed by Brazil's first major yellow fever epidemic, the famous outbreak that began in Recife in 1685, spread the following year to Bahia, and at an uncertain date reached south to Rio de Janeiro.[35]

During the 1690s the smallpox virus punished Brazil from one extremity to the other. In 1690 a ship from Bahia carried the infection to the newly established Portuguese Platine outpost of Colônia do Sacramento (Almeida, 1973: 323). Three years later, Rio de Janeiro's inhabitants, particularly its slaves, suffered heavily from their first reported smallpox epidemic in half a century (Coaracy, 1965: 229). And in 1695 two Jesuit fathers, one an Austrian serving in the Seven Missions of the future Brazilian state of Rio Grande do Sul, the other a Luxembourger who ministered for nearly forty years in the state of Maranhão, watched helplessly as their Indian neophytes were devastated by the disease. One of them, Father João Felippe Betendorf, observed 5,000 of his flock perish during a major regional epidemic.[36]

African drought and smallpox coincided with this extraordinarily lethal episode in the epidemiological history of the Americas. The intensity of the American catastrophe seemed to increase with the severity of the disasters across the ocean. In the 1680s the major West African drought of the entire seventeenth century dessicated regions extending far beyond the apparent limits of earlier failures in the rains along the desert fringe. The dryness spread even to Lower Guinea, where Bahian slavers were then turning in growing numbers in their quest for African labor (Verger, 1968; Curtin, 1975: 2: 3; Nicholson, 1981: 255).[37] It is tempting to speculate that the first large influx of the subsequently famous "Mina" slaves to reach northeastern Brazil from Lower Guinea may have contributed to the unprecedented virulence and persistence of the epidemics of the 1690s there.[38] In Luanda, Bahians accused the local governor of monopolizing the import of foodstuffs at a time of extreme scarcity, no doubt depriving the ships carrying their slaves of provisions essential for a successful middle passage (cf. J. C. Miller, 1985). They also lamented the destructive effects of yet another smallpox epidemic in Angola, this one so devastating that slavers feared the African populations of the mainland would take years to regenerate to the point of supporting slave exports at previous levels. The Bahians turned to their new sources of slaves at Mina in part to escape the tribulations in Angola (Rau, 1956: 60; Verger, 1968: 11, 66–67; J. C. Miller, 1982: 45–46).

As in other parts of the Americas, Brazil remained relatively free from reported major disease outbreaks during the very last years of the seventeenth century and the first decade of the eighteenth century.[39] After abatement of apparently localized drought near the mouth of the Zaire River in 1691 and 1692, these years also proceeded without reported interruptions in the rains or notice of epidemics in Angola. Indeed, in 1701 the municipal council at Luanda complained of the damage done to streets by abundant rains running off through the loose sandy soils on which the town stood (AHU/PA/Angola cx. 18; Venâncio, 1983: 90). Famine along the Niger Bend in 1695 and a possible short-term disruption in food supplies along the Gold Coast in 1696 seem not to have contributed more to the history of Brazilian diseases than possibly to have prolonged the discomforts of the early 1690s (Curtin, 1975: 2: 5; Johnson, c. 1974: 3).

EIGHTEENTH CENTURY

A reference to smallpox aboard a ship reaching Buenos Aires in 1705 may have heralded a renewed upsurge in American diseases originating in Africa (Scheuss de Studer, 1958: 124). Buenos Aires generally received few slaves from Upper Guinea at that time, but the accelerating West African tendency toward aridity had again revealed itself. Failed rains and famine on the upper Niger in 1704, fifteen or sixteen years of prolonged drought in the Cape Verde Islands from 1705 to 1721, and the beginnings of famine in the lower Sénégal River reported later in 1710 may account for the pox arriving at the Plata estuary (Curtin, 1975: 2: 3; Nicholson, 1980b: 188–189).[40]

These seemingly localized sufferings in West Africa became more general throughout in the decade after 1710 (Bathily, 1986: 289), and after 1713 others appeared in central Africa as well. Smallpox ravaged Angola from 1715 to 1720 (AHU/PA/Angola cx. 16; F. Campos, 1982: 98).[41] In the same decade the surgeon of the Royal African Company (RAC) stationed on the Gold Coast described smallpox as so common there during his thirteen or fourteen years of residence that "thousands of Men have been swept away" by the disease (Bosman, 1721: 108, as

cited in Herbert, 1975: 545). A Portuguese ship reached Rio de
Janeiro in 1715 with many of its 116 slaves suffering from smallpox, and four dead (Lisanti, 1973: 2: 62). Copious and direct
evidence demonstrates the slave-born transfer of the central African epidemic to South America. Smallpox appeared in Pernambuco in 1715, precisely on schedule. English South Seas Company
ships brought slaves and smallpox together to Buenos Aires from
the coasts just north of the mouth of the Zaire River and from
Angola in the very same year (Scheuss de Studer, 1958: cuadro
V). A year later in 1716 "great losses to slave mortality" at Angola hit a ship reaching Bahia. The outbreak had assumed serious
proportions in the backcountry of the Brazilian captaincy of Bahia,[42] and also in the city itself, ruining several merchants. Word
of other losses among merchants in Rio de Janeiro came to Lisbon
in 1718 (Lisanti, 1973: 1: 91–92; 2: 131). The smallpox introduced in 1715 at Buenos Aires may have spread all the way up
the tributaries of the Plata to Córdoba and to southern Peru,
where "killer epidemics" had broken out by 1718–1720 (Scheuss
de Studer, 1958: cuadro V).[43] Smallpox also appeared in Pará
by 1720, thus distributing outbreaks of documented African origin
from the most southern to the most northern ports of South
America.

The 1720s, 1730s, and 1740s saw frequent and severe epidemics continue in various parts of Brazil, at first seemingly supported
by Angolan sources and later, by mid-century, coinciding with the
most severe drought to afflict West Africa during the entire eighteenth century. After reports of West African drought and famine
in 1721–1722 and 1723 stretching from the Sénégal River valley
to the Niger Bend, though without immediately recorded epidemiological consequences in Portuguese America, sickness soon appeared in both northern Brazilian captaincies, Maranhão and Pará,
in 1724.[44] The port of São Luis do Maranhão was already infected when Dom Bartholomeu do Pilar, newly confirmed bishop
of Pará, arrived from Lisbon that year. He continued on to Belém, capital of Pará, after transferring to a large seagoing canoe.
En route and in the Paranense city his crewmen unwittingly dis-
seminated the pox. From Belém other canoes carried it to upriver
plantations and mission stations, causing a serious shortage of
Indian laborers.[45]

During the same decade epidemics also afflicted the east coast of Brazil. In 1724, coincident with the north coast smallpox outbreaks, another hit São Paulo. Though it appears to have been spent by 1725, it was immediately followed by a massive attack of measles that also visited Bahia the same year (1726) (Taunay, 1949–1950: 2: 101–103).[46] While measles was still raging on the plateau of São Paulo, its principal seaport, Santos, was struck by smallpox in 1727 (Lisanti, 1973: 4: 19, 27).

The Angolan origins of this southern Brazilian outbreak are clear. In the early decades of the eighteenth century, Angola had become a major source for burgeoning slave miner populations brought in through Rio de Janeiro to the south-central Brazilian gold fields in Minas Gerais adjoining São Paulo. The rains failed totally along the Angolan coast in 1724–1726, and scarcities of food at Luanda drove grain prices in the town up to unprecedentedly high levels. Smallpox broke out in the Angolan port in 1725, with slave mortality ruining an entire generation of merchants by 1727 (AHU/PA/Angola cxs. 16–18).

The years 1729–1732 witnessed low rainfall and famine along the Sénégal River (Curtin, 1975: 2: 4),[47] and these dry conditions in West Africa coincided with bad years for illness in Maranhão and Pará in the late 1720s and early 1730s. Between 1730 and 1732 smallpox returned also to the city of São Paulo, as well as to Bahia, Pernambuco, and Pará (Taunay, 1949–1950: 3: 161–164; Accioli, 1930–1940: 2: 378).[48] These epidemics must have spread southward with the slaves then being drawn from all Brazilian captaincies toward the ravenous labor markets in the booming mining districts of Minas Gerais.

Reports from Angola at that time noted only a minor failure of the rains in 1731 but no ensuing epidemic. By 1734 a more severe drought had set in along Angolan shores, leading to famine again by 1735 at Luanda and throughout the interior at least by 1736 (Venâncio, 1983: 90; AHU/PA/Angola cx. 20). In 1736 an epidemic of an undesignated nature broke out in Angola (AHU/PA/Angola cx. 20), and another outbreak of disease, also without specification as to its nature, appeared in Rio de Janeiro in 1737 and claimed 3,000 lives.[49] Possibly it was smallpox, which again afflicted Bahia in that year, paving the way for additional attacks by fevers and catarrhs the following year.[50] But the Luanda and Rio diseases were probably not the highly visible pox, since eighteenth-century observers were deeply afraid of the disease and usually quite explicit in identifying its disfiguring pustules. In this case witnesses failed to diagnose smallpox on either side of the Atlantic.

Infectious diseases on the American side of the Atlantic seem to have reached their eighteenth-century zenith during the 1740s. Once again, weather anomalies in Africa coincided with sickness among arriving slaves, who would seem to have spread the pox from the eastern shores of the ocean to the west. In French Canada there were three major smallpox epidemics, while others occurred in New York, Philadelphia, Maryland, and Virginia in 1745, 1747, and 1748 (Heagerty, 1928: 1: 73–74; Duffy, 1953: 84–85).[51]

The same decade saw catastrophic losses from several afflictions in Brazil from São Paulo to the Amazon, though more intensively in the north than in the south. Three separate smallpox epidemics struck São Paulo in the 1740s, and in 1745 a Jesuit estate manager reported from Bahia that measles, introduced by slave ships from the Mina Coast, infested the entire central and northeastern coastal area of Brazil, especially Bahia.[52] Even more grievously affected was the State of Maranhão. In August 1743 Belém do Pará was visited by its first serious outbreak of smallpox reported in two decades. On its heels came debilitating secondary infections of catarrhs, pleurisy, and bloody flux. Then in 1749, just as those maladies seem to have run their course, the cities of Belém and São Luis and the vast Amazonian interior were hit by a lethal epidemic of measles. By 1750 confirmed deaths in the captaincy of Pará alone reached over 18,000, but officials predicted that total losses would exceed 40,000.[53] During most of the 1750s "waves" of smallpox continued to wash over Maranhão and, according to other reports, over the entirety of Brazil (Rocha, c. 1954: 53).

The intercontinental scale and unprecedented virulence of these epidemics corresponded to the similarly severe and prolonged great West African drought of 1738–1756 (Curtin, 1975: 1: 110). The calamity there attained proportions sufficient to infect the entire Western Hemisphere, and in Brazil, particularly the northerly regions of Maranhão and Pará that were taking slaves from Bissau and Cacheu. The middle decades of the eighteenth century saw widespread drought, hunger, and diseases among both Africans and Europeans in West Africa. Supposedly, half the population of the Niger River valley perished in this prolonged arid episode (Curtin, 1975: 2: 5). Food supplies ran short along the Gold Coast in 1743 and again in the early 1750s (Johnson, c. 1974: 4). The drought-prone Cape Verde Islands, always a sensitive barometer of climate on the adjacent West African mainland, experienced serious famine in the late 1740s and again in 1754 (Freeman et al., 1978: table 2.1; Moran, 1982: table 1; Carreira, 1966: 38, citing Senna Barcelos, n.d.: 904). At the French post near the mouth of the Sénégal River, slaves died of malnutrition in 1751–1752 (Curtin, 1975: 2: 4; Donnan, 1930–1935: 4: 321). Finally, yellow fever outbreaks hit that and other European settlements in Upper Guinea throughout the 1750s (Curtin, 1975: 2: 5). Probably more than coincidentally, imports of West African slaves to the North American ports, where smallpox appeared in the 1740s, had risen to significant levels for the first time in the late 1730s (Coughtry, 1981: 35).[54]

COMPANY TRADE AND SMALLPOX

Smallpox remained the principal scourge of Brazil during the second half of the eighteenth century. By our count Brazil suffered nine significant epidemics during those fifty years, compared with ten for Peru. But, whereas smallpox seems to have figured prominently in only two of the Peruvian epidemics, it remained the principal killer in all of the Brazilian contagions (Polo, 1913: 80–84).[55]

The administration and patterns of slaving to Brazil changed to feature two monopoly trading companies, the Pará Company (i.e., the Companhia Geral do Grão Pará e Maranhão, or the CGGPM) and the Pernambuco Company (or the Companhia Geral de Pernambuco e Paraíba, the CGPP)[56] chartered to support agricultural development in northeastern and northern Brazil. Their records allow detailed analysis of the interaction between drought and disease in Africa and epidemic smallpox in America.

After some years of generally sufficient rains in central Africa before about 1754 (although Bahia had reported the arrival of an Angolan ship with smallpox aboard in 1750 [J. C. Miller, 1982: 49; Goodyear, 1981: 5]), an otherwise unidentified but particularly deadly disease swept away Luandans in 1755. It was probably a southerly prolongation of the contemporaneous West African yellow fever outbreak, carried there aboard Portuguese ships, but it was preceded by indications of food scarcities in 1753 (AHU/PA/Angola cx. 27, maço 18 [D.O.]; Venâncio, 1983: 90–91). The later 1750s in Angola seem to have become intermittently droughty, with widespread aches and stiffness but few deaths reported around Luanda in 1757 (AHU/PA/Angola cx. 27).[57] The first CGGPM ship sailed from Luanda to Maranhão in 1756. Food shortages became critical toward the end of the 1758 dry season, when people were starving in Luanda and Africans were assaulting the trade routes throughout the interior of the colony (J. C. Miller, 1982: 49; Brásio, 1979: 212, 213). Smallpox was reported from a company slaver bound from Luanda to Pernambuco in 1759 (Carreira, 1968–1969: 349; BNL, cód. 617).

Northern Brazil, until 1774 the State of Maranhão, became a major theater of smallpox infection after mid-century with intensified company deliveries of slaves at São Luis and Belém from both Upper Guinea and Angola after 1756, the year of a smallpox epidemic in nearby Pará and a year with smallpox probable in West Africa.[58] It would be surprising if the recurrent outbreaks of smallpox in the state were unrelated to the slave trade, since the slave ships frequently brought diseased chattel to those northern ports.[59] During the winter months (June through August) of 1756, Belém was beset by "a terrible epidemic of catarrhs," which had not fully abated before the city was afflicted by a smallpox outbreak, which typically sickened Indians and second-generation Portuguese (*filhos da terra*).[60] Three years later the contagion reached the Xingu River, where Indians living near the town of Portel became its chief victims.[61] During the following decade the neighboring state of Maranhão experienced a series of calamities. First, smallpox resurged in 1762–1763 (Alencastro, 1981: 46, fn. 112);[62] drought followed in 1763 (AHU/PA/Maranhão cxs. 40, 41; E. de S. Campos, 1956: 145); pox broke out in 1766 and 1767; and finally a second drought recurred in 1769.

The eastern littoral also suffered intermittent contagion between the late 1760s and the early 1780s. Smallpox, along with jaundice and leprosy, raged in São Paulo in 1768 (Marcilio, 1968: 166). Eleven years later smallpox caused hundreds of persons to be admitted to Salvador's two hospitals, where most of them died (Accioli, 1930–1940: 5: 513–514). Outbreaks also occurred in

Pernambuco and adjoining Rio Grande do Norte sometime just after 1774 (Duarte, 1956: 71; Andrade, 1956: 13; Rocha, c. 1954: 55). In 1780 São Paulo experienced another smallpox outbreak, while Pernambuco apparently suffered a series of eruptions of the pox between 1774 and 1787 (Andrade, 1956: 13; E. de S. Campos, 1956: 146).

The great West African drought had relented during the 1760s,[63] but in that same decade the familiar lethal combination of dryness and disease recurred twice again in Angola. In this case the company records show reduced slave prices in Angola, increased purchases, and higher slave mortality at sea coinciding during years when government officials at Luanda or Benguela reported drought, famine, and epidemic. Although the companies' shareholders and directors in Lisbon resisted the trading losses implicit in their agents' apparent strategy of buying up diseased and starving Africans for sale in Brazil, the unreliable and self-interested local administrators in Africa seem nonetheless to have minimized their acquisition costs just that cynically[64] and thus to have dispatched to the New World large numbers of pathogen-bearing slaves.

Company agents at Luanda paid relatively low prices for the apparently sick slaves they sent to Pará in 1762 and 1763, which were bad years for sickness at Luanda,[65] but the connection of these Angolan practices to the smallpox outbreaks of the 1760s and 1770s in Brazil is less clear. Smallpox reappeared in those years only in Maranhão. However, Pará Company ships from Cacheu and Bissau recorded deaths from smallpox among slaves from West Africa throughout these years (Mettas, 1975: 357; cf. M. Nunes Dias, 1971: 389–390). Even though the destinations of the company ships from Luanda do not match the Brazilian captaincies in which epidemics broke out in these cases, the close coincidences in timing hint at possible other, unrecorded connections between West African infections and smallpox in Brazil.

Angola experienced another siege of drought and epidemic smallpox between 1765 and 1767,[66] with the result reflected in the records of the chartered companies, and perhaps indirectly again in Brazil. The Pará Company agents paid lower prices for the slaves they embarked in 1765 and 1766, at the beginning of the drought, and their superiors in Lisbon bore the costs of their recklessness with "epidemic" smallpox aboard one of the ships sent in 1765 (Carreira, 1968–1969: 375). The 1766–1767 outbreaks in Maranhão may have been a further cost borne in Brazil. The Pará Company directors then shifted away from the disastrous mismanagement of the Luanda administrators and bought West African slaves, making no further shipments from Angola in the late 1760s. However, its chartered sister firm, the Pernambuco Company, which lacked the CGGPM's alternative sources in Upper Guinea, continued to buy in central Africa. It realized reduced costs of slave acquisition there in 1767, 1768, and 1769, apparently buying weak and afflicted survivors of the Angolan drought, who must have flooded Luanda in those years (Carreira, 1968–1969: 99). These indications of suffering in Angola coincided with the 1768 outbreak of smallpox in São Paulo, not carried there by Pernambuco Company slaves, of course, most of whom went to northwestern Brazil, but perhaps transmitted by other captives from Luanda and Benguela then being sent aboard private ships to central and southern Brazil.

The northern Brazilian smallpox outbreaks of 1774 and after may have sprung in part from slaves introduced via Pará Company ships then loading mostly in Upper Guinea, where droughts occurred from 1773 to 1776.[67] Pará Company directors seem to have shifted their buying back to Angola between 1775 and 1778, apparently to avoid the fatal consequences of the drought of those years in West Africa (Mettas, 1975: 357).

In Angola, Pernambuco Company agents similarly paid higher prices in the moist and relatively healthy early 1770s but lowered their slave acquisition costs in the following years, when drought there again seemed to correlate with disease in America. A brief price dip in 1776 is unexplained in the African data but coincided with the major Brazilian smallpox eruptions in Belém, in which more than a thousand persons, "principally Indians and slaves," died (AHU/PA/Pará cx. 37) in Pernambuco and in Rio Grande do Norte. Pernambuco Company acquisition costs in Angola then rose to their all-time peaks in the climatically uneventful later years of that decade. Slave prices at Benguela dropped again with particular abruptness in 1781, the same year in which that southern Angolan port reported food shortages and high mortality among its slaves (AHMF/CGPP, livro 126), but this indication of distress seems too late to account for the 1779–1780 epidemics of smallpox in Bahia and São Paulo (AHU/PA/Angola cxs. 39, 40). After a failed harvest near Luanda in 1782–1783,[68] Pernambuco Company agents purchased slaves at less than two-thirds of previous high levels. Though not perfectly correlated, rising company purchases of slaves in Africa, lowered slave prices there, Angolan droughts, and smallpox in the Americas produce a suggestively grim composite linking weather, slave mortality, disease on two continents, and the economic and political tribulations of the chartered Pombaline companies between 1755 and 1785.

THE LATE EIGHTEENTH-CENTURY PANDEMIC

Brazil's third major pandemic of smallpox began in the late 1780s and continued almost uninterrupted into the first years of systematic inoculation and vaccination there after the turn of the nineteenth century. It may have approached those of the 1560s and the 1660s in ferocity and formed part of a continent-wide flare-up of the virus, imported through infected Angolan slaves sold by Africans hoping to survive the longest and most severe central African drought since the persistent failures of the rains from the 1570s through the 1620s. Short droughts began at both Benguela and Luanda in the early 1780s and became generalized and continuous after a fleeting interlude of abundant rains near Luanda during the 1784–1785 rainy season. Famine and smallpox spread in 1786, as banditry began to disrupt the slaving trails of the interior (AHU/PA/Angola cx. 40). Typically, for a period of distress among African populations, slave prices fell, yet quantities of captives offered for sale remained high (cf. note 65). By 1787 food shortages forced the Luanda governor to resort to the extraordinary emergency measure of requesting provisions from the island of São Tomé, long a refreshment station for slavers of all nations dropping down off the Guinea Coast of West Africa on their way to Brazil or the Caribbean (AHU/PA/Angola cx. 40). A slave ship headed for Pernambuco acknowledged the pox on board in 1787 (AHMF/CGPP, livro 125).

From 1789 through 1794 relentless drought and disease threw Angola into near chaos from the mouth of the Zaire River to the southern deserts and far into the interior. The widespread unrest provoked military authorities in Luanda to send an army out to clear the bandit-infested roads in 1793, but the troops themselves fell victims to the epidemics sweeping the country (J. C. Miller, 1982: 52–53).[69] Swarms of locusts, not reported from Angola since the decades following the great droughts of the early seventeenth century, fell on Luanda and consumed growing plants down to their roots. Ironically, a similar—perhaps part of the same—swarm saved the Portuguese army in the field from starvation in 1793, since the largely African soldiers survived by eating the insects (AHU/PA/Angola cx. 42; Corrêa, 1937: 2: 228–229). Packs of dogs, driven to savagery by the famine, roamed the city, and rodents scuttled everywhere. Lions and other large wild cats became a serious threat to people. Starving refugees from the interior flocked into Luanda, and 63 of the 90 patients at the town's Santa Casa de Misericórdia were suffering from starvation by 1798 (Venâncio, 1983: 255, fn. 51). The governor had fruitlessly begged his colleagues in Brazil and São Tomé to dispatch emergency relief for the Angolan port, pleading once again that "the pox . . . this year have been extremely cruel throughout this continent" (AHU/PA/Angola cx. 43).[70]

The Angolan governor's words almost exactly anticipated those of Dom Rodrigo de Sousa Coutinho, Portuguese minister of the marine, who looked back in 1799 over the similarly trying 1790s in Brazil and lamented to his father (the renowned former governor of Angola who had overseen the African colony during its serious drought of 1765–1767), "the great damage that the pox have been causing, and continue to cause, all over Brazil . . ." (BAPP, cód. 685).[71] These two illustrious servants of the Portuguese crown, father and son, must have understood the transatlantic disease connection, though without making explicit reference to it. The smallpox that had appeared in 1786 at Luanda and had made its way aboard a slaver to Pernambuco in 1787 had assumed epidemic form in Maranhão in 1788, as the drought intensified in central Africa. Jamaica reported smallpox in 1785, a cargo of infected slaves spread the disease in Louisiana in 1787 (Sheridan, 1985: 118–119, 256, 264, 266–267), and other epidemics of unknown provenience hit New Granada in 1788–1789 (Chandler, 1981: 122–123). Smallpox was mentioned also in 1789 at Buenos Aires, the landing spot for numerous Angolan slaves smuggled through Rio de Janeiro and other ports in southern Brazil to Spanish territories upstream from the Río de la Plata estuary (Socolow, 1978: 140). "Febres miasmáticas," not necessarily smallpox but also not impossibly the same virus, since some medical opinion of the time viewed the disease as a type of tropical fever (Azeredo, 1799: 22), appeared in Ceará in the Brazilian north in 1791, and from 1793 onward epidemics of smallpox, exacerbated by American droughts (Bauss, 1977: 60; Brown, 1985), struck everywhere in South America, "incessantly" in Pará, and from Buenos Aires to São Luis do Maranhão by 1799.[72] This pandemic, after final flare-ups in Maranhão and in Piauí, and possibly in New Granada in 1801–1802 (E. de S. Campos, 1956; Chandler, 1981: 122), seems to have subsided in the first decade of the nineteenth century.

Mortality statistics aboard the slave ships leaving Angola for Rio de Janeiro during that decade and the following unequivocally establish the tides of death that overwhelmed pox-ridden slaves as they bore the infecting African viruses to Brazil. The epidemics reported around 1793–1795 in Pará, then linked directly to Angola by slaving ships, arose from pathogens originating at Luanda, wracked by the epidemic peaking in 1793.[73] The records of slave mortality at sea, though beginning only in 1795, suggest a peak in 1795 or just before (J. C. Miller, 1975: 57). Losses at sea quadrupled from background levels of 3% to 5% on the crossing to Rio to around 14% in both 1796 and 1797 to spark the Brazilian epidemics of the later 1790s. The 1799–1802 American outbreaks have no immediate sources in soaring middle-passage slave mortality from Benguela or Luanda, but the famished slave populations that had poured into Brazil during the preceding decade could have spontaneously generated further American recurrences, particularly when the New World droughts of those years extended their sufferings.

The African sources of these contagions, while primarily Angolan, may also have included malnourished and diseased West African slaves. The 1780s had seen a remarkable number of wet years in West Africa (Nicholson, 1980b: 188–189), and so the 1787 report of smallpox at Porto-Novo on the Lower Guinea coast might have referred to sickness imported from Angola, perhaps via Bahian slavers working their preferred Mina sources of labor (Verger, 1968: 215–216).[74] However, by 1790 the Cape Verdes once again suffered from lack of rainfall, and after 1795 the long-term deterioration in the moisture regime of West Africa began to reassert itself. North American slavers along the Gold

Coast reported both measles and smallpox there in 1795 (Wax, 1968: 482ff), and an Asante army there abandoned an 1807 campaign because of smallpox and dysentery in its ranks (Fynn, 1971: 143).

THE EARLY NINETEENTH CENTURY: VACCINATION

If the pace of Brazilian epidemics slackened after 1802, it was not because the virulence of the central African sources of pathogens declined in those years.[75] In the first three decades of the nineteenth century, epidemics were reported all over Angola in nearly every year. Sources implied smallpox in 1805, 1819, and 1825 and specified it in 1811, 1814–1816, 1822, and 1826. Deaths reported aboard the slave ships heading for Rio de Janeiro reached what must have been their apogee, nearly 20% losses for three straight years from 1806 to 1808, and regularly returned to the 10% to 15% range throughout the 1810s and 1820s. Middle passage mortality among Benguela slaves rose back to about 10% from 1806 to 1810 and again crossed the 10% threshold intermittently throughout the 1820s (J. C. Miller, 1975: 157–158). The general picture in Angola during those years was one of irregular resumptions of drought, atmospheric aftershocks of the extreme aridity of the 1780s and 1790s, that sustained continuing sickness among the debilitated survivors in the ports and their hinterlands and at sea (J. C. Miller, 1982: 55–59).

On the other hand, the influence of West African climate and diseases on the history of smallpox in Brazil may have lessened after 1811 or so, as the efforts of British antislavery patrols began to hinder slaving north of the equator.[76] However, significant numbers of slaves from Lower Guinea continued to reach Bahia and other parts of northern Brazil. The deterioration of West African rains that had set in during the 1790s continued into the nineteenth century, with two more years of hunger in the Cape Verde Islands in 1803–1804, drought from 1810 to 1814, and again in 1825 (Freeman et al., 1978: table 2.1; Moran, 1982: table 1).[77] Poor rainfall and famine hit extensive regions along the lower Sénégal River in 1812 (Curtin, 1975: 2: 4). A report possibly indicating dearth came from the Gold Coast in 1816, and crops surely failed there in 1824 (Johnson, c. 1974: 4–5).[78] Southeastern Africa entered the picture as a substantial source of Brazil's slaves at the end of the eighteenth century, probably more than coincidentally beginning with failures of the rains there from 1791 to 1796 and again from 1799 to 1803 and continuing through a series of early nineteenth-century droughts that parched the Zambezi valley and adjoining source regions for slaves boarded at Mozambique Island, Quelimane, and Inhambane (Liesegang, 1982; Nicholson, 1980a: 104, 111, 119; Hall, 1977: 16–17). After the British antislavery patrols began to drive Brazilian slavers off West African shores in the 1810s, Rio suppliers of labor to southern Brazil in particular began to develop sources in southeastern Africa, importing increasing numbers of captives from there down through the 1820s. The generally undependable weather of that entire period culminated in an extended drought from 1822 to 1832 (Isaacman, 1972: 450–451, 458–459; Isaacman and Isaacman, 1977: 115–117; Vail and White, 1980: 28).[79] Wars, violence, and famine in the Zambezi valley once again coincided with rising quantities of captives sent to Brazil.[80]

Systematic inoculation and vaccination finally broke the lethal connection between continuing drought-provoked smallpox in Africa and Brazilian epidemics beginning in 1803. The alacrity with which European governments, including that of Portugal, adopted the so-called Jenner method at the turn of the nineteenth century was remarkable, and their actions apparently insulated Brazil from African smallpox almost at once. In Brazil acute consciousness of the dangers of smallpox aboard African slave ships had previously prompted municipal councils and other authorities to impose quarantines intended to protect their vulnerable inhabitants from arriving cargoes of infected slaves (Goodyear, 1982; Santos Filho, 1977: 313–314). However, owners of the quarantined slaves had sometimes refused to accept the financial losses they stood to incur from public health measures that effectively assigned to them the costs of holding the suffering and dying slaves—often the only ones they could buy in Africa. Rather they preferred to spread the losses, along with the pox, among their customers and the Indians and the slaves already settled in Brazil. Hence, quarantines had seldom successfully contained the African contagion entering Brazil via the trade in slaves, as the frequency of smallpox in colonial Brazil demonstrated so gruesomely.[81]

Variolation, an earlier method of combating smallpox by inoculating potential victims with live virus obtained from human lesions, had been extensively adopted in eighteenth-century Europe and even in New England but was long opposed by Portuguese medical authorities. The Chinese have been credited with developing the procedure in the eleventh century. It was introduced to New England by African slaves about 1706 (Herbert, 1975: 539–540) and to England from Turkish sources after 1713 (Dixon, 1962: 117–121).

Inoculation had been used on West Indian slaves since the 1720s and 1730s, where, supplemented by quarantine measures after 1732 in Jamaica, it reduced the incidence of smallpox until the massive epidemics of the 1780s overwhelmed its limited efficacy (Stewart, 1985; Sheridan, 1985; 118–119, 367, fn. 16). Sporadic early efforts to inoculate slaves at sea became general and effective by the end of the eighteenth century. The Court of Assistants of the Royal African Company in 1721–1722 expressed its interest in inoculation, which "would be of great advantage to Us, could it be put in practise by saving the lives of great Numbers of Slaves . . ." (Stewart, 1985: 65). Their effort came to no known effect, but the practice evidently became more widely applied in the late 1760s and early 1770s. It was reported aboard an unidentified ship (presumably English) making for Charleston in 1769 (Donnan, 1928: 819), and a French ship in the Indian Ocean made use of it in 1770 (Herbert, 1975: 546–547), though it may not have been entirely "standard . . . by the second half of the eighteenth century" among both the French and British (Klein and Engerman, 1975: 271, citing a source from 1790; Klein, 1978: 202, 229). Thomas Winterbottom, physician to the colony of Sierra Leone at the turn of the nineteenth century, confirmed that by then "Inoculation has been frequently practised to a considerable extent on board of slave vessels, and though no instance has fallen under my observation, it has always proved successful" (1969: 2: 136). John Duffy found that the "extent and virulence" of smallpox diminished sharply in England's North American colonies after the 1760s, attributing the reduction in the incidence of smallpox in the English settlements largely to widespread adoption of variolation (1953: 105).

No comparable later eighteenth-century decline occurred in Brazil, since the technique was attempted only rarely there. In 1728 or 1729 a Carmelite missionary in the lower Amazon had been perhaps the first person in Latin America to experiment with variolation. His experiments, conducted only a few years after inoculation began to receive widespread publicity in England and New England, were emulated by other Carmelite fathers but without reported success (Sweet, 1974: 88–89; Condamine, 1747: 92–93). Jesuit fathers in Pará, on the other hand, achieved considerable local success with inoculation in the early 1740s (Araujo, 1972).

In spite of later improvements in the technique (Razzell, 1977a), as late as 1761 a standard Portuguese medical text advised against its use, and the author noted that it was rarely employed in Portugal (Saldanha, 1761: 1: 351ff).[82] By the 1790s, however, both the crown and its agents overseas became increasingly interested in the prophylactic possibilities of variolation. Their interest may have been sparked by Pernambucan-born Francisco Arruda Camara, who graduated from the French medical school at Montpellier in 1790 after writing a thesis on smallpox inoculation (Araujo, 1972). A few years later the government, confronted by alarming reports of renewed Brazilian outbreaks of the pox, founded a special hospital in Lisbon to treat its victims.

Interest in variolation also rose in Brazil in the 1790s, especially in the afflicted far north. In 1798 Diogo de Sousa, governor of Maranhão, undertook a program to promote inoculation and enjoyed some success among whites and blacks but less among Indians (E. de S. Campos, 1956: 147–149; BNRJ, 2: 34, 15, 32).[83] That year also the governor of neighboring and smallpox-ridden Pará received instructions from the crown to offer inoculation at state expense to all persons in Belém willing to receive it (A. Vianna, 1975: 45–46, fn. 12). At the same time, in the south at Rio de Janeiro, a military surgeon, Francisco Mendes Ribeiro de Vasconcellos, won public acclaim for his efforts to variolate against the "smallpox . . . [that had] alarmed sugar planters and other agriculturalists at seeing their slaves die" (Piragibe, 1881). By a general circular of 9 July 1799, the crown directed all colonial governors to undertake inoculation programs, especially among young black and Indian children, "since experience has shown this to be the only effective defense (*preservativo*) against the scourge . . . which has caused such considerable devastation in the Portuguese colonies" (Botelho, 1927: 203; E. de S. Campos, 1956: 148, 152, 156).

That circular was issued one year after Dr. Edward Jenner, an

English physician, privately published a pamphlet based upon his experience with cowpox inoculations. Jenner demonstrated that a long-standing country folk belief was correct: persons inoculated with cowpox became immune to smallpox. Jenner's vaccination technique proved to be a vast improvement over traditional remedies that included special prayers to Christian and non-Christian deities, bloodletting, the drinking of horse-manure tea, the imbibing of tar water, the burning of tar in public places, quarantine, and more risky methods of variolation.[84]

It is unlikely that the inoculation program announced by the Portuguese crown in 1799 involved the use of cowpox; it is more probable that the then traditional variolation method was intended. However, it is known that vials of Jenner's cowpox lymph were sent from London to the University of Coimbra and to Lisbon the same year, and the following year the crown advised overseas authorities of the existence of the new preventive procedure. Two years later copies of an account of the Jenner method by Manoel Joaquim Henriques de Paiva, a popularizer of current medical knowledge, were sent to Brazil (Araujo, 1972: 26; Paiva, 1806).[85]

If Carlos da Silva Araujo is correct, the Jenner vaccine first arrived in Brazil in 1804 (1972: 25). In May of that year Portugal's prince regent directed the surgeon-general of the kingdom, Brazilian-born, Paris-trained José Correa Picanço, to vaccinate two royal princes, Pedro (destined to become Brazil's first emperor) and Miguel (Araujo, 1972: 22). At the same time a wealthy Brazilian landowner, Francisco Caldeira Brant (1772–1841), the future Marquis of Barbacena, sent seven of his slaves to Lisbon to be vaccinated and returned to provide fresh human reservoirs of the protective lymph. The slaves were vaccinated by the chief surgeon of the royal fleet, who demonstrated the so-called arm-to-arm procedure to an accompanying Brazilian physician. Upon their return the vaccinated slaves were met at the dockside of Salvador by the marquis, whose young son became the first person in Bahia to be inoculated on 31 December 1804, an experience that he obviously survived, since he died in 1906 at the remarkable age of 104 (BNRJ, 1: 31, 30, 49; Costa, 1970: 145; Araujo, 1972: 26).

News of the Jenner method spread rapidly along the Brazilian littoral. It was first tried in Rio de Janeiro and Pernambuco in

1804 and 1805. Enlightened administrators elsewhere, hearing of the apparent successes obtained by the new method, sent children to Bahia to obtain the life-saving lymph for the protection of their citizens and slaves (E. de S. Campos, 1956: 153–157; Andrade, 1956: 14; Sigaud, 1844: 182). In Bahia, backland communities also dispatched youths to Salvador to be vaccinated so that they might become future arm-to-arm donors.[86] In 1806 the crown distributed throughout the empire copies of a pamphlet prepared to reassure doubters about the effectiveness of vaccination. It was written by the surgeon-general of Portuguese India, who demonstrated the advantages of vaccination over other forms of prophylaxis.[87]

Very likely the same successes ensued in other parts of Brazil, even though not always with uniform effectiveness. The imported lymph was sometimes weak and failed to confer the intended immunity.[88] Some whites believed the Africans' black skin was too thick to penetrate (Rout, 1976: 155). Nonetheless, in Rio the staff of a Vaccine Commission (*Instituição Vacínica*) created on 4 April 1811 later claimed to have applied the technique to 102,719 people, perhaps a third of them slaves, going through the city of 50,000 to 100,000 residents between 1811 and 1835 (Sigaud, 1844: 540; ANRJ, cód. 368).[89] The Vaccine Commission clearly concentrated its efforts on the slave population of the city, applying 74% of its doses to black arms in a four-and-a-half-month period in 1811 in conformity with standing royal orders. The linguistic and cultural ignorance of the newly arrived slave patients, sometimes not yet even baptized, who flocked to its Wednesday and Sunday clinics at the Church of the Rosary provoked a complaint in 1822 from the commission's dedicated but frustrated personnel that they could not learn the names of their subjects and thus could not complete the records that bureaucratic regulations required them to maintain (Silva, 1975: 51–55).

The slaveowners of Rio were exquisitely sensitive to smallpox among their human chattel, and so slaves—and only secondarily free children—formed the main focus of the public vaccination program of the *Instituição Vacínica*. If around 500,000 slaves entered Rio in the twenty-four years between 1811 and 1835, the 102,719 vaccinations performed by the Vaccine Commission might have immunized as many as a sixth of the new Africans in this

public program alone.[90] Public officials at Santos, one of the major
entry points for slaves headed for São Paulo's expanding agricultural estates, established its own vaccination program for entering
Africans in 1822 (E. de S. Campos, 1956: 158). In 1826 a
British traveler confirmed that all slaves were vaccinated upon
their arrival at Rio (Karasch, 1987: 152–153; citing MacDouall,
1833: 20). John Mawe, the first English traveler to write his impressions of Brazil after the court's arrival (1808), appears to
have felt that vaccination measures in São Paulo were already
proving effective there (1812: 69).

Vaccination in Brazil, despite occasional public resistance,
medical and administrative ineptness, and failure to preserve the
potency of the delicate lymph, clearly dampened the effects of
imported smallpox. Although the smallpox-bearing ship *Sertório*
from Angola reached Maranhão in 1806, where Jennerian vaccine had been received in 1805, no ensuing epidemic was reported
(A. Vianna, 1975: 17).[91] Only six reported outbreaks of smallpox
occurred in Brazil between 1803 and 1831, the year when the
legal slave trade between Africa and Brazil came to an end and the
year that marks the conclusion of this survey. We have no details
concerning the severity of a reported epidemic in São Paulo in
1808, but it came during the period of extremely high mortality
aboard ships carrying Angolan slaves between 1806 and 1810 (Marcilio, 1968: 166, 201).[92]

There can be no question that the second was a major outbreak.
In 1819 the contagion reentered Belém, that oft-victimized city,
via a slave ship from Africa. Between April and September of
that year 2,200 persons—nearly a sixth of the city's inhabitants—
perished (A. Vianna, 1975: 46–50).[93] The third epidemic was
apparently a localized one in the northeastern province of Paraíba
in 1825 (AMAE, CC, Pernambouc, 3). Smallpox also appeared
in that year in Rio, and these widely separated outbreaks corresponded to reports of disease and famine in all three African
source regions for Brazil's slaves. The last two epidemics, apparently minor ones, occurred in Rio de Janeiro in 1828 and 1831
(Karasch, 1982: 7, 12).[94] Clearly, the disfiguring scourge of the
colonial period was on its way to extermination in Brazil as the
newly independent empire moved along many paths toward modern medicine and up-to-date public health policies (Sigaud, 1844:
110–111; Santos Filho, 1977: 316–321) and—though belatedly—

finally to termination of the illegal African slave trade after 1851.[95]

Reports of Angolan epidemics and repeated surges in deaths aboard slavers making their way from Africa to America revealed that efforts to contain smallpox through vaccination in Africa had not worked as effectively as they had in Brazil. In Luanda, Dom Fernando António Soares Noronha (1800–1806), the Angolan governor in office when royal vaccination instructions of 24 October 1802 and 26 April 1803 reached the African colony, had welcomed news of the promised salvation. Feelings no doubt ran high in the wake of the disastrous epidemics of the 1790s and even more so after a French ship in the vicinity had demonstrated the efficacy of the vaccine by limiting losses among its 250 slaves to a single death (AHU/PA/Angola cx. 54). Angolan government officials, anxious about opposition among suspicious townspeople and among practitioners of local medical techniques, had carefully avoided experiments with the new procedures among moribund patients in the Luanda military hospital, whom the colonial surgeon-general feared might discredit the vaccine by dying of other causes (AHU/PA/Angola cx. 54).

The difficulty of transporting the live viral matter from Europe through Brazil to Angola by the arm-to-arm method, however, delayed implementation of these hopeful good intentions for several years. As at Bahia in 1804, proponents of vaccination gathered groups of small boys young enough not to have acquired immunities during the recent spate of epidemics, sent them off to the nearest city with a supply of potent vaccine, had one infected, and then transferred the lymph from youth to youth as pustules formed around the sites of the successive vaccinations. Thus they were to travel until one of them reached Luanda with an active source of the lymph. Attempts to tap the transfer of the vaccine to Bahia failed first in 1806, on the fortieth day out to sea on the usual sixty-day voyage from Bahia to Benguela, with another four or five days beyond that to reach Luanda (AHU/PA/Angola cx. 57; Feo Cardoso, 1825: 365).

The arrival at Luanda in 1807 of a new governor, António de Saldanha da Gama, brother of the Bahian governor of the time, the Conde da Ponte, brought a renewed effort but one that also culminated in failure in 1809. The 1807 enterprise, initiated during a three-year siege of raging epidemics in 1806–1808, maintained the vaccine matter active in Indian boys until the fiftieth day at sea, but it once again failed to bring live vaccine to the people of Luanda.[96]

The Angolans made no further reported efforts to introduce vaccination in Africa during the turmoil that followed transfer of the Portuguese court from Lisbon to Rio de Janeiro after 1808, thus allowing the epidemics of the 1810s to rage unabated and provoking protests from Brazil, where public health measures were otherwise making headway against epidemic smallpox (Rebelo, 1970: 29–30). However, probably early in that decade prudent traders had begun vaccinating their slaves immediately upon debarkation in Brazil (Spix and Martius, 1938: 2: 153, fn. V), evidently to good effect in view of the records of the Rio Vaccine Commission and the decreasing incidence of smallpox outbreaks reported from other provinces through those years.

Public smallpox vaccination finally began in Luanda on 24 November 1819, this time to the same enthusiastic acclaim it had received eight years earlier in Rio. By January 1821 no less than 12,292 persons, including slaves, had received immunity in the town of 2,000 to 3,000 inhabitants (AHU/PA/Angola cxs. 66, 67; Rebelo, 1970: 30, 390). The Luanda authorities had succeeded in transmitting the vaccine to Benguela by August 1820 (AHU/PA/Angola cx. 66; Delgado, 1940: 76) and rejoiced at the year's end at reports from Pernambuco that their efforts had already dramatically reduced mortality aboard ships entering Recife (AHU/PA/Angola cx. 66). Royal officials at Rio confirmed the "very sensible diminution" in middle passage mortality achieved that same year aboard ships reaching the southern Brazilian port (Rebelo, 1970: 403).

Methods of controlling smallpox at sea during those years must have applied late eighteenth-century improvements in the practice of inoculating from human sources once the infection had appeared on board, rather than extending true preventive vaccination with cowpox matter as at Luanda. It was difficult to preserve active lymph and virtually impossible to keep the matter available on the high seas or at the several remote outports north of Luanda then contributing larger and larger shares of the slaves sent from the Angolan coast to Brazil (J. C. Miller, forthcoming). Mortality figures for the 1820s from all Angolan ports fell to levels below those of the horrendous epidemics of 1795–1811. Although they still showed wavelike year-to-year fluctuations characteristic of African epidemics afflicting the slave cargoes on their way to the Americas, the generally reduced toll may have represented a significant achievement in view of the nearly continuous smallpox reported on the mainland and the high volume of slaves shipped in those years (J. C. Miller, 1975: 157–158). Nonetheless, the combination of vaccination at Luanda and Benguela, shipboard inoculation, and private and public antismallpox programs in American port cities, pursued with obvious relief by slavers able for the first time to limit epidemic mortality among their human property, sufficed to contain the continuing African epidemics in the middle passage and to dampen their impact on the New World.[97]

Mozambique slavers may also have used inoculation successfully to limit smallpox aboard the ships they sent to Brazil, twenty years earlier than vaccination reached Angola. One report had it that general inoculation had successfully suppressed an epidemic of smallpox in southeastern Africa early in 1796 (E. de S. Campos, 1956: 148–149).[98] Circumstances surrounding high fatalities aboard a slaver reaching Buenos Aires from southeastern Africa in May 1804 confirmed the effective employment of "vaccine" (in fact, probably inoculation from human sources) in Mozambique at the end of 1803. Gross neglect of provisioning the vessel in question had led to the deaths of 316 of the 376 slaves taken on board, but smallpox had not broken out under circumstances that elsewhere constituted ideal incubators of epidemic (Scheuss de Studer, 1958: 309–310). Later crude mortality levels aboard ships entering Rio from Mozambique and other southeastern African ports ran higher than contemporaneous figures from Angola, but these figures reflected longer voyage lengths and the difficulty of carrying provisions adequate for the long journey around the Cape of Good Hope. They may or may not have represented reductions from the earlier preinoculation period, for which no mortality data are available (J. C. Miller, 1976).

Illegalization of West African slaving after 1815, and the consequent virtual absence of subsequent public health supervision of this segment of Brazil's slave trade, left the continuing outflow of slaves from Lower Guinea subject only to such inoculation measures as furtive Portuguese evaders of the British West Africa Squadron might find time to administer to their captives. We know of no data on this question for the years from 1808 to 1830, although African inoculation techniques—never before of much effectiveness, to judge from the lurid epidemiological history of the slave trade from West Africa—probably remained in effect in selected localities. By the 1840s, however, smallpox seems no longer to have contributed significantly to the complex mortality equation of the illegal trade of that decade (Eltis, 1983: 276).

The effectiveness of the inoculation and vaccination measures employed in the last two decades of the legal slave trade received explicit acknowledgment from Brazil's most sophisticated physician in the 1830s, Dr. Joseph François Xavier Sigaud. Sigaud, looking back on what he regarded as the virtual absence of smallpox from Rio de Janeiro for five full years from 1829 to 1834 (cf. Karasch, 1987: 152), attributed the city's relief to the effectiveness of these practices, but he went on to lament the reappearance of the disease among raw African youths in the city in 1834. It was clear to Sigaud that suppression of legal slaving in 1830–1831 had temporarily ended the importation of Africans, and also of the pathogens they bore in their bodies, but that the subsequent clandestine trade that arose by about 1834 had reintroduced the dreaded affliction through new illegal channels that escaped not only the watchful eyes of British abolitionists but also the anti-smallpox institutions that Brazilians had designed to police the earlier legal trade. With drought and smallpox reported again from all parts of Africa, the illegal slavers were failing to vaccinate the captives they brought from across the Atlantic, and the seemingly inexhaustible African storehouse of disease had once again dispatched the terrible pox to Brazil.

CONCLUSION

Early European records from or about Brazil were lavish in their praise of its beauty, economic potential, and salubrious ambience. Francisco Guerra, an able medical historian, has accurately summarized the glowing impressions conveyed by this literature to suggest that Brazil became a less healthy land after the arrival of the Europeans and Africans (Guerra, 1979: 472). We would not dispute that conclusion. Indeed, the evidence we have cited reinforces Guerra's argument. It is apparent that on many occasions contagious infections, especially smallpox, ravaged the land from end to end from the middle of the sixteenth century onward. Space limitations have not permitted us to discuss in detail the effects of measles, yellow fever and other fevers of many sorts, influenza, pleurisy, dysentery, and nutritional deficiencies of all types that, while present in Brazil, did not exhibit the frequency or virulence of epidemic smallpox outbreaks. Yet when these afflictions were in ascendancy and immediately preceded or followed epidemics of the malady discussed here, they contributed to the resulting loss of life.

We would contend that because of the prevalence of all these disorders, as well as of poor sanitation, malnutrition, and the brutalizing consequences of the Europeans' enslavement of Amerindians and Africans, the quality of life in Brazil during the centuries we have surveyed did deteriorate. But while the state of public health was abysmal everywhere at this time, it may have been less so in Brazil than in Europe or even in English colonial America. It is estimated that during the seventeenth century there was a four-year span between epidemics in Europe and that in the eighteenth century that interval decreased to only two years (G. Miller, 1957: 33, fn. 22, app. C). In the English mainland colonies of North America, Duffy found that between 1675 and 1775 smallpox was "absent . . . for as long as five years only on two occasions" (1953). In Greater London, where smallpox became endemic during the seventeenth century, 6.1% of all deaths between 1661 and 1700 were attributed to smallpox, a percentage that increased to 8.4% between 1721 and 1760.[99] In smaller English rural communities smallpox accounted for one out of four deaths during the eighteenth century (Duffy, 1953). During the same century it was blamed for the deaths of one out of four persons in Geneva above age five and in The Hague for 37% of those above that age who perished (Creighton, 1891–1894: 2: 623).

Although our evidence for Brazil is far less detailed than the quantitative data that can be derived from the famous mortality bills in England or from other European sources, and although the epidemiology of smallpox in the tropics differs from patterns of the disease in temperate latitudes, it is our impression that smallpox may have been less devastating in Brazil during the centuries we have surveyed. The best explanation of why the malady, though occasionally catastrophic, was less common in Brazil than elsewhere during those centuries may simply be that Brazil's population was more dispersed and its communities smaller than those of Europe or North America, for certainly it was the urban centers that were always primary dissemination points for contagious diseases.

As in English and French North America, Brazilian outbreaks of contagion began in the seaports and moved rapidly from there to the interior via trails and waterways. Though how smallpox reached the seaports in the first place is a difficult question to answer definitively, our comparison of African climate and epidemiological history with the parallel record from Brazil shows suggestive coincidences between drought and epidemics in Africa and smallpox outbreaks in South America. It thus confirms the general impressions of contemporary observers that slave traders often transported the unwanted smallpox virus to Brazil and adds a historical explanation of how African disease, fanned to epidemic proportions by the drought, malnutrition, and pervasive crowding, traveled along the path, through the barracoons, and across the middle passage.

The data marshaled here in support of the general argument do not trace the first outbreaks of American smallpox in the sixteenth-century Caribbean to African sources and fail to document the presence of the disease in Angola at the time the first pandemic swept through Brazil in the 1560s. Explicit reports of Angolan smallpox, beginning in the 1620s, correlate intermittently with the main outbreaks of the disease in seventeenth-century Brazil, and Brazilian and other sources for that century explicitly attributed epidemics to arriving slaves. The African sources of Brazilian epidemics become clearer early in the eighteenth century, and the widespread prevalence of the disease at the end of the century in Brazil seems clearly connected to the drought and sickness then ravaging central Africa. Reports of diseases from West Africa are generally tied less conclusively to epidemics in Brazil, perhaps owing in part to their incompleteness. The introduction of effective inoculation and vaccination programs in Brazil after 1803 effectively limited the unwanted cargoes of smallpox virus that slaving had carried from Africa to Brazil before that date, nearly a half century before the slave trade itself finally ended early in the 1850s. If one is willing to rely on the apparent general association of failed rains in the semiarid parts of the tropical world with epidemic outbreaks of smallpox, the far more plentiful data on droughts in both West Africa and the Angolan regions of central Africa might offer additional support for the hypothesized lethal connection, back to the first reported Brazilian epidemics in the 1560s.

The complexity of the epidemiology of smallpox, its relatively unknown behavior under tropical conditions, our inability to control for the possibility of shipboard infections of African slaves from European sources during the middle passage, and the uncertainties of scattered and incomplete data from two continents allow no more than the qualified—though suggestive—conclusion that African drought and smallpox were among the great variety of factors influencing the history of the disease in the lowland parts of the Americas receiving significant members of slaves in the centuries before 1800. The tendency for endemic African smallpox to take epidemic form in the aftermath of drought seems both theoretically likely and frequently documented, either directly by African sources or indirectly in the form of epidemics noted aboard the slave ships or in the Americas. The tendency of the virulence of the disease aboard the slave ships from the southwestern parts of the continent to rise and fall in synchrony with African droughts also seems reasonably clear in the 1620s, the 1760s, and 1795–1811, the periods for which data have been analyzed in a manner calculated to reveal the pattern. The timing, intensity, duration, and generality of smallpox outbreaks in Brazil give the impression of following the periods of African drought, and also of documented smallpox in Africa, more closely than sheer chance would allow. Although we have made almost no effort to evaluate numerous American conditions that also influenced the spread of epidemic smallpox in Brazil, the arrival of hundreds and thousands of infected slaves provides a plausible trigger for most of the outbreaks recorded there during the colonial period.

Appendix   Summary Chronology of Droughts and Epidemics in Africa and Brazil, c. 1550–c. 1840

Time line	West Africa	Angola	Mozambique	Brazil	Other American
1510					1518: Smallpox appeared first in Hispaniola, probably from Spain. 1518–1520: Transfer of smallpox from Caribbean to Mexican mainland.
1520					1520s: Smallpox epidemics in highland Mexico and Peru.
1530					
1540	1541–1542: Famine on Upper Guinea mainland. 1549: Drought in Cape Verde Islands.			1549: sick slaves (disease unknown) at Bahia.	1546: First smallpox epidemic in New Granada, via slaves from Santo Domingo.
1550		1558–1560: Hunger (?) and high mortality at São Tomé.			1558–1560: Smallpox at the Río de la Plata and elsewhere in Spanish South America.

1560		1561–1563: Drought and famine in interior.		1562–1565: Smallpox pandemic, Pernambuco to São Vicente.
1570		c. 1574–1588: Drought, continuing intermittently.		
1580	c. 1580–1582: Drought in Cape Verdes.	(Drought.) 1584: Sickness noted at Luanda.	1585: Smallpox in Ilhéus.	1581: Smallpox in Peru.
1590	1594: Drought in Cape Verdes.		1597: French vessel from Arguin (West Africa) introduced smallpox in Rio Grande do Norte.	
1600				
1610	1609 (to 1614?): Drought in Cape Verdes. 1617: Drought along the Niger Bend.	1614–1619: Serious drought.	1611: Smallpox at São Paulo (?). 1613: Smallpox at Pernambuco. 1616: Smallpox in the northeast, attributed to slaves from both West Africa and Angola.	

Appendix Summary Chronology of Droughts and Epidemics in Africa and Brazil, c. 1550–c. 1840 (continued)

Time line	West Africa	Angola	Mozambique	Brazil	Other American
1620	1620: Famine and sickness in Cape Verdes.	1625–1628: First recorded smallpox epidemic, also great drought. 1625: Extraordinarily high mortality on board slavers from Luanda.	c. 1620: Possibly a time of great drought.	1621–1623: Smallpox in the north and northeast. 1626: Ship carrying smallpox arrives in Bahia from Angola.	1621: Quarantine measures introduced at Buenos Aires. 1627: Smallpox at Anserma.
1630					1633–1634, 1636, 1639–1641: Epidemics at Panama.
1640	1639–1643: Major drought and famine. Smallpox aboard WIC ships from West Africa.	1639–1645: Drought, no report of sickness, but high shipboard mortality (1643–1644).		1641: Excessive rains and smallpox widespread in north, northeast. 1644: Smallpox in Maranhão.	
1650		1655: Unspecified sickness in Kongo. 1656: Drought and warfare at Benguela.		1655: Angolan slaves quarantined at Bahia.	

1660	1661: Severe but short drought on Gold Coast.	1660–1663: Famine and illness described as *inchação* (swelling).	1662: Smallpox in Pará and Maranhão. 1664–1666: Pandemic smallpox.	1663–1664: RAC ships reach Barbados with smallpox aboard; great mortality among slaves in St. Chistopher's and Nevis.
1670	1669–1670: Very dry years along Niger Bend. 1676: Drought in lower Senegal valley.			
1680	1680s: Major drought all over West Africa. 1682–1683: Famine at Accra. 1687: Famine at Ardra. 1688–1690: Drought and famine in Upper Guinea.	1680s: Famine, also drought(?). 1684–1685: Smallpox, with great loss of life.	1680–1684: Smallpox in Bahia. 1682: Smallpox in Pernambuco. (1685–c. 1692: Yellow fever in Pernambuco, Bahia, etc.). 1686: Angolan slaves with smallpox at Bahia.	1686: Quarantine at Martinique.
1690	c. 1690: Drought in Cape Verdes.	1691–1692: Localized(?) drought near mouth of Zaire River.	1690: Smallpox at Colónia do Sacramento. 1693: Smallpox at Rio de Janeiro.	1690s: Smallpox in Barbados and Jamaica. 1693: Smallpox in Bogotá.

Appendix Summary Chronology of Droughts and Epidemics in Africa and Brazil, c. 1550–c. 1840 (continued)

Time line	West Africa	Angola	Mozambique	Brazil	Other American
	1695: Famine along the Niger Bend. 1696: Possible famine on Gold Coast.			1695: Smallpox in Rio Grande do Sul and Maranhão.	1698: Quarantine measures introduced at Charleston.
1700	1704: Drought and famine along Niger Bend. 1705–1721: Prolonged drought in Cape Verdes.				1700–1702, 1704: Smallpox at New Granada. 1705: Smallpox aboard a ship reaching Buenos Aires. 1708: Smallpox aboard a ship arriving in Jamaica. Epidemics in Guayaquil.
1710	1710: Serious famine in lower Senegal valley. c. 1712–1713: Smallpox at Whydah (Slave Coast, lower Guinea). 1719: Drought at Cape Verdes.	1713–1720: Drought. 1715–1720: Smallpox.		(Drought in Bahia.) 1715–1718: Smallpox widespread in Brazil.	1713: Smallpox aboard RAC ship at Jamaica. 1715, 1717: Smallpox in mainland North American seaports. 1718–1720: Widespread reports of smallpox from southern Spanish colonies.

1720	1721–1723: Famine and drought from Senegal to Niger Bend. 1721–1722: Smallpox on ships from both Whydah and Sierra Leone. 1723: Smallpox in the Gambia.	1724–1727: Drought and smallpox.	1720: Smallpox in Pará (?). 1724: Smallpox in Pará and Maranhão. 1724: Also in São Paulo. 1726: Measles in Bahia and São Paulo. 1727: Smallpox at Santos.	Before 1727: First reports of inoculation in Jamaica (in response to epidemic?).
1730	1729–1732: Hunger and low rainfall along lower Senegal. 1736: Abundant slaves, then famine at James Fort (Gambia). 1738: Beginning of major drought (to 1756).	1734: Drought. 1735–1736: Famine. 1736: Epidemic (disease not specified).	1730–1732: Pandemic smallpox. 1737: Unspecified disease at Rio de Janeiro. 1737: Smallpox at Bahia.	1732: First quarantine at Jamaica. 1738: Smallpox raging at Charleston.
1740	1740s: Major drought continues.		1740s: Three outbreaks of smallpox at São Paulo and elsewhere.	1742–1744: Smallpox in Peru, Córdoba.

Appendix   Summary Chronology of Droughts and Epidemics in Africa and Brazil, c. 1550–c. 1840 (*continued*)

Time line	West Africa	Angola	Mozambique	Brazil	Other American
	1743: Food short along Gold Coast. 1746–1750: Serious famine in Cape Verdes.			1743: Smallpox at Pará. 1745: Measles in Bahia. 1749: Measles in north.	1745–1747: Smallpox in Chesapeake, Philadelphia, New York, and French Canada.
1750	1750s: Yellow fever in Upper Guinea. 1751–1755: Slaves dying of malnutrition at St. Louis (Senegal). 1754: Serious famine in Cape Verdes. 1755: Smallpox in Gambia.	Late 1750s: Intermittent droughtiness.	(Before 1759: widespread drought in Zambezia.)	1750s: Pandemic smallpox. 1756: Smallpox at Pará.	1756: Slaver imports smallpox to Antigua.
1760	1764: Minor drought in Cape Verdes.	1762: Smallpox. 1765–1767: General drought. Smallpox aboard ship leaving Luanda in July 1765.		1762–1763: Smallpox in Maranhão. 1766, 1767: Smallpox in Maranhão. 1768: Smallpox and other diseases in São Paulo.	1763–1764: Suriname epidemic attributed to imported slaves. 1767–1768: Major epidemic in Jamaica.

1770	1770–1771: Drought and famine at Timbuktu. 1773–1776: Serious drought in Cape Verdes. 1773: Smallpox in Sierra Leone. 1774: "Period of starvation" on Gold Coast.	1773 and after: Persistent drought, wars in the interior; burgeoning French slaving from Mozambique coast.		1774: Smallpox in Pernambuco and Rio Grande do Norte. 1776: Smallpox at Belém. 1779: Smallpox at Bahia. 1779: Smallpox at São Paulo.	1778: Smallpox in Louisiana. 1782–1783: Smallpox epidemics in New Granada. c. 1785: Smallpox epidemics in Jamaica (despite use of inoculation).	1773: Smallpox in Antigua.
1780	1786: Smallpox at Upper Guinea. 1787: Smallpox at Porto Novo (Slave Coast).	1781: Food shortages and high mortality at Benguela.	1786: Famine, smallpox. 1787: Extraordinary food shortages, smallpox.	1787: Smallpox at Pernambuco and Maranhão.	1787: Slaves import smallpox to Louisiana. 1788–1789: Epidemics in New Granada (?). 1789: Smallpox in Buenos Aires.	

Appendix Summary Chronology of Droughts and Epidemics in Africa and Brazil, c. 1550–c. 1840 (continued)

Time line	West Africa	Angola	Mozambique	Brazil	Other American
1790	1789–1791: Drought in Cape Verdes. 1790s: Generally dry in West Africa. c. 1790: Smallpox on River Sherbro (Upper Guinea). 1795: Measles and smallpox on the Gold Coast.	1789–1794: Extreme famine and disorder, repeated epidemics. 1793(?)–1794: High mortality aboard slave ships. 1796–1797: Second mortality peak on slavers.	1791–1796: Drought in the south. 1796: Smallpox aboard slave ship, suppressed by inoculation.	1791: "Febres miasmaticas" in Ceará. 1793–1799: Pandemic smallpox throughout Brazil.	
1800	1803–1804: Drought in Cape Verdes. 1804–1805: Drought in Sahara.	Recurrent epidemics. Smallpox implied in 1805 1806–1808: Mortality rises on slavers at sea.	1799–1803: Dry period in Nguniland (Natal).	1808: Smallpox in São Paulo.	1801–1802: Smallpox epidemics in New Granada, "less severe."
1810	1810: Drought in Cape Verdes. 1812: Drought and famine in lower Senegal. 1813–1814: Drought in Cape Verdes.	Smallpox further specified in 1811, 1814. Continuing episodes of drought.			

	1816: Possible dearth on Gold Coast.		1817: Drought and smallpox in Madagascar.	1819: Smallpox at Belém from a ship from Africa.
1820	1822–1823: Serious epidemics in Sahara. 1824: Crop failure on Gold Coast. 1825: Drought in Cape Verdes.	Continuing epidemics. Smallpox specified in 1822 and 1826, implied in 1825.	1822–1832: Widespread drought. 1824: Famine and wars at Delagoa Bay.	1825: Smallpox in Paraíba, Rio de Janeiro. 1828: Smallpox (minor?) at Rio de Janeiro.
1830–1840	c. 1828–1839: Severe drought, climaxing lengthy period of climate deterioration.	1830: Drought.	Drought continues. 1832–1836: Smallpox epidemics.	1831: Smallpox (minor?) at Rio de Janeiro. 1834–1836: Smallpox reappears at Rio de Janeiro.

NOTES

1 Recent broad surveys with an emphasis on demography begin with Curtin, 1969, and, beyond an extensive article and chapter literature taking up specific points raised by Curtin, include Klein, 1978, and Rawley, 1981. Reviews of the literature from fresh angles are Lovejoy, 1982, 1983.

2 See, for example, Crosby, 1972; Curtin, 1964 and 1968; and a great deal of more recent literature focused on slave health, demography, and medicine in specific parts of the Americas. Kiple and King, 1981, have usefully expanded the scope of the discussion to include nutrition, genetics, and ideological issues.

3 Also not an uncommon assertion among medical specialists in other slave-holding parts of the Americas: Chandler, 1981: 69ff; Ashburn, 1947: 28–29; Scott, 1939: 1: 5; Scott, 1943: 185. The Duke of Portland, governor of Jamaica, commented in 1725 "that freshly landed Negroes infected the inhabitants with their 'malignant fevers, small pox, and other dangerous distempers,' " as quoted in Chandler, 1981: 49. Also see Sheridan, 1985: 19.

4 See appendix 1 in Curtin, 1975: 2: 3–7. Nicholson has worked out the broad contours of the climate history of Africa in a series of publications and papers: 1974; 1976; 1979; 1980a; 1980b; 1981. Brooks, 1985, makes the point in general terms for West Africa, as does J. C. Miller, 1982, for southwestern Africa in this period. A broad and suggestive survey of eastern and southeastern Africa appears in Webster, 1979. Liesegang has refined dates for the nineteenth century there in 1978 and 1982. In general, for Africa the research on climate history has proceeded faster than reconstructions of the history of diseases. This study suffers from the relative incompleteness of the record of epidemics for both western and southeastern Africa.

5 For revisionist opinion, see African Historical Demography: II, 1982; J. C. Miller, 1984; and Brooks, 1985.

6 Limited applications of the neo-Malthusian approach to Africa appear in Curtin, 1975: 1: 19–22, and in Lovejoy and Baier, 1975. A regional application is in Matthews, 1976: 46–47. It underlies J. C. Miller, 1981. The great antiquity of food shortages and population pressures is argued in many papers in Williams and Faure (eds.), 1980. See also African Historical Demography: II. Evidence of drought-forced sales of children and other dependents as slaves recurs throughout the primary sources of Africa in the era of the slave trade; J. C. Miller, forthcoming. Cf. the Aztecs (Hassig, 1981: 173, 174); for Indian emigration to escape hard times, Engerman, 1983: 647–648. The Irish flight from famine in the 1840s is well known (and see Eltis, 1983).

7 For an illuminating discussion of the structure and identification of viruses, see Horne, 1963.

8 The literature on smallpox is voluminous. Standard is Dixon, 1962. Particularly valuable for its bibliography as well as its clinical discussion

is Benenson, 1982. Other helpful discussions are in Guslits, 1961; Cahill, 1964; Ackerknecht, 1965: 62ff; Baxby, 1981; and World Health Organization (WHO), 1980. Two classics should be mentioned also: Creighton, 1891–1894, and Ricketts and Byles, 1910, the latter of which is especially valuable for its abundance of vivid photographs of victims of smallpox and diseases mistaken for smallpox. The most recent study of early postconquest Andean epidemics is Cook, 1981.

9 Carmichael, 1983, in a nuanced discussion of the complex interactions of disease, parasites, nutrition, and sociology, notes the difficulty of documenting lethal smallpox in Europe before the 1570s.

10 Africans reaching northeast Brazil with smallpox, allegedly of Angolan origin, though possibly infected en route by European sailors, were reported a decade earlier in the mid-1610s; Brandão, 1966: 62. Africans in some regions also knew techniques of inoculation by at least the early seventeenth century; Herbert, 1975.

11 For an extension of this notion, axiomatic in studies of pastoralist transhumance, to agricultural populations in semiarid zones on longer time scales, see J. C. Miller, 1981. It is our admittedly lay impression that the epidemiology of smallpox in the tropics differs significantly from the course of the disease in temperate climates, and that much of the fine professional work done on post-vaccination smallpox in England and other nontropical parts of the world bears only limited relevance to the history of epidemics in precolonial Africa and colonial Brazil. See Rogers, 1926. For modern Africa, see Breman et al., 1977; Imperato et al., 1972; Dumbell and Huq, 1975.

For similar reasons, we do not generalize from recent literature on early modern Europe that attempts, sometimes too crudely, to separate epidemics from famine. See, for example, Appleby, 1973.

12 See Bathily, 1986: 276–277. Kiple and King, 1981: 8–11, generally for West Africa; Mendes, 1812: 20–24, for details in eighteenth-century Angola. Winterbottom, 1969: 2: 27, emphasized the "very scanty and wretched diet with which they [the slaves] are fed in the *path,* as they term the journey, and which, from the distance they are brought inland, often lasts for many weeks, at the same time that their strength is further reduced by the heavy loads they are obliged to carry." Also see Schotte, 1782: 89–91. Medical historians have long emphasized pre-embarkation hardships, e.g., Scott, 1943: 171; Hoeppli, 1969: 20.

13 See, for example, BPP, 1790: XXIX (698): 494, testimony of Captain William Sherwood on an incident aboard the brig *Joshua* in 1777.

14 Contemporary observers of the slave trade usually emphasized dysentery as the most striking symptom of the complex causes of slave deaths at sea, and Eltis informs us in a personal communication based on forthcoming work that aggregate slave mortality did indeed rise significantly during the African rainy seasons when dysentery (but also, it should be noted, fevers of several sorts) flourished on the mainland. The evidence on dysentery is not incompatible with our stress on smallpox that varied in intensity over the longer term, rather than seasonally,

and that in its virulent forms, according to medical sources, also produced dysenterylike symptoms. See Creighton, 1891–1894: 1: 627; also Carmichael, 1983.

15 Smith, 1974: 6, cites the early chroniclers, records the doubts of some historians about this story, and alludes to the possibility of an earlier mainland introduction of smallpox from Cuba in 1518.

16 For the preliminary infections of 1558–1559, see Cabral, 1931: 207, 258, anon. Jesuit to (Jesuits in Portugal), Espirito Santo, c. 1559, and Rui Pereira, S.J., to same, Bahia, 15 Sept. 1560, the former of which notes the deaths of 600 slaves, "huns com prioris a outros com camaras do sangue."

17 Freitas, 1935: 25, accepts this as the first epidemic identified specifically as smallpox but dates it erroneously to 1565.

18 The only contemporary reports of Brazil's first pandemic come from the Jesuits, for it was strangely ignored by secular chroniclers such as Pero Magalhães de Gandavo and Gabriel Soares de Sousa. The key accounts are Leonardo do Vale, S.J., Bahia, to P. Gonçalo Vaz de Melo, 12 May 1563; José de Anchieta to P. Diego Lianes, São Vicente, 8 Jan. 1655, and P. Pedro da Costa to the fathers in Lisbon, Espírito Santo, 27 July 1565. The first and third are in Leite (ed.), 1956–1968: 4: 9–22 and 178–181, while the second and fourth are in Cabral (ed.), 1931: 458, 462. See, too, José de Anchieta, "Informação dos primeiros aldeiamentos da Baia" (c. 1587), in Machado (ed.), 1933: 359, and Vasconcelos, 1977: 2: bk. 3: paras. 38–39. For modern interpretations, see J. M. da Fonseca, 1946: 83–94, and Leite, 1938–1950: 2: 575. Previous historians to note these epidemics include Sigaud, 1844: 108–109; Rocha, 1954: 18; Andrade, 1956: 13; Duarte, 1956: 69–70; Santos Filho, 1966: 45. Other general lists of epidemics in Brazil, mostly less complete, include E. de S. Campos, 1956: 138–160, Lima, 1949: 5: 253–268; A. Vianna, 1975, 35–54.

19 Schwartz, 1978: 72–76, dates the first formal request for African labor to 1558, though he emphasizes that the numbers of African slaves remained small until around 1600. For Maranhão, see Alden, 1983. Nonetheless, Africans were clearly present and had already been blamed for at least one epidemic. Rout, 1976: 134, cites shipments in 1538 and 1545 and petitions requesting shipments in 1539 and 1549. Freitas, 1935: 22–24, mentions an unidentified epidemic at Bahia in 1549, reportedly breaking out among slaves being disembarked: "foi acabar de baptisar-se a primeira centena que descer sobre ella tal fogo de doença que parece peste." In 1552 a "peste terrivel de tosse e catarrho mortal" befell the town. Sickness was also reported from São Vicente in 1554.

20 Epidemics also spread through western South America in 1558 and 1562; Chandler, 1981: 121ff. For São Tomé, Garfield, 1971.

21 Personal communication from Professor Stuart Schwartz, whose information is based upon a Jesuit account from Ilhéus.

22 This was not the only military campaign aborted because of an outbreak of smallpox. Almost a century later, an intended English attack

on Quebec with Indian allies was canceled because of the ravages of the pox. Duffy, 1951: 331.

23 Famine had also been reported on the mainland of Upper Guinea in western Africa in 1541–1542, and drought had struck the offshore islands of Cape Verde in 1549; see Jorge Vaz (factor at Cabo Verde), 10 June 1542, abstracted in Senna Barcelos, n.d.: 1: 119, and translated in Blake, 1942: 173; Fyfe, 1981: 6. We are indebted to George Brooks for references to these sources.

24 During the seventeenth century there were fifteen epidemics in Andean America compared with eight the previous century and with another fifteen in the mainland colonies of England. Polo, 1913: 50–74; Dobyns, 1963: 493–510; and Duffy, 1953: chs. 2, 4, and 5. See also Cook, 1981: esp. ch. 5.

25 Unfortunately, the author supplies no documentation or additional details. Also: E. de S. Campos, 1956: 143, says that Taunay, 1926–1929 (no volume or page given), identifies the 1611 "doença" in São Paulo as smallpox.

26 There was also smallpox in Bahia in 1615, but whether it existed in epidemic form is unknown. Vasconcellos, 1943: 2: 161. It was evidently the 1616–1617 epidemic in the Northeast to which Willem Piso, the great Dutch specialist on tropical diseases and remedies, referred, in Piso, 1957: 68–69.

27 At the same time, quarantine regulations were introduced at Buenos Aires (1621) and in Peru (1622); Moll, 1944: 75–78.

28 See the extraordinarily high mortality (50.8%) aboard five ships that the Angolan governor João Correa de Souza sent to Brazil in 1625; cited in Mattoso, 1979: 52. Goodyear, 1981: 2, notes the arrival of a "navio de Engola, que vem impedido de Bexigas" at Bahia in 1626; also Goodyear, 1982: 5.

29 Chandler, 1981: 121–122, reports epidemics in Ansermo, New Granada, in 1627.

30 So much so that Piso appears to have regarded smallpox as an insignificant problem and measles as one unworthy of comment, though he wrote extensively about cholera (not the nineteenth century, Asiatic variety), syphilis, dysentery, and other disorders. See note 26.

31 Much of which is quoted in Hemming, 1978: 338–339. There are brief accounts of the smallpox epidemic in Berredo, 1905: 2: 178–179, para. 1109, and in an anonymous eighteenth-century Jesuit memoria written after the 1724 epidemic in BPE, cód. CXV/2–14, fls. 49ᵛ–50ʳ.

32 Two eighteenth-century descriptions of the pandemic exist: Rocha Pita, 1950: 227–228, and Couto (1903[1904]): 180–181. There is a brief modern reference to the pandemic in Godinho, 1970: 6: 510. In addition there is the coeval documentation for Santos cited in E. de S. Campos, 1956: 138–139.

33 Cf. the first report of a smallpox-bearing slaver at Jamaica in 1663; Sheridan, 1985: 250.

34 Preceded by an informed essay by Duarte, 1956: 37–72. It is interesting to note that Morão's treatise was published about four years after the

appearance of Thomas Thatcher's pamphlet, "A Brief Rule to Guide the Common People of New England how to order themselves and theirs in the Small Pox, or Measles," the first medical work published in English America; Duffy, 1953: 47.

35 Guerra, 1965, provides an introduction to the abundant literature on this epidemic, and there is a good modern edition of the basic source in Morão, Rosa, and Pimenta. Martinique, in the French Antilles, imposed quarantine measures on arriving slaves in 1686; Hoeppli, 1969: 16.

36 Translated with an incorrect reference by Hemming, 1978: 467–468; Betendorf, 1901: 585–595, states that the pox swept through Indian villages in the lower Amazon for four months beginning in late August or early September and that the infection was brought by a canoe loaded with Indians from the Tapajoz River. They arrived infected, but buyers demanded their release, and the infection spread rapidly thereafter. The epidemic appears to have recurred during each of the next two years. Total casualties are reported in a document cited by L. da Fonseca, 1940: 11: 215.

37 Also Johnson, c. 1974: 3. We are grateful to Johnson for furnishing this paper and for her helpful comments on our approach to this essay.

38 Smallpox raged in the 1690s in Barbados and Jamaica, then the major slave-importing islands of the British West Indies; Sheridan, 1985: 250.

39 In the English mainland colonies there was a mild attack of smallpox in the interior of New York province in 1702, but a major epidemic did not occur until 1715, joined in 1717 by measles that struck Virginia. Duffy, 1953: 49, 74, 76, 169.

40 See Palmer, 1981: 49, for mention of smallpox aboard South Seas Company ships bound for Jamaica in 1708 and 1713 with slaves destined, at least in part, for the Spanish Main. The 1708 outbreak in Guayaquil is discussed in Dobyns, 1963: 511.

41 This outbreak occurred in still another period of serious drought in Angola; J. C. Miller, 1982: 46. Walter, 1957: 53, cites a *certidão* of the Santa Casa de Misericórdia de Luanda specifying epidemics of 1717 and 1718 as "grandes contágios de sarampo [measles], catolo tolo [glossed by Walter as "biliosa"] e outros diversos achaques."

42 Petition of Col. Garcia de Avellar Pereira cited in a report by former magistrate Manoel Gomes de Oliveira, 1 July 1716, AMB, Cartas de senado a sua magestade, 28: 9, fl. 12. The 1710s were a decade of devastating drought in Bahia, and the aridity must have exacerbated the suffering; Pinto, 1979: 193.

43 Smallpox and apparently typhus ravaged the viceroyalty of Peru from Buenos Aires to southern Peru in 1718–1720; Dobyns, 1963: 511–515. See also Cushner, 1980: 88, 168. Cf. the epidemics of 1715 and 1717 in New York and Virginia, note 39.

44 But smallpox appeared in those years aboard RAC ships from both Upper and Lower Guinea making for the Caribbean; Stewart, 1985.

45 Joseph Borges (ouvidor geral) to king, 8 September 1725, AHU/PA/Maranhão cx. 5 (orig.); João da Maia da Gama (governor) to king,

13 September 1726; petitions of M.^{el} de Sousa, Hyeronimo Vaz Vieira, and Domingos Serzão de Castro to king, 15 August 1726, and n.d., *provisão* of 1 March 1727, AHU/LR 270, fl. 16^r. The best account of the Maranhão epidemic is Sweet, 1974: 82–84.

46 Vasco Fernandes da Cunha Menezes (viceroy) to Diogo de Mendonça Corte Real (secretary of state), 22 August 1726, APB/OR, 20, no. 102.

47 The Spanish briefly quarantined South Seas Company ships at Buenos Aires in the early 1730s (?); Palmer, 1981: 72.

48 By 1733 the Bahian epidemic was over, but the tone of the viceroy's reports suggests that by the eighteenth century smallpox was seasonally expected in Bahia. For Pernambuco, see Couto (1903 [1904]): 184; the Pará epidemic is mentioned in a petition by Sor. Mariana Bernarda and Sor. M.ª Margarida Bittancourt to king, ca. 1733, AHU/PA/Pará cx. 7. See also MacLachlan, 1974: 134–135.

49 Gomes Freire de Andrada (governor, Rio de Janeiro) to Antonio Guedes Pereira (secretary of state), 9 June 1737, ANRJ col. 60/6/224^r.

50 Conde das Galveas (viceroy) to king, Bahia, 15 May 1738, APB/OR/ 35, no. 75, informing the king that Salvador and All Saints Bay continued to suffer from fevers and catarrhs.

51 By contrast, the Andean lands saw only two epidemics between 1730 and 1756, including spotted fever or typhus (1746) and measles (1749). Polo, 1913: 78–80.

52 Epidemics in São Paulo are reported for 1744, 1746, and 1749. Holanda, 1966: 77. An extensive outbreak of measles, which killed six to eight and incapacitated 100 out of 184 blacks on the Jesuit estate of Engenho do Conde, is reported in the slave inventory, "Escravos pertencentes ao eng.º do Conde . . . Abril de 1745," ANTT/CJ maço 15, no. 25.

53 The epidemics of the 1740s are the most fully reported of all the scourges that afflicted colonial Brazil. Most important are João Antonio de Castelbranco (governor) to Antonio Guedes Pereira (secretary of state), 30 November 1744, AHU/PA/Maranhão cx. 29 (orig.); Francisco Pedro de Mendonça Gorjão (Castelbranco's successor) to king, Belém, 26 April 1749, AHU/PA/Pará maço 1; both contain valuable annexes, as does Gorjão to king, 13 August 1750, AHU/PA/ Maranhão maço 1. Other accounts are scattered throughout AHU/PA/ Pará cxs. 3 and 12. News of the epidemic caused concern as far south as Rio de Janeiro. Gomes Freire de Andrada (governor) to Conde de Atouguia (viceroy), 7 June 1750, ANRJ col. 84/12/57^v. Secondary accounts include MacLachlan, 1974: 134–135; Sigaud, 1844: 109; A. Vianna, 1975: 10; and M. N. Dias, 1971: 137.

54 Significantly, Charleston, where new import duties had virtually shut off the slave trade in the 1740s, had reported smallpox in 1738 but not again until 1760; Donnan, 1928: 818–819.

55 Except for the epidemic in northern Brazil during the late 1740s and early 1750s, measles does not appear to have been a significant factor in any of the Brazilian eruptions during the second half of the century.

56 Generally, on the Pombaline chartered companies: Carreira, 1968–1969; M. Nunes Dias, 1971; Ribeiro, 1976.

57 BNL/CP cód. 617/221, José da Costa Pereira, 20 March 1759. Also Carreira, 1968: 349.

58 That year, a "French PawPaw [Popo, on the Slave, or Mina, Coast] Guinea man" introduced smallpox to Antigua in the Caribbean; Sheridan, 1985: 252.

59 For example, on 10 August 1765, a slaver arrived from Angola with 470 slaves, of whom 50 had become mortally ill with smallpox. The remainder were quarantined, but buyers usually became so anxious to procure slaves that continuous isolation of infected slaves was rarely enforceable. Joaquim de Melo Póvoas (governor, Maranhão) to Francisco Xavier de Mendonça Furtado (colonial secretary), 11 August 1765, AHU/PA/Maranhão cx. 40 (orig.). For other examples of slavers arriving in Maranhão with the pox, see A. Vianna, 1975: 36–37, fn. 3.

60 The previous year the city was struck by another "terrible epidemic" brought by two war frigates whose crews were diseased and communicated their malady to the city, where "a formidable epidemic" of unidentified type began; Miguel de Bulhões e Sousa (Bishop of Pará) to Francisco Xavier de Mendonça Furtado (as Governor, State of Maranhão), 16 September 1755, BNL/CP cód. 627/230ʳ; Bulhões e Sousa to Paulo de Carvalho e Mendonça, 7 November 1755, ANTT/MR cód. 598 (orig.).

61 Portel was formerly the Jesuit mission of Arucará.

62 A 1762–1763 epidemic in Suriname was attributed to imported slaves, and government health inspectors were appointed to regulate arrivals; Hoeppli, 1969: 16.

63 Only a minor episode reported from the always hypersensitive Cape Verde Islands in 1764; Carreira, 1966, summarizing Senna Barcelos, 1904; also Freeman et al., 1978: table 2.1.

64 As Pernambuco Company directors in Lisbon realized at least as early as 1763; AHMF/CGPP, livro 125 (copiador de Angola), letters of 15 February 1763, fls. 9ᵛ–11ᵛ; 7 November 1766, fls. 5ᵛ–6; 9 January 1775, fls. 57–57ᵛ; 9 April 1783, fls. 92–94; livro 126 (copiador de Benguela), letter of 17 May 1782; AHMF/CGPP, livro 125. For the complexities of this veritable economics of mortality, see letter of 4 July 1769, AHMF/CGPP, fls. 40ᵛ–43; MacLachlan, 1974: 134–135, introduces this idea.

65 AHU/PA/Angola cx. 29, letter from Miguel de Almeida e Vasconcelos (governor, Angola), 18 June 1762, remarking that it had been a bad year for sickness. Compare the volume figures in Carreira, 1968: 311; BNL/CP cód. 617/221, letter from José da Costa Pereira, 20 March 1759; and J. C. Miller, 1982: 49–51. The locally rather stronger Pernambuco Company also experienced a similar drop in the cost of acquiring slaves at Luanda in the same years; Carreira, 1969: 99.

66 AHU/PA/Angola cx. 30, letters from Francisco Inocêncio de Sousa Coutinho (governor, Angola), 30 June 1765 and 18 December 1765;

cx. 31, letters from Sousa Coutinho, 28 May 1766, 4 June 1766, 24 December 1766, 3 April 1767, 15 August 1767, 30 October 1767, 16 December 1767, 15 October 1768; cf. Matos, 1963: 301; Venâncio, 1983: 90. Governor Sousa Coutinho remarked that good supplies of slaves continued to reach Luanda at that time, in spite of declining prices in Brazil; AHU/PA/Angola cx. 31, letter of 18 May 1766.

67 Reports of dryness in the 1770s generally in West Africa and hunger near the Danish castle on the Gold Coast in 1774 may also have contributed; Nicholson, 1979: 47–48; Johnson, c. 1974: 4. Winterbottom, 1969: 2: 133, recalled smallpox along the upper branches of the Sierra Leone River in Upper Guinea in 1773.

68 But cf. the smallpox epidemics in New Granada in 1782–1783; Chandler, 1981: 122.

69 The military expedition is described in detail in Corrêa, 1937: 2: 193–228.

70 See also the serious problems that Rio and Pernambuco, similarly beset by droughts, faced in feeding their own populations in that decade; we are grateful to Larissa Brown for her generous sharing of research in progress on this and related issues.

71 Dom Rodrigo de Sousa Coutinho to Francisco Inocêncio de Sousa Coutinho, 29 July 1799, BAPP, cód. 685, no. 3 (orig.). See also Marcilio, 1968: 166, 203, who found that between 1799 and 1809 smallpox was the third ranking (13.2%) cause of death among the free population of the cathedral parish of São Paulo.

72 The Maranhão epidemic is mentioned in Pachêco, 1968: 87–88. That Pará was also afflicted is implied by A. Vianna, 1975: 37–38. Francisco Inocêncio de Sousa Coutinho (by then governor, Pará) to Luis Pinto de Sousa (secretary of state), 7 June 1796 and 12 February 1797, BAPP, cód. 682, no. 103; cód. 702, no. 14. See also MacLachlan, 1974: 135; Scheuss de Studer, 1958: 300, notes smallpox in Buenos Aires in 1799; E. de S. Campos, 1956: 148–149, 152; A. Vianna, 1975: 16–18. Inoculation may have been widespread enough in the British West Indies by this date that potential outbreaks were dampened there; Sheridan, 1985: 255ff.

73 E. de S. Campos, 1956: 152, explicitly states that the pox arrived on the slave ships and, 156, confirms for São Paulo generally in this period. The Benguela governor had reported "unprecedented" mortality in 1792–1793 but had attributed it to famine rather than to disease at that time; AHU/PA/Angola cx. 43, letter from Francisco Paim da Câmara Ornellas (governor, Benguela), 19 January 1793.

74 Although there are references to an "epidemic" at Cape Coast Castle on the Gold Coast in 1789; Herbert, 1975: 546–547. Smallpox had appeared also in 1786 in the Gambia and the Sherbro River in Upper Guinea; Winterbottom, 1969: 2: 133; BPP, XXV (635), 206, testimony of Captain William Littleton.

75 Nor, indeed, have they until the very recent past; J. R. Dias, 1981.

76 Generally, on the abolition of the Brazilian slave trade, Bethell, 1970, and Eltis, 1978.

77   Droughts also afflicted the desert regions in 1804–1805; McDougall, 1980: 320–321.

78   McDougall, 1980: 320–321, reports drought in the desert in 1822–1823.

79   Brazilian shipping data from PRO/FO/63 and FO/84, partially published (with errors) in BPP, XLIX, 593–633, and discussed in J. C. Miller, 1976.

80   Harries, 1981: 313, 322, has the connection for southeastern Africa in 1824. Campbell, 1981: 208, 219, has the opposite: prices rising and exports falling, from Madagascar in 1817. Clearly, beyond a certain level of mortality depopulation reversed the supply/demand relationship.

81   Corrêa, 1937: I: 80, mentions the refusal of Luanda merchants to isolate or quarantine slaves suffering from smallpox. New customs regulations forbade, but probably did not prevent, this practice only in 1799: AA, 1936: 418. Cf. J. C. Miller, 1986: 172–189. For parallel problems in the Spanish empire, Chandler, 1981: 262 (Lima); Scheuss de Studer, 1958: 312–313 (Buenos Aires); Palmer, 1981: 113–114.

82   An earlier physician, the Carmelite Manoel de Azevedo (1680), advised the use of bezoar stones to cure smallpox. In the Near East and East Indies bezoar stones, derived from the stomachs of wild goats and other animals, were widely used as remedies for various ailments although they possessed no real therapeutic qualities: Burkhill, 1935: I: 321–323. For reasons unclear, smallpox does not seem to have been a major health hazard in Portugal, as it was in England and elsewhere in Europe. Medical treatises rarely refer to it. In addition to those cited above, see Abreu, 1707, Leitão, 1738. All are available in the National Library of Medicine, but we have been unable to see others cited by Lemos, 1899: I: 62, fn. I. It may be that the comparative rarity of the pox in the kingdom explains why the only verifiable instance that we found when it was introduced to Brazil directly from Portugal was in 1562. See above p. 43.

83   "Representação de moradores do Rio de Janeiro sobre a vantagem da vacina," 15 June 1798, BNRJ, II/32/16/9 (orig. signed by 36 persons); petition by 31 others to viceroy, Rio de Janeiro, 20 Feb. 1800, BNRJ, II/34/15/32 (orig.). Santos Filho, 1977: 316–317, wrongly says that these inoculations involved vaccine.

84   In addition to authorities cited in note 8, see G. Miller, 1957, and Baxby, 1981. For a recent effort that sets his achievement in the context of other eighteenth-century medical advances, see Razzell, 1977a and 1977b.

85   Henriques de Paiva was also the author of 1785 and the editor of 1792. These two are unavailable in the National Library of Medicine, but we have been able to see the first treatise.

86   Costa, 1970: 147, citing the example of the municipal council of Cachoeira, which sent two youths to the capital in 1805 for that purpose. See also Conde dos Arcos (governor, Bahia) to priest in charge of the village of Massarandupió, 4 October 1811, directing him to send

four Indian youths of sturdy constitution, ten to fifteen years of age, and previously unexposed to smallpox to be inoculated in Salvador. Accioli, 1930–1940: 3: 197.

87 Visconde de Anadia to governor of Bahia, 29 March 1806, enclosing forty copies of the report for distribution. The original is in BNRJ, II/33/28/23, and was conveniently published or "reprinted" in Costa, 1970: 147.

88 We are grateful to Larissa Brown for having called the Silva study to our attention. Sigaud, 1844: 540–541, apparently erred in ascribing the creation of this institution to the same year as the arrival of the Jenner vaccine, 1804. Matos, 1963: 334–335, writing as late as 1835–1836, mentioned smallpox in Angola and notes that vaccine had been tried many times (presumably during his service there and in São Tomé 1797–1816) but without benefit. He may have confused the vaccine with inoculation (below).

89 Polícia-Instituição de Vaccínica, 1811–1821, ANRJ. See also the plans announced in 1819 for a similar "Instituição Vaccínica" in São Paulo; E. de S. Campos, 1956: 159.

90 PRO data on slave imports being analyzed, and allowing for slaves already in the city among those vaccinated.

91 E. de S. Campos, 1956: 153–155, casts some doubts on the claims of efficacy.

92 The 1808 is the last smallpox outburst she reports for São Paulo in her study, which extends to 1850.

93 A. Vianna, 1975: 46–50. Barata, 1973: 177, adds that as many as fifty persons a day died of the disease.

94 Karasch, 1982: 7, 12, notes that by the late 1820s and after smallpox no longer seemed to be a killer disease.

95 Goodyear, 1982, for further commentary on the African-Brazilian epidemiological link.

96 Conde de Anadia to Conde da Ponte, Rio de Janeiro, 4 March 1809, Accioli, 1930–1940: 3: 196–197, documents the departure of the ships bearing the boys and the vaccine; AHU/PA/Angola cx. 54, Noronha, 2 August 1804; Feo Cardoso, 1825: 3: 304.

97 Cf. Dias, 1981: 16, for the later nineteenth century in Angola. Also the other public health reforms introduced in the Portuguese trade after 1810; J. C. Miller, 1985; J. C. Miller, forthcoming; H. Vianna, 1962; Spix and Martius, 1938: 2: 153.

98 As early as November 1800, the governor of Mozambique had assured the crown that it was "rare" that a slave ship left his ports "sem que primeiro os faça vacinar a todos" (though surely meaning inoculation rather than true vaccination); quoted by Botelho, 1927: 202–203.

99 Calculated from the summaries of the Bills of Mortality in Creighton, 1891–1894: 2: 456, 531.

96   DAURIL ALDEN AND JOSEPH C. MILLER

REFERENCES

AA. Argivos de Angola.
Abreu, J. R. de (1707) Luz de cirurgioens embarcadissos, que trata das doenças epidemicas, de que costumaõ enfermar ordinariamente todos, os que se embarcaõ para as partes ultramarinas. Lisbon: Antonio Pedrozo Galram.
Accioli de Cerqueira e Silva, I (1930–1940) Memorias historicas da Bahia. Ed. Braz do Amaral. 6 vols. Salvador: Imprensa Official do Estado.
Ackerknecht, E. H. (1965) History and Geography of the Most Important Diseases. New York: Hefner.
African Historical Demography: II (1982) Edinburgh: University of Edinburgh, Centre of African Studies.
AHMF. Arquivo Histórico do Ministério das Finanças (Lisbon). Companhia Geral do Pernambuco e Paraíba (CGPP). Livros nos. 125, 126.
AHU. Arquivo Histórico Ultramarino (Lisbon). Papeis avulsos (PA) Angola cxs. 16–18, 20, 27, 31, 39, 40, 43, 54, 57, 66, 67, maço 18(DO). Livro de Registo (LR) 270. Maranhão cxs. 29, 40, 41, maço 1. Pará cxs. 3, 5, 7, 12, 29, 37, maço 1.
Alden, D. (1983) "Indian versus Black Slavery in the State of Maranhão during the Seventeenth and Eighteenth Centuries." Biblioteca Americana 1: 91–142.
Alencastro, L.-F. de (1981) "La traite négrière et les avatars de la colonisation portugaise au Brésil et en Angola (1550–1825)." Cahiers du Centre de recherches ibériques et ibéro-américaines de l'Université de Rouen (C.R.I.A.R.) 1: 9–76.
——— (1984) "Prolétaires et esclaves: immigrés portugais et captifs africains à Rio de Janeiro—1850–1872." Cahiers du Centre de recherches ibériques et ibéro-américaines de l'Université de Rouen (C.R.I.A.R.) 4: 119–156.
Almeida, L. F. de (1973) A Colônia do Sacramento na época da sucessão de España. Coimbra: Faculdade de Letras da Universidade de Coimbra.
AMAE. Archives du Ministère des Affaires Etrangères (Paris). Correspondance consulaire et commerciale (CC), Pernambouc, 3.
AMB. Arquivo Municipio da Bahia. Cartas de senado a sua magestade, 28: 9.
Andrade, G. O. de (1956) "As bexigas em Pernambuco," in E. Duarte (introduções históricas, interpretações e notas) and G. O. de Andrade (estudo crítico) Morão, Rosa, e Pimenta: Notícia dos três primeiros livros em vernáculo sôbre a medicina no Brasil. Pernambuco: Arquivo Público Estadual: 11–34.
ANRJ. Arquivo Nacional do Rio de Janeiro.
Anstey, R. T. (1975) The Atlantic Slave Trade and British Abolition. London: Macmillan.
ANTT. Arquivo Nacional da Torre do Tombo (Lisbon). Cartorio Jesuitico (CJ). Ministério do Reino (MR), cód. 598.
APB. Arquivo Público da Bahia. Ordens regias (OR), 20.

Appleby, A. B. (1973) "Disease or Famine? Mortality in Cumberland and Westmoreland 1580–1640." Economic History Review 26: 403–432.

Araujo, C. da S. (1972) The Immortalized Cow: Smallpox Vaccine and Wright's Vaccines in Brazil. Rio de Janeiro: Gráfica Olímpia Editôra.

Ashburn, F. D. (1947) Ranks of Death: A Medical History of the Conquest of America. Ed. P. M. Ashburn. New York: Coward-McCann.

Azeredo, J. P. de (1799) Ensaios sobre algumas enfermidades d'Angola. Lisbon: Oficina Typografica.

Azevedo, M. de (1680) Correcçam de abusos introduzidos contra o verdadeiro methodo da medicina & farol medicina para medicos, cyrurgiones, & boticarios. 2 vols. Lisbon: Joam da Costa.

BAPP. Biblioteca e Arquivo Público do Pará. Cód. 385.

Barata, M. (1973) Formação histórica do Pará. Repr. Belém: Universidade Federal do Pará.

Barleu[s], G. (1940) Historia dos feitos recentemente praticados durante oito anos no Brasil. Tr. and ed. C. Brandão. Rio de Janeiro: Ministério da Educação.

Bathily, A. (1986) "La traite atlantique des esclaves et ses effets économiques et sociaux en Afrique: le cas du Galam, royaume de l'hinterland sénégambien au dix-huitième siècle." Journal of African History 27: 269–293.

Bauss, R. (1977) "Rio de Janeiro: The Rise of Late Colonial Brazil's Dominant Emporium, 1777–1808," Ph.D. dissertation, Tulane University.

Baxby, D. (1981) Jenner's Smallpox Vaccine: The Riddle of Vaccinia Virus and its Origin. London: Heinemann.

Becker, C. (1985) "Notes sur les conditions écologiques en Sénégambie aux 17e et 18e siécles." African Economic History 14: 167–216.

Benenson, A. S. (1982) "Smallpox," in A. S. Evans (ed.) Viral Infections of Humans: Epidemiology and Control. 2d ed. rev. New York: Plenum Medical Books: 541–568.

Berredo, B. P. (1905) Annaes historicos de Berredo (1749). 3d ed. 2 vols. Florence: Typographia Barbèra.

Betendorf, J. F., S.J. (1901) "Chronica da missão dos padres da Companhia de Jesus no estado do Maranhão." Revista do Instituto Histórico e Geográfico Brasileiro 72: 1–697.

Bethell, L. (1970) The Abolition of the Brazilian Slave Trade: Britain, Brazil, and the Slave Trade Question 1807–1869. Cambridge: Cambridge University Press.

Blake, J. W. (1942) Europeans in West Africa, 1450–1560. 2 vols. London: Hakluyt Society. (2d series, nos. 86–87.)

BNL. Biblioteca Nacional (Lisbon). Coleção Pombalina (CP). Códs. 617, 627, 628.

BNRJ. Biblioteca Nacional de Rio de Janeiro.

Boogaart, E. van den and P. Emmer (1979) "The Dutch Participation in the Atlantic Slave Trade, 1595–1650," in H. A. Gemery and J. S. Hogendorn (eds.) The Uncommon Market: Studies in the Economic History of the Atlantic Slave Trade. New York: Academic Press: 353–375.

Bosman, W. (1721) A New and Accurate Description of the Coast of Guinea. 2d ed. London: J. Knapton.

Botelho, J. J. Teixeira (1927) "Acerca da vacinação e das bexigas." Boletim da Academia das Sciencias de Lisboa—Segunda Classe 17: 202–203.

BPE. Biblioteca Pública de Evora. Cód. CXV/2–14, fls. 49ᵛ–50ʳ.

BPP. British Parliamentary Papers.

Brandão, A. F. (1956) Diálogos das grandezas do Brasil (1618). Ed. R. Garcia. Salvador: Imprensa Nacional.

—— (1966) Diálogos das grandezas do Brasil (1618). Ed. J. A. G. de Mello. Recife: Imprensa Universitária.

Brásio, A. [ed.] (1951–1985) Monumenta missionaria africana—Africa Ocidental. 14 vols. Lisbon: Agência Geral do Ultramar.

—— (1979) "Descripção dos Governos dos Ill.ᵐᵒˢ e Ex.ᵐᵒˢ Snr.ᵉˢ António de Vasconcellos, e D. Francisco Innocencio de Souza Coutinho." Studia 41–42: 205–226.

Breman, J. G., A. B. Alécaut, and J. M. Lane (1977) "Smallpox in the Republic of Guinea, West Africa." American Journal of Tropical Medicine and Hygiene 26: 256–264.

Brooks, G. E. Jr. (1985) Western Africa to c.1860 A.D.: A Provisional Historical Schema Based on Climate Periods. Bloomington: African Studies Program, Indiana University.

Brown, L. V. (1985) "Internal Commerce in a Colonial Economy: Rio de Janeiro and Its Hinterland, 1790–1822," Ph.D. dissertation, University of Virginia.

Burkhill, I. H. (1935) A Dictionary of the Economic Products of the Malay Peninsula. 2 vols. London: Isaac Henry.

Cabral, A. do V. [ed.] (1931) Cartas avulsas (1550–1568). Rio de Janeiro: Officina Industrial Graphica.

Cadornega, A. de O. de (1940–1942) História geral das guerras angolanas (1680). 3 vols. Lisbon: Agência Geral das Colonias.

Cahill, K. M. (1964) Tropical Disease in Temperate Climates. Philadelphia: G. Lippincott.

Campbell, G. (1981) "Madagascar and the Slave Trade, 1810–1895." Journal of African History 22: 203–227.

Campos, E. de S. (1956) "Considerações sobre a ocorrência de variola e vacina nos séculos XVII, XVIII e XIX vistas sob a luz de documentação coeva." Revista do Instituto Historico e Geográfico Brasileiro (RIHGB) 231: 138–160.

Campos, F. (1981–1982) "A data da morte da Rainha Jinga D. Verónica I." Africa (São Paulo) 4: 79–103 and 5: 72–104.

Carmichael, A. G. (1983) "Infection, Hidden Hunger and History." Journal of Interdisciplinary History 14: 249–264.

Carreira, A. (1966) "Crises em Cabo Verde nos séculos XVI e XVII." Geográphica (Sociedade de Geografia de Lisboa) 6: 35–45.

—— (1968–1969) "As companhias pombalinas de navegação, comércio e tráfico de escravos entre a costa africana e o nordeste brasileiro." Boletim cultural da Guiné Portuguesa 23: 5–88, 301–454 and 24: 59–188, 284–474.

Cavazzi de Montecuccolo, Pe J. (1965) Descrição histórica dos três reinos de Congo, Matamba e Angola. 2 vols. Lisbon: Junta de Investigações do Ultramar.

Chandler, D. L. (1981) Health and Slavery in Colonial Colombia. New York: Arno Press.

Cissoko, S.-M. (1968) "Famines et épidémies à Tombouctou et dans la boucle du Niger du XVIe au XVIIIe siècle." Bulletin de l'Institut Français d'Afrique Noire Sér. B, 30: 806–821.

Coaracy, V. (1965) O Rio de Janeiro no século 17. Rio de Janeiro: Livraria José Olympio Editôra.

Condamine, M. de la (1747) A Succinct Abridgement of a Voyage. 2d ed. Paris, 1746. Trans. London: E. Withers.

Cook, N. D. (1981) Demographic Collapse: Indian Peru 1520–1620. New York: Cambridge University Press.

Corrêa, E. A. da Silva. (1937) História de Angola. 2 vols. Lisbon: Agência Geral das Colonias.

Costa, L. M. da (1970) "A introdução da vacina jeneriana na Bahia." Anais do Arquivo do Estado da Bahia 39: 145–148.

Coughtry, J. (1981) The Notorious Triangle: Rhode Island and the African Slave Trade 1700–1807. Philadelphia: Temple University Press.

Couto, D. de L. (1903 [1904]) "Desagravos do Brazil e glorias de Pernambuco (1757)." Annaes da Biblioteca Nacional do Rio de Janeiro (ABNRJ) 25: 1–366.

Creighton, C. (1891–1894) A History of Epidemics in Britain. 2 vols. Cambridge: The University Press.

Crosby, A. W. (1972) The Columbian Experiment: Biological and Cultural Consequences of 1492. Westport, CT: Greenwood Press.

——— (1976) "Virgin Soil Epidemics as a Factor in the Aboriginal Depopulation in America." William and Mary Quarterly, 3d series, 33: 289–299.

Curtin, P. D. (1964) The Image of Africa: British Ideas and Action, 1780–1850. Madison: University of Wisconsin Press.

——— (1968) "Epidemiology and the Slave Trade." Political Science Quarterly 83: 190–216.

——— (1969) The Atlantic Slave Trade: A Census. Madison: University of Wisconsin Press.

——— (1975) Economic Change in Pre-Colonial Africa: Senegambia in the Era of the Slave Trade. 2 vols. Madison: University of Wisconsin Press.

Cushner, N. P. (1980) Lords of the Land: Sugar, Wine, and Jesuit Estates of Coastal Peru, 1600–1767. Albany: State University of New York Press.

Dawson, M. H. (1979) "Smallpox in Kenya, 1880–1920," in J. M. Janzen and S. Feierman (eds.) The Social History of Disease and Medicine in Africa (Special issue of Social Science and Medicine: Part B—Medical Anthropology) 13-B: 245–250.

——— (1983) "Socio-Economic and Epidemiological Change in Kenya: 1880–1925," Ph.D. dissertation, University of Wisconsin, Madison.

Delgado, R. (1940) A famosa e histórica Benguela: Catálogo dos governadores (1779–1940). Lisbon: Edições Cosmos.

——— (1945) O Reino de Benguela (do descobrimento à criação do governo subalterno). Benguela: Imprensa Beleza.

Dias, G. S. (1934) Relações de Angola. Coimbra: Imprensa da Universidade.

Dias, J. R. (1981) "Famine and Disease in the History of Angola, c. 1830–1930." Journal of African History 21: 349–378.

Dias, M. Nunes (1971) A Companhia Geral do Grão Pará e Maranhão (1755–1778). São Paulo: Universidade de São Paulo.

Dixon, C. W. (1962) Smallpox. London: J. and A. Churchill.

Dobyns, H. F. (1963) "An Outline of Andean Epidemic History to 1720." Bulletin of the History of Medicine 37: 493–515.

Donnan, E. (1928) "The Slave Trade into South Carolina Before the Revolution." American Historical Review 28: 804–828.

——— (1930–1935) Documents Illustrative of the History of the Slave Trade to America. 4 vols. Washington, D.C.: Carnegie Institution of Washington.

Duarte, E. (1956) "Introdução histórica [to the 'Tratado único das bexigas e sarampo'']," in E. Duarte (introduções históricas, interpretações e notas) and G. O. de Andrade (estudo crítico) Morão, Rosa, e Pimenta: Notícia dos três primeiros livros em vernáculo sôbre a medicina no Brasil. Pernambuco: Arquivo Público Estadual: 37–72.

Duffy, J. (1951) "Smallpox and the Indians in the American Colonies." Bulletin of the History of Medicine 25: 324–341.

——— (1953) Epidemics in Colonial America. Baton Rouge: Louisiana State University Press.

Dumbell, K. R. and F. Huq (1975) "Epidemiological Implications of the Typing of Variola Isolates." Transactions of the Royal Society of Tropical Medicine and Hygiene 69: 303–306.

Eltis, D. (1978) "The Transatlantic Slave Trade, 1821–43," Ph.D. dissertation, University of Rochester.

——— (1983) "Free and Coerced Transatlantic Migrations: Some Comparisons." American Historical Review 88: 251–280.

Engerman, S. L. (1983) "Contract Labor, Sugar, and Technology in the Nineteenth Century." Journal of Economic History 43: 635–659.

Fage, J. D. (1975) "The Effect of the Export Slave Trade on African Populations," in R. J. A. R. Rathbone and R. P. Moss (eds.) The Population Factor in African Studies. London: University of London Press: 15–23.

Feo Cardoso de Castello Branco e Torres, J. C. (1825) Memórias . . . contendo . . . a história dos governadores capitaens generaes de Angola desde 1575 até 1825. 3 vols. Paris: Fantin.

Fonseca, J. M. da (1946) "Anchieta e a medicina." Anais do IV centerario da Companhia de Jesus. Rio de Janeiro: Ministério da Educação e Saude: 83–94.

Fonseca, L. da [ed.] (1940) "O Maranhão (Roteiro dos papeis avulsos do século XVII do Arquivo Histórico Colonial)." Publicações do Congresso lusobrasileiro de história. 19 vols. Lisbon.

Freeman, P. H., V. E. Green, R. B. Hickok, E. F. Moran, and M. D. Whitaker (1978) "Preliminary Report: Cape Verde, Assessment of the Agricultural Sector." Submitted to AFR/RA/PSA, U.S. Agency for International Development.

Freitas, O. de (1935) Doenças africanas no Brasil. São Paulo: Editora Nacional.

Fyfe, C. (1981) "The Cape Verde Islands." History Today 31 (May): 5–9.

Fynn, J. K. (1971) Asante and Its Neighbours 1700–1807. London: Longman.

Garfield, R. (1971) "A History of São Tomé Island, 1470–1655," Ph.D. dissertation, Northwestern University.

Geografia y descriptión universal de las Indias . . . desde . . . 1571 al . . . 1574. (1894). Madrid: Fortanet.

Godinho, V. M. (1970) "Portugal and Her Empire, 1680–1720," in J. S. Bromley (ed.) The New Cambridge History. Cambridge, Eng.: Cambridge University Press: vol. 6.

Goodyear, J. D. (1981) "A Preliminary Epidemiology of the Bahian Slave Trade, 1780–1810." Draft paper.

—— (1982) "The Slave Trade, Public Health, and Yellow Fever: The Image of Africa in Brazil." Paper delivered at American Historical Association, Washington, D.C.

Guerra, F. (1965) "Early Texts on Yellow Fever." Clio medica (Oxford) 1: 59–60.

—— (1979) "Medicine in Dutch Brazil," in E. van den Boogaart, H. R. Hoetink, and P. J. P. Whitehead (eds.) Johan Maurits van Nassau-Siegen 1604–1679: A Humanist Prince in Europe and Brazil. Essays on the Occasion of the Tercentenary of his Death. The Hague: Johan Maurits van Nassau Stichting: 472–493.

Guslits, S. V. (1961) "Smallpox," in I. I. Elkin (ed.) A Course on Epidemiology. New York: Pergamon Books: 369–372.

Hall, M. (1977) "Ethnography, Environment, and the History of the Nguni in the Eighteenth Century." Collected Seminar Papers on the History of Southern Africa in the Nineteenth and Twentieth Centuries (Institute of Commonwealth Studies, University of London) 8: 11–20.

Harries, P. (1981) "Slavery, Social Incorporation, and Surplus Extraction: The Nature of Free and Unfree Labour in South-East Africa." Journal of African History 22: 309–320.

Hassig, R. (1981) "The Famine of One Rabbit: Ecological Causes and Social Consequences of a Pre-Columbian Calamity." Journal of Anthropological Research 39: 172–182.

Heagerty, J. J. (1928) Four Centuries of Medical History in Canada and a Sketch of the Medical History of Newfoundland. 2 vols. Toronto: Macmillan, 1928.

Heintze, B. (1981) "Das Ende des unabhängigen Staates Ndongo (Angola)." Paideuma 27: 197–273.

Hemming, J. (1978) Red Gold: The Conquest of the Brazilian Indians, 1500–1760. Cambridge, MA.: Harvard University Press, 1978.

Henige, D. (1986) "When Did Smallpox Reach the New World (And Why

102 DAURIL ALDEN AND JOSEPH C. MILLER

Does It Matter)?" in P. E. Lovejoy (ed.) Africans in Bondage: Studies in Slavery and the Slave Trade. Madison: African Studies Program, University of Wisconsin: 11–26.

Herbert, E. W. (1975) "Smallpox Inoculation in Africa." Journal of African History 16: 539–559.

Hielkema, J. U., J. Roffey, and C. J. Tucker. (1986) "Assessment of Ecological Conditions Associated with the 1980/81 Desert Locust Plague Upsurge in West Africa Using Environmental Satellite Data." International Journal of Remote Sensing 7: 1609–1622.

Hoeppli, R. (1969) Parasitic Diseases in Africa and the Western Hemisphere: Early Documentation and Transmission by the Slave Trade. Basel: Verlag für Recht-und Gesellschaft AG.

Holanda, S. B. de (1966) "Movimentos da população em São Paulo no século XVIII." Revista do Instituto de Estudos Brasileiros 1: 55–111.

Hopkins, D. (1983) Princes and Peasants: Smallpox in History. Chicago: University of Chicago Press.

Horne, R. W. (1963) "The Structure of Viruses." Scientific American 208 (January): 48–69.

Imperato, P. J., O. Sow, and F. Fofaria (1972) "The Epidemiology of Smallpox in the Republic of Mali." Transactions of the Royal Society of Tropical Medicine and Hygiene 66: 176–182.

Inikori, J. E. (1980) "Introduction," in idem (ed.) Forced Migration: The Impact of the Export Slave Trade on African Societies. London: Hutchinson: 13–60.

Isaacman, A. (1972) "The Origin, Formation and Early History of the Chikunda of South Central Africa." Journal of African History 13: 443–461.

Isaacman, B. and A. Isaacman (1977) "Slavery and Social Stratification among the Sena of Mozambique," in S. Miers and I. Kopytoff (eds.) Slavery in Africa: Historical and Anthropological Perspectives. Madison: University of Wisconsin Press: 105–120.

Jaboatão, A. de S. M. (1858–1862) Novo orbe seráfico brasílico. 5 vols. Rio de Janeiro: Typ. Brasiliense de M. Gomes Ribeiro.

Johnson, M. [c. 1974] "Drought on the Guinea Coast." African History Seminar paper, University of London, School of Oriental and African Studies, Institute of Commonwealth Studies.

Joralemon, D. (1982) "New World Depopulation and the Case of Disease." Journal of Anthropological Research 38: 108–127.

Karasch, M. (1982) "African Mortality and Epidemic Disease in 19th Century Rio de Janeiro." Paper delivered at American Historical Association.

——— (1987) Slave Life in Rio de Janeiro, 1808–1850. Princeton: Princeton University Press.

Kiemen, M. C. (1954) The Indian Policy of Portugal in the Amazon Region, 1614–1693. Washington, D.C.: Catholic University of America Press.

Kiple, K. F. (1985) The Caribbean Slave: A Biological History. New York: Cambridge University Press.

———— and V. H. King (1981) Another Dimension to the Black Diaspora: Diet, Disease, and Racism. New York: Cambridge University Press.

Klein, H. S. (1978) The Middle Passage: Comparative Studies in the Atlantic Slave Trade. Princeton: Princeton University Press.

———— and S. L. Engerman (1975) "A Note on Mortality in the French Slave Trade in the Eighteenth Century," in H. A. Gemery and J. S. Hogendorn (eds.) The Uncommon Market: Essays in the Economic History of the Atlantic Slave Trade. New York: Academic Press: 261–272.

[Knivet, A.] (1906) "The Admirable Adventures and Strange Fortunes of Master Antonie Knivet," in S. Purchas, Hakluytus Posthumus or Purchas His Pilgrimes. Glasgow: Maclehose: 16: 177–289.

Koster, H. (1817) Travels in Brazil. 2d ed. London: Hurst, Rees, Orme, and Brown.

Leitão, M. da S. (1738) Arte com vida, ou vida com arte, muy curiosa necessaria e proveitosa naõ so a medicos e cirurgioens, mas ainda a toda a pessoa de qualquer estado. Lisbon: A Pedrozo Galrão.

Leite, S. (1938–1950) História de Companhia de Jesús no Brasil. 10 vols. Rio de Janeiro: Civilização Brasileira.

———— [ed.] (1956–1968) Monumenta brasiliae. 5 vols. Rome: "Monumenta Historica Societatis Iesu."

Lemos, M. (1899) Historia de medicina em Portugal. 2 vols. Lisbon: Gomes.

Liesegang, G. (1978) 'Famines and Smallpox in South Eastern Africa, 18th to 20th Centuries." Paper delivered at Universidade Eduardo Mondlane, Maputo.

———— (1982) "Famines, Epidemics, Plagues and Long Periods of Warfare: Their Effects in Mozambique 1700–1795." Paper delivered at Conference on Zimbabwean History, Progress, and Development, University of Zimbabwe.

Lima, A. P. de (1949) "Nota sobre algumas epidemias na cidade da Bahia," in Anais do IV Congresso de história nacional. Rio de Janeiro: 5: 253–268.

Lisanti, L. (1973) Negócios coloniaes (Uma correspondência do século XVIII). 5 vols. São Paulo: Ministerio da Fazenda and Visão S/A Editorial.

Lovejoy, P. E. (1982) "The Volume of the Atlantic Slave Trade: A' Synthesis." Journal of African History 23: 473–502.

————. (1983) Transformations in Slavery: A History of Slavery in Africa. London: Cambridge University Press.

———— and S. Baier (1975) "The Desert-Side Economy of the Central Sudan." International Journal of African Historical Studies 13: 551–581.

MacDouall, J. (1833) Narrative of a Voyage to Patagonia and Terra del Fuégo. London: Renshaw and Rush.

McDougall, E. A. (1980) "The Ijil Salt Industry: Its Role in the Pre-Colonial Economy of the Western Sudan," Ph.D. dissertation, University of Birmingham.

Machado, A. de A. [ed.] (1933) Cartas, informações, fragmentos historicos e sermões de Joseph de Anchieta, S. J. (1554–1594). Rio de Janeiro: Civilização Brasileira.

MacLachlan, C. M. (1974) "African Slave Trade and Economic Development in Amazonia, 1700–1800," in R. B. Toplin (ed.) Slavery and Race Relations in Latin America. Westport, CT: Greenwood Press: 112–145.

Manchester, A. K. (1953) British Preeminence in Brazil: Its Rise and Decline. Chapel Hill: University of North Carolina Press.

Marcilio, M. L. (1968) La ville de São Paulo: Peuplement et population 1750–1850. Rouen: l'Université, Faculté des lettres et sciences humaines: Paris: Nizet.

Matos, R. J. de Cunha (1963) Compêndio histórico das possessões de Portugal na Africa. Rio de Janeiro: Arquivo Nacional.

Matthews, T. I. (1976) "The Historical Tradition of the Peoples of the Gwembe Valley, Middle Zambezi," Ph.D. dissertation, University of London.

Mattoso, K. M. de Q. (1979) Être esclave au Brésil, XVIe–XIXe siècle. Paris: Hachette.

Mauro, F. (1956) "L'Atlantique portugais et les esclaves (1570–1670)." Revista da Faculdade de Letras (Universidade de Lisboa) 22: 5–55.

Mawe, J. (1812) Travels in the Interior of Brazil, Particularly in the Gold and Diamond Districts of that Country. London: Longman, Hurst, Rees, Orme, and Brown.

May, J. M. (1958) The Ecology of Human Diseases. New York: MD Publications.

Mendes, L. A. de O. (1812) "Discurso academico ao programma." Memórias económicas da Academia Real das Sciencias de Lisboa 4: 1–64.

Mettas, J. (1975) "La traite portugaise en Haute Guinée, 1758–1797." Journal of African History 16: 343–363.

Miller, G. (1957) The Adoption of Inoculation for Smallpox in England and France. Philadelphia: University of Pennsylvania Press.

Miller, J. C. (1975) "Legal Portuguese Slaving From Luanda, Angola—Some Preliminary Indications of Volume and Direction, 1760–1830." Revue française d'histoire d'outre-mer 62: 135–176.

——— (1976) "Sources and Knowledge of the Slave Trade in the Southern Atlantic." Paper delivered at Pacific Coast Branch of the American Historical Association, La Jolla.

——— (1981) "Lineages, Ideology, and the History of Slavery in Western Central Africa," in P. E. Lovejoy (ed.) The Ideology of Slavery in Africa. Beverly Hills: Sage: 41–72.

——— (1982) "The Significance of Drought, Disease, and Famine in the Agriculturally Marginal Zones of West-Central Africa." Journal of African History 23: 17–61.

——— (1984) "Demographic History Revisited (review article on African Historical Demography—Volume II)." Journal of African History 25: 93–96.

——— (1985) "Overcrowded and Undernourished: The Techniques and Consequences of Tight-Packing in the Portuguese Southern Atlantic

Slave Trade." Paper delivered at the Colloque International sur la Traite des Noirs, Nantes.

────── (1986) "Imports at Luanda, Angola: 1785–1823," in G. Liesegang, H. Pasch, and A. Jones (eds.) Figuring African Trade: Proceedings of the Symposium on the Quantification and Structure of the Import and Export and Long Distance Trade of Africa in the 19th Century (c. 1800–1913) (St. Augustin 3–6 January 1983) Berlin: Kölner Beiträge zur Afrikanistik, 11: 165–246.

────── (forthcoming) Way of Death: Merchant Capitalism and the Angolan Slave Trade, 1730–1830. Madison: University of Wisconsin Press.

Moll, A. A. (1944) Aesculapius in Latin America. Philadelphia and London: Saunder.

Moran, E. F. (1982) 'The Evolution of Cape Verde's Agriculture." African Economic History 11: 63–86.

Morão, Rosa, e Pimenta: Notícia dos três primeiros livros em vernáculo sôbre a medicina no Brasil. (1956) Pernambuco: Arquivo Público Estadual. With introductions, historical notes, and notes by E. Duarte and critical study by G. O. de Andrade.

Nicholson, S. E. (1974) "Climatic Variations in the Sahel and other African Regions During the Past Five Centuries." Journal of Arid Environments 1: 3–24.

────── (1976) "A Climatic Chronology for Africa: Synthesis of Geological, Historical, and Meteorological Information and Data," Ph.D. dissertation, University of Wisconsin, Madison.

────── (1979) "The Methodology of Historical Climate Reconstruction and its Application to Africa." Journal of African History 20: 31–49.

────── (1980a) "African Climatic and Environmental Changes During the Past Five Centuries." National Science Foundation Final Report. ATM 77-21547.

────── (1980b) "Saharan Climates in Historic Times," in M. A. J. Williams and H. Faure (eds.) The Sahara and the Nile. Rotterdam: Balkema: 173–200.

────── (1981) "The Historical Climatology of Africa," in T. M. L. Wigley, M. J. Ingram, and G. Farmer (eds.) Climate and History: Studies in Past Climates and Their Impact on Man. Cambridge: Cambridge University Press: 249–270.

Nieuhof, J. (1942) Memorável viagem marítima e terrestre ao Brasil. Tr. M. N. Vasconcelos. Ed. J. H. Rodrigues. São Paulo: Livraria Martins.

Pachêco, Don F. C. (1968) Historia eclesiastica do Maranhão. São Luís: Departamento de Cultura do Estado.

Paiva, M. J. H. de (1785) Farmacopéa lisbonense ou Collecção dos simplices, preparações, e composições mais efficazes, e de maior uso. Lisbon: Filippe da Silva e Azevedo.

────── [ed.] (1772) Instituições ou elementos de farmacia extrahidos dos de Baume. Lisbon.

────── (1806) Preservativo das bexigas: ou a história da origem e descobrimento da vacina, e dos efeitos ou sintomas, e do método de fazer a vacinação. 2d ed. Lisbon.

Palmer, C. (1981) Human Cargoes: The British Slave Trade to Spanish America 1700–1739. Urbana: University of Illinois Press.

Pinto, V. N. (1979) O ouro brasileiro e o comércio anglo-português (uma contribuição aos estudos da economia atlântica no século xviii). São Paulo: Nacional.

Piragibe, Dr. A. (1881) A primeira página da historia de vaccina no Brasil. Rio de Janeiro: Typ. de Oliveira e Cia., 1881.

Piso, G. (1957) Historia natural e medica da India ocidental. Tr. Mario Lobo Leal, et al. Rio de Janeiro: Ministério da Educação e Cultura, Instituto Nacional do Livro.

Polo, J. T. (1913) "Apuntes sobre las epidemias en el Peru." Revista histórica (Lima) 5: 50–109, 207–209.

PRO. Public Record Office (London). FO/35, FO/84.

Purchas, S. (1906) Hakluytus Posthumus or Purchas His Pilgrimes. Glasgow: Maclehose.

Rau, V. (1956) O "Livro de razão" de António Coelho Guerreiro. Lisbon: Publicações Culturais do "DIAMANG."

Rawley, J. A. (1981) The Transatlantic Slave Trade: A History. New York: Norton.

Razzell, P. (1977a) The Conquest of Smallpox: The Impact of Inoculation on Smallpox Mortality in Eighteenth Century Britain. Firle, Sussex: Caliban Books.

——— (1977b) Edward Jenner's Cowpox Vaccine: The History of a Medical Myth. Firle, Sussex: Caliban Books.

Rebelo, M. dos A. da S. (1970) Relações entre Angola e Brasil (1808–1830). Lisbon: Agência Geral do Ultramar.

Reinegg, A. S. von (1910) Viagem as missões jesuitas e trabalhos apostolicos (1698). Tr. A. R. Schneider. Repr. São Paulo: Livraria Martins Editora.

Ribeiro, J., Jr. (1976) Colonização e monopólio no nordeste brasileiro: A Companhia Geral de Pernambuco e Paraíba (1759–1780). São Paulo: HUCITEC.

Ricketts, T. F. and J. B. Byles (1910) The Diagnosis of Smallpox. New York: Funk and Wagnalls.

Rocha, L. de Assis [c. 1954] Efermérides médicas pernambucanas, séculos XVI, XVII e XVIII. Recife: Prefeitura Municipal, Departamento de Documentação e Cultura.

Rocha Pita, S. da (1950) Historia da America portuguesa (1730). Salvador: Livraria Progresso Editora.

Rogers, Sir L. (1926) Smallpox and Climate in India: Forecasting of Epidemics. Medical Research Council, Special Report Series, no. 106. London: HMSO.

Rout, L. B. (1976) "The African in Colonial Brazil," in M. L. Kilson and R. I. Rotberg (eds.) The African Diaspora: Interpretive Essays. Cambridge, MA: Harvard University Press: 132–172.

Saco, J. A. (1832) "Análisis de una obra sobre el Brasil." Revista bimestre cubana. Reprinted in Colección de papeles científicos, históricos, politicos y de otros ramos sobre la isla de Cuba. 3 vols. Havana (1962): 2: 30–69.

Saldanha, D. R. de ("medico nesta corte") (1761) Illustração medica. 2 vols. Lisbon: J. de Aquino Bulhocus.

Salvador (Bahia), Prefeitura do Municipio do [c. 1950] Cartas do senado 1684–1692 (Documentos historicos do Arquivo Municipal). 6 vols. Salvador.

Salvador, Frei V. do (1954) Historia do Brasil 1500–1627. Eds. J. Capistrano de Abreu and R. Garcia. 4th ed. São Paulo: Edições Melhoramentos.

Santos Filho, L. de C. (1966) Pequena história da medicina brasileira. São Paulo: DESA.

——— (1977) Historia geral da medicina brasileira. São Paulo: HUCITEC.

Scheuss de Studer, E. F. (1958) La trata de negros en el Río de la Plata durante el siglo XVIII. Buenos Aires: Universidad de Buenos Aires.

Schotte, Dr. J. P. (1782) A Treatise on the Synochus Atrabiliosa, A Contagious Fever Which Raged in Senegal in the Year 1778. London: M. Scott.

Schwartz, S. B. (1978) "Indian Labor and New World Plantations: European Demands and Indian Responses in Northeastern Brazil." American Historical Review 83: 43–79.

——— (1986) Sugar Plantations in the Formation of Brazilian Society: Bahia, 1550–1835. New York: Cambridge University Press.

Scott, H. H. (1939) A History of Tropical Medicine. 2 vols. London: E. Arnold and Sons.

——— (1943) "The Influence of the Slave-Trade in the Spread of Tropical Disease." Transactions of the Royal Society of Tropical Medicine and Hygiene 36: 169–188.

Senna Barcelos, C. J. (1904) Cabo Verde: alguns apontamentos sobre as fomes em Cabo Verde desde 1717–1904. Lisbon: Typ. da Cooperativa Militar.

——— (n.d.) Subsidios para a história de Cabo Verde e Guiné. 3 vols. Lisbon: Imprensa Nacional.

Sheridan, R. B. (1985) Doctors and Slaves: A Medical and Demographic History of Slavery in the British West Indies, 1680–1834. New York: Cambridge University Press.

Sigaud, Dr. J. F. X. (1844) Du climat et des maladies du Brézil, ou statistique médicale de cet empire. Paris: Masson.

Silva, M. B. N. da (1975) Análise de estratificação social (O Rio de Janeiro de 1808 a 1821). São Paulo. Boletím no. 7, nova série, Departamento de História, Faculdade de Filosofia, Letras e Ciências Humanas, Universidade de São Paulo.

Silva Rebelo, M. dos A. da (1970) Relações entre Angola e Brasil (1808–1830). Lisbon: Agência Geral do Ultramar, 1970.

Smith, M. M. (1974) The "Real Expedición Maritima de la Vacuna" in New Spain and Guatemala. Philadelphia: American Philosophical Society, Transactions. Vol. 64, pt. 1.

Socolow, S. M. (1978) The Merchants of Buenos Aires 1778–1810: Family and Commerce. London: Cambridge University Press.

Spix, J. B. von and C. F. P. von Martius. (1938) Viagem pelo Brasil. Tr. Lucia F. Lahmeyer. 3 vols. Rio de Janeiro: Imprensa Nacional.

Stewart, L. (1985) "The Edge of Utility: Slaves and Smallpox in the Early Eighteenth Century." Medical History 29: 54–70.

Studart, G. [ed.] (1904–1921) Documentos para a historia do Brasil e especialmente a do Ceará. 4 vols. Fortelaza: Typ. Studart.

Sweet, D. G. (1974) "A Rich Realm of Nature Destroyed: The Middle Amazon Valley, 1640–1750," Ph.D. dissertation, University of Wisconsin, Madison.

Taunay, A. de E. (1926–1929) Historia seiscentista da Vila de São Paulo. 4 vols. in 2. São Paulo: H. L. Canton.

——— (1949–1950) Historia da cidade de São Paulo no século XVIII. 2 vols. São Paulo: Divisão do Arquivo Histórico.

Thornton, J. K. (1979) "The Kingdom of Kongo in the Era of Civil Wars, 1641–1718," Ph.D. dissertation, University of California, Los Angeles.

Vail, L. and L. White (1980) Capitalism and Colonialism in Mozambique: A Study of Quelimane District. London: Heinemann.

Vasconcellos, S. de (1943) Vida do venerável Padre José de Anchieta. Ed. S. Leite. 2 vols. Rio de Janeiro: Imprensa Nacional.

Vasconcelos, S. de (1977) Crônica da Companhia de Jesus (1663). 3d ed. 2 vols. Petrópolis: Editora Vozes.

Venâncio, J. C. G. (1983) "A economia de Luanda e hinterland no século XVIII: um estudo de etnologia histórica." Dissertação inaugeral, Universidade de Johannes Gutenberg em Mogúncia.

Verger P. (1968) Flux et reflux de la traite des nègres entre le Golfe de Bénin et Bahia de Todos os Santos du dix-septième au dix-neuvième siècle. Paris: Mouton.

Vianna, A. (1975) As epidemias no Pará. Pará: Imprensa do "Diário Oficial," 1906. 2d ed. Belém.

Vianna, H. (1962) "Um humanitário alvará de 1813, sôbre o tráfico de africanos em navios portuguêses." Revista do Instituto Histórico e Geográfico Brasileiro 256: 79–88.

Walter, J. (1957) "A propósito de uma doença de Angola de há mais de três séculos: doença do bicho ou maculo." Boletim clínico e estatistico do Hospital do Ultramar 7: 47–68.

Wax, D. D. (1968) "A Philadelphia Surgeon on a Slaving Voyage to Africa." Pennsylvania Magazine of History and Biography 94: 465–493.

Webster, J. B. (1979) "Drought and Migration: The Lake Malawi Littoral as a Region of Refuge," in M. T. Hinchey (ed.) Proceedings of the Symposium on Drought in Botswana. Durham, NH. University of New Hampshire Press: 148–157.

Wheeler, D. (1964) "A Note on Smallpox in Angola, 1670–1875." Studia 13–14: 352–362.

Williams, M. A. J. and H. Faure [eds.] (1980) The Sahara and the Nile. Rotterdam: Balkema.

Winterbottom, T. (1969) An Account of the Native Africans in the Neighbourhood of Sierra Leone. 2 vols. London: Cass. Original edition London: Whittingham, 1803.

Worden, N. (1985) Slavery in Dutch South Africa. Cambridge: Cambridge University Press.

WHO. World Health Organization. (1980) The Global Eradication of Smallpox: Final Report. Geneva: WHO.

African Health at Home and Abroad

PHILIP D. CURTIN

IN THE NINETEENTH century, annual reports of European military medical authorities usually carried some such title as "The Health of the Army at Home and Abroad." Though historians have recently studied the health of slaves in transit and the demographic patterns of slave populations in the New World, they have not paid much attention to these military data.[1] For the West Indies they begin in 1803, for West Africa in 1810. After 1819, it is possible to trace the disease patterns of West Indian and West African populations in the last decades of the slave trade and on into the early twentieth century. These records help to show what happened epidemiologically to populations of African descent that crossed the Atlantic in both directions.[2]

FROM AFRICA TO THE WEST INDIES

These records cover two quite different circumstances. For the period 1817–1836, they deal with Africans who were originally enslaved, shipped out through the slave trade, and then recaptured at sea by British naval vessels. Many were landed in Sierra Leone,

Philip D. Curtin is a professor in the department of history, Johns Hopkins University, 312 Gilman Hall, Baltimore, MD 21218. The author would like to thank Arthur C. Aufderheide, Jerome Handler, and Kenneth Kiple for their suggestions.

Social Science History 10:4 (Winter 1986). Copyright © 1986 by the Social Science History Association. CCC 0145-5532/86/$1.50.

where some were persuaded to enlist in one of the West India Regiments. Some of these recruits served in Sierra Leone and vicinity. Others served in the West Indies. From 1836 until 1859, the detailed time-series break off for both the West Indies and West Africa. By then, the recruitment of the West India Regiments had changed. Africans were no longer enticed into the service in Sierra Leone and sent to the West Indies. Instead, Afro-West Indians enlisted in the West India Regiments, and the British sent some of these units to serve in West Africa under European officers and non-coms. From the 1890s, they recruited numbers of Africans to serve in Africa itself alongside the Afro-Americans, and in the early twentieth century, Africans again appear in the medical records—though not with the detailed reporting they were accorded in the 1820s and 1830s.

The Africans recruited in Sierra Leone came from many different parts of Africa, their origins shifting with the changing source of supply to the slave trade. A reasonable picture for the early nineteenth century, however, can be constructed from the Freetown census of 1848, which reflects the general origins of slave recaptives landed in Sierra Leone over the past two or three decades (Curtin, 1969: 244–260). The important point for epidemiological purposes is that comparatively few came from the immediate vicinity of Sierra Leone. The great majority—at least 80% of the total—came from the forest country further east, in what is now Nigeria and the People's Republic of Benin. Recruits for the army no doubt fitted a similar pattern, which means they were strangers to the specific disease environment of Sierra Leone, though not to the more extended disease environment of the West African forest belt—and they were strangers still more to the distant disease environment of the West Indies.

For 1817–1836, the patterns of mortality were nearly what epidemiological theory would predict. Morbidity and mortality are expected to increase as people move away from an isolated disease environment into a more ecumenical setting where they come into contact with new diseases and new strains of familiar diseases. In this instance, the black soldiers in the Cape Coast Command, serving mainly in what is now present-day Ghana, had an annual average mortality a little under 20 per thousand. Those serving in the Sierra Leone Command had a mortality rate just over 30 per thousand, while those sent across the ocean to serve in the Wind-

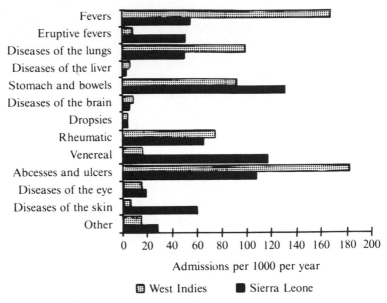

Figure 1   Morbidity of African troops serving in West Indies and Sierra Leone, 1819–1836

ward and Leeward Command died at 40 per thousand (PP, 1840 [c.228]:15, 21; PP, 1837–1838 (138):11, 50, 73).[3]

We have no conventional measure for this epidemiological phenomenon of rising death rates or morbidity rates as a result of movement. For convenience, a measure for the cost of movement from one disease environment to another can be called *relocation cost*—expressed as the percentage of change in mortality or any of the other conventional measures of health, such as morbidity, the incidence of medical discharge, or repatriation. Thus, the relocation cost in mortality for troops in the Gold Coast was small but unmeasurable, for those in Sierra Leone it was about 50%, and for the West Indies, 100%. Though this doubling of the death rate may seem excessive, it was far from unusual for this period, when the death rates of European troops serving overseas in the tropical world were normally two to four time those of similar troops serving in Britain itself. (See also Appendix Tables 1 and 2, which differ because they give relocation costs from Sierra Leone to the West Indies—not home territory to Sierra Leone.)

The causes of death were not recorded for the Cape Coast Command, but changes in morbidity after the Atlantic passage outline patterns of immunity which the African soldiers took with them (or failed to take with them) into a new environment. (See Figures 1 and 2, based on numeric data in Appendix Tables 1 and 2.) These are contemporaneous classifications of disease, which may disguise reality. Fevers, for example, were mainly malaria on either side of the Atlantic, but the category could also have included typhus, typhoid, and yellow fever, to mention only the most obvious. Later data provide at least some suggestion as to the prevalence of the various fevers. By 1859–1863, the official classification for deaths in the West Indies distinguished deaths from at least three kinds of fever, "continued fever" (mainly typhoid and typhus) making up about 29% of the "febrile group," "yellow fever" and "paroxysmal fevers" (malaria) at 71% of deaths in that group. Deaths from malaria continued in the range of 53% to 92% of fever deaths for the rest of the century.[4]

Curiously enough, yellow fever figured only in the 1860s and 1870s. This should not be so surprising, however, in spite of the

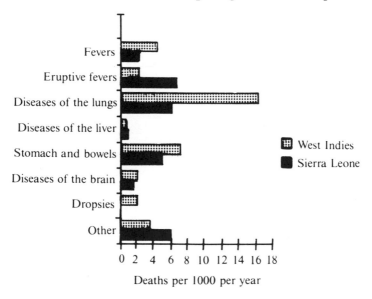

Figure 2   Mortality of African troops serving in Sierra Leone and the West Indies, 1817–1836

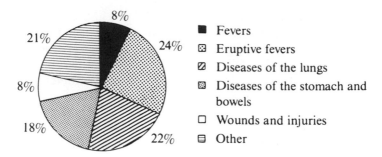

Figure 3   African troops serving in Sierra Leone, 1817–1836 (percentage of all deaths)

notorious death rate from yellow fever among European troops. The disease occurred in the West Indies in epidemic form, especially among new arrivals from elsewhere. Local people were often infected in youth with sub-clinical cases, which nevertheless provided lifelong immunity (Burnet and White, 1972: 242–249).

"Diseases of the lungs" was another aggregate hard to disentangle. The two largest components were obviously pneumonia and tuberculosis. Alexander Tulloch, like other authorities of the early nineteenth century, noted that tuberculosis was far more common in Europe than it was in Africa. Figures 3 and 4 certainly demonstrate that the disease was more prevalent in the West Indies than in Africa (PP, 1840 [c.288]: 17). Indeed, the most significant difference between the two sides of the ocean was the greater number of deaths from smallpox in Africa and the increase in pneumonia and tuberculosis in the New World. This pattern was normal for the time, at least in popular medical opinion. Smallpox appeared in epidemic form in West Africa, though epidemics were comparatively rare in Sierra Leone. This occurrence was therefore unusual, and smallpox never again accounted for as many as a quarter of all deaths among British troops stationed in West Africa. Diseases of lungs, on the other hand, were a chronic problem in the centuries of the slave trade for Africans who found themselves in the new disease environment in the New World, and later on for Africans who went to work in new surroundings like the South African mines (Packard, 1983; Kiple and Kiple, 1980: 213–214).

Their transatlantic experience with malaria also fits the patterns of recent medical knowledge. West Africans lived in a holoendemic region, where *Plasmodium falciparum* was the dominant species of the parasite. The African pattern of heavy infestation from infancy implied a true morbidity rate of close to 100%, but, since clinical symptoms were comparatively uncommon, this fact would not show up either in the hospital admissions or in the death rates of adults. When Africans moved to the West Indies, on the other hand, they show the high morbidity rates indicated in Figure 2, probably from strains of *Plasmodium falciparum* new to them, since falciparum malaria is notorious for its immunities that are valid only against specific strains. *Plasmodium vivax,* which does not occur in Africa, probably did not enter the picture since people of African descent are resistant to vivax on account of inherited blood characteristics (Kiple, 1984: 17).

A large part of the "abcesses and ulcers" on the African side would have been Guinea worm (*Dracunculus medinensis*), possibly acquired by the recaptive slaves even before they had arrived in Sierra Leone, since the rates of infestation by this parasite reached as high as 25% in the Gold Coast region later in the century. They tended to be much lower in Sierra Leone. The spectacular increase in morbidity from abcesses and ulcers in the West Indies, without much influence on death rates, would be hard to identify out of the wealth of comparatively unfamiliar parasites in the West Indies. As for the spectacular improvement in both morbidity and mortality from venereal diseases, it appears to be more a matter of social than environmental conditions. The African troops in the West Indies were allowed or even encour-

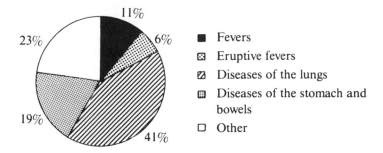

Figure 4   African troops serving in the West Indies, 1817–1836 (percentage of all deaths)

aged to marry. The "dropsies" mentioned here were mainly heart conditions.

"Diseases of the brain" would have included epilepsy and the whole range of nervous disorders, but it nevertheless shows a puzzlingly high death rate for men of military age—2.2 deaths per thousand among troops serving in the West Indies, and 1.6 per thousand among those serving in Africa. Some recent inter-disciplinary work by anthropologists and medical investigators provides a probable explanation (Handler et al., 1986; Aufder-heide et al., 1985). Lead poisoning was very prevalent in the West Indies and in North America in the late eighteenth and early nine-teenth centuries. The principal cause was the use of lead con-tainers for liquids, especially among the upper class in North America, but also among slaves in the Caribbean. One of the principal culprits was apparently lead piping used in the distilla-tion of cheaper grades of rum. And the evidence of lead poisoning is readily detectable from the skeletal material of slave cemeteries. As medical authorities gradually became aware of the nature and source of lead poisoning, lead dropped out of use. Death rates of West Indian troops at home from "diseases of nervous system" dropped accordingly, to 1.47 per thousand in 1869–1873, 0.46 per thousand in 1879–1884, and 0.25 in 1905–1910 (AMSR reports for 1864: 65; 1874: 77–78; 1885: 203; 1900: 289; 1911: 151).

FROM THE WEST INDIES TO AFRICA

When the supply of recruits among the recaptured slaves began to dry up after the 1850s, the West India Regiments began to be recruited in the West Indies themselves. Some recruits served there, but the British Army began in the 1860s using West Indian units as the principal British force in West Africa. With the re-sumption of statistical publication from 1859, it becomes possible to follow the health of West Indians in Africa, but not of Africans themselves until the early twentieth century. With the resumed data after 1859, the most striking fact is the sharp decline in death rates on either side of the ocean (see Figure 5). The West Indian death rate dropped from 64 per thousand in 1803–1816, the last years of the Napoleonic Wars, to 3.06 per thousand in 1909–1913 —for non-European troops in West Africa it dropped from 28.81 to 4.29 per thousand.[5]

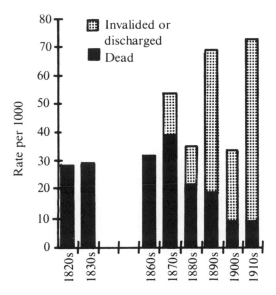

Figure 5   West Indian troops serving in West Africa—dead and in-valided—1820s to 1910s

These mortality rates are probably accurate enough to point up such gross changes, but their interpretation poses some problems. Death in action or from wounds received in action was uncommon in the nineteenth-century West Indies or West Africa, but death from disease could increase enormously under campaign conditions. Death rates of soldiers in Britain itself were higher than those of civilians of the same age group, simply because of crowded barracks and easy transmission of whatever diseases were around. When soldiers left barracks and went into action, their death rates from disease rose steeply, even if they never saw a shot fired in anger. The high rates for 1803–1816 were mild for European troops campaigning in the West Indies, but they were higher than those of the slave population which, in 1816–1830, was around 30 per 1000 for males and 25 per 1000 for females (PP, 1837: XL (138), Appendix, p. 5 [Abstract III]). By that measure, the mortality of West Indian troops after 1817—in the 30s per thousand—would have been just a little higher than the civilian rate and hence "normal" for military forces of that period. There is some reason to believe that death rates of troops in the

West Indies had fluctuated mildly during recent decades, but with no pronounced trend until the nineteenth century.

Although West Indians at home escaped the high mortality of campaigning, it was not so in West Africa. It is possible, however, to avoid the periods of most active fighting by choosing five-year samples of relative peacetime as surrogates for a whole decade. This works out reasonably well by using the first five years of resumed reporting (1859–1863) and similar data at five-year intervals. This leaves out the Asante campaign of 1874 (but not the preliminary fighting of late 1873). It also leaves out the further Asante campaign of 1885–1886. By the 1890s, when the scramble for West Africa was at its height, it is hard to distinguish a period without fighting, so the whole of 1890–1899 was used. Then, with the first decade of the new century, the period 1903–1908 can be taken to reflect conditions after the worst of the conquest period was over. Data for 1909–1913 are all we have for the 1910s, and reporting was discontinued in mid-1914, for obvious reasons.

A second problem of measurement comes from the changing technology of transportation and health care. In the early part of the century, for example, medical authorities recorded only hospital admissions and deaths. Later they added a category for those who were repatriated—"invalided" in the terminology of the time—for those discharged on account of illness, and for the average number of hospitalized soldiers per 1000—called "constantly sick" in the British records. Some invaliding took place even in the early part of the century, but it became much more common after the 1850s, when regular steamship service was available. This meant those who would have died on the spot a decade or so earlier were "invalided" instead and may well have died elsewhere. In comparing data on West Indian troops at home with those in Africa, repatriation from Africa was not quite equivalent to a medical discharge at home. Some of those repatriated were not finally discharged for that cause, but treating "invalided" and "discharged" as equivalent is as close as one can come. Figures 5 and 6 therefore include a category for soldiers discharged in the West Indies or invalided home from West Africa. (Tables 3 and 4 in the Appendix show all four basic indicators.)

Even while recognizing the invaliding problem as a distortion of the long-term mortality index, it is clear that the mortality of West Indian troops serving in the West Indies dropped consis-

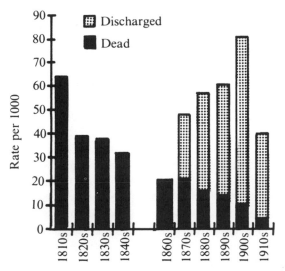

Figure 6   West Indian troops serving in the West Indies—dead or discharged on account of disease, 1810s to 1910s

tently over this century, from 64 per thousand in the 1810s to 3.06 per thousand in the 1910s (see Figure 5). For West Africa, on the other hand, the mortality of West Indian soldiers in the 1860s and 1870s remained as high as that of their African-born predecessors in the 1820s and 1830s. Then, when the drop in mortality began in earnest over the half-century from the 1860s to the 1910s, the percentage decrease was nearly the same on both sides of the ocean—87% in West Africa, 86% in the West Indies (see Figure 6 and Appendix Table 5.) This drop followed a pattern similar to that of European troops in tropical service.

It is hard to assess the extent of distortion produced by increasing rates of invaliding and medical discharge. The increased invaliding in Africa while death rates went down is certainly owing to more frequent opportunities for transportation home. For the West Indies, the rate of discharge per 1000, which almost doubled between the 1870s and the 1900s, is harder to account for. The annual reports of army doctors in the West Indies are generally silent on the matter. (They have far more to say about British than about West Indian health in any case.) The change could easily represent a slow rise in physical and medical standards, rather than actual change in the health of the troops. For similar reasons, the other two measures of health—admissions and constantly sick—are too dependent on professional judgment and medical policy to be useful measures across time, though they tell something about the health differences within the same army in the same decade (see Appendix Tables 3 and 4).

While the sharp drop in mortality was expected and worldwide among soldiers on European service, the relocation costs did not change as much as one might have expected from the overall improvement in mortality figures (see Figure 7 and Appendix Table 5). The relocation cost stood at 51% in the 1860s and remained at 40% in the 1910s. The long term trend was nevertheless downward, though much less steeply than the decline in mortality rates. This seems to demonstrate the tenacity of childhood immunities or lack thereof, but it may also reflect the fact that the West African disease environment was one of the worst in the world for human beings of any origin.

The striking improvement in mortality and morbidity has to be seen in the light of similar trends elsewhere. The vastly decreased mortality in nineteenth-century Europe has been subject to controversy among demographers, nutritionists, and historical epidemiologists. It began with Thomas McKeown's (1976) observation that the decline of mortality in nineteenth-century England and Wales cannot be accounted for by known discoveries of medical science. He concluded that it must have begun with improved nutrition, helped along in the late century by piped water supplies and other works of sanitary engineering.[6]

After the 1860s, the West India Regiments received the same rations as other British troops, which was not the case, say, of "native" troops in British India or of black troops in the West Indies in earlier times. It therefore seems unlikely that current nutrition could explain these differences, but childhood nutrition could have an influence. It would be nearly impossible to measure this kind of influence. We are left with an undifferentiated childhood background that combined nutrition, disease, and perhaps other environmental factors (see Appendix Tables 6 through 9).

A more detailed, if incomplete explanation emerges if the data are assembled according to cause of death, though to do so raises the problem of changing disease classification. The classification of Figures 1 and 2 and Appendix Tables 1 and 2 was that of the

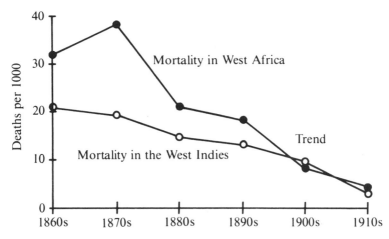

Comparative mortality of West Indian troops serving in the West Indies and in West Africa, 1860s to 1910s

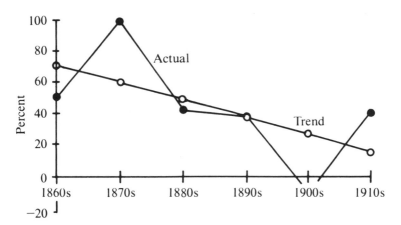

Figure 7   Relocation cost—West Indies to Africa, 1860s to 1910s

late 1830s. By the mid-century, the classification had changed, and diseases were grouped in classes and sub-classes. Malaria, for example, was no longer simply part of an amorphous group of fevers. It came under the heading of "paroxysmal fevers" within the sub-group of "myasmatic diseases," which in turn belonged to a larger class of "zymotic disease." The zymotic category was, in turn, one of five prime categories that included constitutional diseases like tuberculosis, local diseases like those of the circulatory or digestive system, "conditions," such as general debility, and finally accidents or violent death. The names of the principal groups changed again in the 1870s, but the system of classes and sub-classes continued to evolve until the list of causes that could be assigned for illness or death rose to more than 600 on the eve of the First War (see, for example, AMSR, 1914: 144–156 [Abstract VIII]). Of all these diseases, however, the principal killers remained the air-borne pneumonia and tuberculosis, the water-borne dysentery and diarrhea and the mosquito-borne malaria (see Figures 7, 8, 9 and Appendix Tables 6 through 9 for numerical data).

But their influence was different on either side of the Atlantic. The only defense against the air-borne diseases was general sanitation, attention to the placement, construction, and ventilation of barracks, isolation of those who became ill, and the other policies associated with mid-Victorian ideas about contagion, ideas still associated in the public mind with the name of Florence Nightingale (see, for example, Rosenberg, 1979). Many of these ideas were quite wrong in the light of the germ theory of disease that was to follow, but many of them worked empirically, whatever their theoretical merit. In the early century, "lung disease" (including tuberculosis in the classification of that period) had been the principal killer of African expatriates in the West Indies (Figure 2), and it continued so, accounting for half of the death of troops in the West Indies during the 1870s.

In the early century, however, it is uncertain whether most deaths were from tuberculosis or pneumonia. Both pneumonia and tuberculosis were extremely uncommon in Africa at that period, hence soldiers sent to the West Indies lacked the appropriate immunities. Furthermore, the tubercle bacillus is comparatively inactive. It multiplies much less rapidly than most ordinary bacteria. This means that the time required to produce symptoms in infected individuals is comparatively long, and (for the disease to spread through an entire community may require several generations. But also, human beings who have received an initial infection can become sensitized to further infection, which then proceeds much more rapidly. Infants sometimes died in their first months on that account, and African troops in France in the

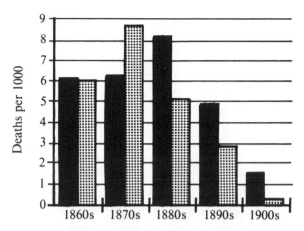

West Indian troops—incidence of death from tubercular disease—1820s to 1900s

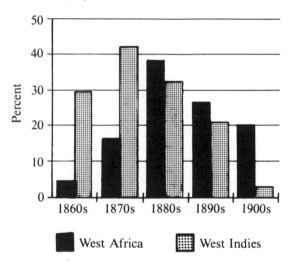

Figure 8   West Indian troops—tubercular disease—1860s to 1900s (percentage of all causes of death)

1914–1918 war died in large numbers from a form of tuberculosis similar to that of European children—in contrast to the slow-acting "consumption" more frequently fatal to adults (Burnet and White, 1972: 213–214; Kiple, 1984: 140–148). The easily recog-

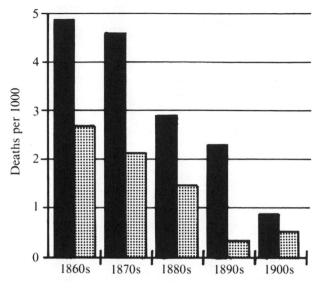

West Indian troops—incidence of death from respiratory disease—1860s to 1910s

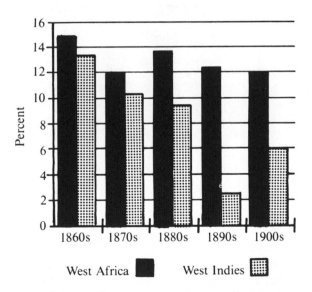

West Africa ■   West Indies ▦

Figure 9   West Indian troops—respiratory disease as a percentage of all causes of death, 1860s to 1900s

nized pulmonary form of the disease tended to appear only gradually in New World slave populations. And the countervailing immunities also required several generations to become effective. These generally expected patterns are supportd by the data on tuberculosis among West Indian troops. The disease increased gradually to reach a peak in the West Indies themselves in the 1870s, the same peak for West Indians serving in Africa coming a decade later. Thereafter, it declined systematically on both sides of the tropical Atlantic, even as it did simultaneously on both sides of the North Atlantic (see Figure 8).

Deaths from other diseases of the respiratory track behaved quite differently over time. They were less in number than tubercular infection, though they were more serious in West Africa than in the West Indies. They also declined significantly from one decade to the next—possibly because West Indians were gradually building up an immune defense, possibly because of improved general sanitation in barracks conditions. Of the major causes of death, only respiratory diseases and tuberculosis declined so systematically and regularly, not merely in deaths per thousand, but also in their contribution to all deaths, even though medical science discovered no new specific cure or means of prevention (see Figure 9).

Nor did spectacular cures for intestinal diseases appear during this period, but military doctors (like civilian doctors) *did* learn about water supply, and the germ theory helped to confirm the role of impure water in carrying disease—which many had already suspected. After the 1880s, filtered water was generally available to troops in barracks when not campaigning. The results of filtering water are revealed in the drop of the death rate from water-borne illnesses to less than one per thousand on both sides of the ocean. Though morbidity and mortality from this cause remained higher in the West Indies than in Africa in the first decade of this century, these diseases still accounted for nearly a fifth of all deaths— if only because the other principal killers had been reduced even more (see Figure 10).

Malaria was far and away the hardest to control. Quinine had been isolated from the raw cinchona bark in 1820, and it began to be widely used by the 1850s both as a cure for malaria and as a prophylactic against possible attack (Smith, 1976). Quinine had its followers and its opponents. It was not universally used, but it

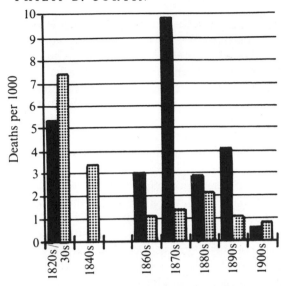

West Indian troops—incidence of death from dysentery and diarrhea, 1820s–1900s

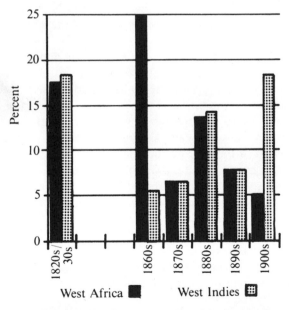

Figure 10   West Indian troops–death from dysentery and diarrhea as a percentage of all causes of death, 1820s–1900s

was certainly the most widely recommended remedy. On the other hand. European army doctors also believed that "Negroes" were immune to malaria. They may well have been less than absolutely strict in enforcing regular prophylactic use. In fact, there is no secure evidence that prophylactic quinine was systematically given to Afro-American troops. After the 1860s, for whatever cause, malaria increased as a cause of death on both sides of the Atlantic, rising in Africa from a killer of less than 4% of total dead in the 1860s to 54% by the 1890s. On the American side, however, its toll never again equalled the 5 per thousand of the early century, and it dropped to zero after 1905 (see Figure 11).

Any attempt to account for this pattern is bound to be largely speculative. One possibility is that West Indians gradually lost whatever immunities their ancestors might have brought from Africa. The number of African-born soldiers in the West India Regiment was greatly reduced, if not eliminated, by the 1870s. The high death rates from the 1870s through the 1890s were therefore those of outsiders to the disease environment of holoendemic falciparum malaria. By the 1890s, whatever protection their predecessors had had in the 1860s was very likely gone, though the hereditary protection against *plasmodium vivax* would have continued in the West Indies, though without effect in West Africa where *P. vivax* was absent. One possibility might be that the sickle-cell trait, which protects against falciparum malaria but exacts a price in the form of higher death rates from anemia, had been bred out of the Afro-American population. North American experience with sickle-cell trait, however, suggests that the time interval was far too short to produce a threefold increase in malaria over a period of three or four decades. Nevertheless, the Afro-West Indians seem to have kept some degree of protection in West Africa. In 1897–1899, for example, their European noncoms died of malaria at more than twice the rate of the Afro-West Indians serving under them.[7]

The striking improvement in malaria rates came, however, after 1900, when both European and West Indian troops profited from more careful quinine prophylaxis—and possibly to some degree from mosquito control. By the quinquenniel period 1904–1908, the overall death rate of European troops in West Africa had dropped to 11.19 per thousand (compared to 9.54 for West Indians). The death rate of European troops from malaria alone was

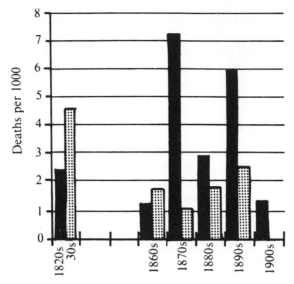

West Indian troops—incidence of death from malaria, 1820s-1900s

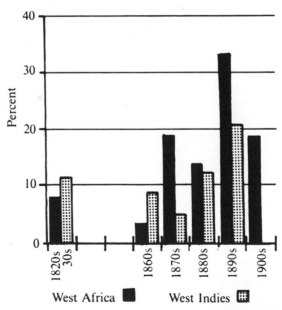

Figure 11   West Indian troops—malaria deaths as a percentage of all deaths, 1820s–1900s

down to 5.8 per thousand (compared to 1.35 for West Indians) (ANSR, 1909: 193). In short, the relocation costs in mortality for European troops remained high—at 170% for Jamaica and 164% for British West Africa in 1910–1914—considerably higher than the 40% extracted for movement from the West Indies to West Africa.[8]

TENTATIVE CONCLUSIONS

This paper is a partial report on a larger project exploring similar data in several parts of the world, but concentrating on tropical Africa. Conclusions at this point must be tentative, but some of the main lines of demographic change seem clear enough. First of all, mortality dropped dramatically over this century, apparently more steeply than at any equivalent period either before or since. Relocation costs in mortality also declined, though they remained greater for Europeans in the tropics than for Afro-West Indians serving in Africa. In time, the most spectacular decrease in mortality rates occurred at two points. The absolute rate per 1000 dropped most between the 1870s and 1880s for West Indians in Africa and the West Indies alike. The percentage decrease, however, was greater in both between 1903–1908 and 1909–1913 (see Appendix Tables 3 and 4).[9] The drop of the 1880s in the West African death rate is overwhelmingly associated with a decrease in deaths from dysentery, diarrhea, and malaria. In the West Indies, however, the decrease was smaller and was associated with lower death rates from both forms of lung disease in a period when deaths from both malaria and intestinal infections were actually rising.

Table 1   African troops serving in the Sierra Leone command, 1819–1836

Disease	Rate per 1000 mean strength:		Percentage of total:	
	Admissions	Deaths	Admissions	Deaths
Fevers	54	2.4	7.7	8.0
Eruptive fevers	52	6.9	7.4	22.9
Diseases of the lungs	51	6.3	7.3	20.9
Diseases of the liver	4	1.1	0.6	3.7
Stomach and bowels	131	5.3	18.7	17.6
Diseases of the brain	6	1.6	0.9	5.3
Dropsies	5	0.3	0.7	1.0
Rheumatic	65		9.3	0.0
Venereal	117		16.7	0.0
Abscesses and ulcers	107		15.3	0.0
Diseases of the eye	19		2.7	0.0
Diseases of the skin	60		8.6	0.0
Other	28		4.0	0.0
Total disease	699			
				0.0
Wounds and injuries	59	2.2		7.3
Punishment	44			0.0
Wounds in action	10	1.4		4.7
Other disease and accidents		2.6		8.6
Grand total	812	30.1	100	100

Source: Great Britain Parliamentary Papers [PP], 1840, xxx [C.288]: 16.

Table 2   African troops serving in the West Indies, 1817–1836

Disease	Rate per 100 mean strength:		Percentage of total:	
	Admissions	Deaths	Admissions	Deaths
Fevers	168	4.6	23.9	11.50
Eruptive fevers	9	2.5	1.3	6.25
Diseases of the lungs	99	16.5	14.1	41.25
Diseases of the liver	7	0.9	1.0	2.25
Stomach and bowels	93	7.4	13.2	18.50
Diseases of the brain	10	2.2	1.4	5.50
Dropsies	5	2.1	0.7	5.25
Rheumatic	74	11.7	10.5	
Venereal	17		2.4	0.00
Abscesses and ulcers	182		25.9	0.00
Diseases of the eye	16		2.3	
Diseases of the skin	7		1.0	0.00
Other	15		2.1	0.00
Total disease	702		100.0	
Wounds and injuries		3.8		
Punishment	80			
Other disease and accidents	38			9.5
Grand total	820	40		100

Source: PP, 1837–1838, xl (123): 11–12.

Table 3   British West Indies, 1816–1914.
Basic health indicators for West Indian troops

Years	Represent-ing	Per thousand mean strength			
		Admis-sions	Dead	Invalided/discharged	Constantly sick
1803–16	1810s		64.00		
1819–28	1820s	856.75	39.42		
1829–36	1830s	699.88	37.50		
1837–46	1840s	768.20	32.16		
	1850s				
1859–63	1860s	896.50	20.13		
1870–79	1870s	1071.50	19.28	27.23	
1880–89	1880s	1132.70	14.94	42,65	64.39
1890–99	1890s	1191.90	13.34	47.70	77.55
1903–08	1900s	866.50	9.54	71.44	64.77
1909–13	1910s	693.90	3.06	37.11	46.73

Sources: PP, 1837–1838; xl (138), 11–12. (Windward and leeward)
    AMSR for 1859: 74. (windward and leeward for 1840s)
    AMSR for 1864: 68. (windward and leeward command)
    AMSR for 1874: 77. (windward and leeward command)
    AMSR for 1880: 103. (West Indies)
    AMSR for 1890: 225. (West Indies)
    AMSR for 1900: 189. (Jamaica)
    AMSR for 1909: 191. (Jamaica, omitting 1906 on account of earth-quake.)
    ASMR for 1914: 58. (Jamaica)

Table 4   British West Africa, 1819–1914.
Basic health indicators for non-European troops

Years	Represent-ing	Admis-sions	Dead	Invalided/discharged	Constantly sick
		Per thousand mean strength			
1819–28	1820s	690.80	28.81		
1829–36	1830s	782.63	29.35		
	1840s				
	1850s				
1859–63	1860s	1061.57	31.95		42.58
1869–73	1870s	1579.00	38.48	15.70	
1879–84	1880s	1511.70	21.26	13.98	64.11
1890–99	1890s	1788.40	18.41	51.03	83.64
1904–08	1900s	870.70	8.46	25.59	46.57
1909–13	1910s	1144.10	4.29	28.06	48.44

Note: Rates exclude killed in action or from wounds received in action.
Sources: PP, 1840: xxx [C. 288], 15 (mainly African); AMSR for 1864: 80–83. (mainly West Indian; AMSR for 1874: 81–85. (mainly West Indian); AMSR for 1885: 205. (includes some African); AMSR for 1900: 293. (includes some African); AMSR for 1909: 195. (West Indian Regiment only); ASMR for 1914: 54.

Table 5   British West Indies, 1816–1914.
Relocation costs in mortality

Decade:	West Africa mortality per 1000	West Indies mortality per 1000	Relocation cost West Africa to West Indies (percentage)	Relocation cost West Indies to West Africa (percentage)
1810s		64.00		
1820s	28.21	39.42	36.80	
1830s	29.35	37.50	27.77	
1840s		32.16		
1850s				
1860s	31.95	21.15		51.06
1870s	38.48	19.28		99.59
1880s	21.26	14.94		42.30
1890s	18.41	13.34		38.01
1900s	8.46	9.54		−11.32
1910s	4.29	3.06		40.20

Source: Appendix Tables 3 and 4.

Table 6   Tubercular disease

Years	Standing for:	Rate per 1000		Percentage of total	
		Admissions	Deaths	Admissions	Deaths
West Indies					
1859–63	1860s	15.60	5.93	1.74	29.46
1869–73	1870s	27.30	8.79	2.76	41.91
1879–83	1880s	13.30	5.10	1.22	32.14
1890–99	1890s	14.80	2.77	1.24	20.76
1905–10	1900s	11.10	0.25	1.28	2.92
West Africa					
1859–63	1860s	11.40	6.13	1.19	4.40
1869–73	1870s	15.10	6.30	0.96	16.37
1879–84	1880s	21.50	8.15	1.42	38.28
1890–99	1890s	12.70	4.90	0.71	26.47
1906–10	1900s	5.50	1.45	0.70	19.81

Note: The table picks up "tubercular disease" for 1859–1863, "scrofula, phthisis, etc." for 1869–1873, "tubercular" for 1879–1884 and 1890–1899, and "tubercule of the lung" plus "other tubercular" for 1905–1910.
Sources for Tables 6, 7, 8, and 9: PP, 1837–1838: xl (123), 11–12; PP, 1840: xxx [C. 288], 16; AMSR for 1859, 74–75, 150–151; for 1860: 172–173; for 1861: 172–173; for 1862: 196–197; for 1864: 14–15; for 1871: 385; for 1872: 492–493; for 1873: 88–89; for 1874: 77–78, 84–85; for 1885: 203–205; for 1900: 289–291; for 1911: 151, 155.

Table 7 Diseases of the Lungs

Years	Standing for:	Rate per 1000		Percentage of total	
		Admissions	Deaths	Admissions	Deaths
West Indies					
Including tuberculosis					
1817–36	1820s/30s	99.00	16.50	12.07	41.04
1937–46	1840s	87.00	9.90	10.82	30.75
Other than tubercular					
1859–63	1860s	77.10	2.69	8.60	13.36
1869–73	1870s	60.40	2.14	6.11	10.31
1879–84	1880s	58.70	1.48	5.37	9.33
1890–99	1890s	71.60	0.32	6.01	2.40
1905–10	1900s	48.30	0.50	5.58	5.85
West Africa					
Including tuberculosis					
1817–36	1820s/30s	54.00	2.40	7.70	8.00
Other than tubercular					
1859–63	1860s	63.17	4.87	6.57	14.95
1869–73	1870s	82.30	4.57	5.21	11.88
1879–84	1880s	135.70	2.91	8.98	13.67
1890–99	1890s	55.80	2.30	3.12	12.43
1906–10	1900s	29.00	0.87	3.71	11.89

Note: Table picks up "diseases of the lungs" for 1817–36, "diseases of the respiratory system" for 1837–46 through 1890–99, and "respiratory" plus "pneumonia" and "sore throat" for 1906–10.

Table 8 Dysentery/Diarrhea

Years	Standing for:	Per 1000 strength		Percentage of total	
		Admissions	Deaths	Admissions	Deaths
West Indies					
1817–36	1820s/30s	93.00	7.40	13.20	18.50
1837–46	1840s	49.40	3.36	6.43	
	1850s	17.90		2.00	
1859–63	1860s	35.90	1.08	4.00	5.37
1869–73	1870s	86.90	1.34	8.79	6.45
1879–84	1880s	91.70	2.13	8.62	14.14
1890–99	1890s	100.20	0.96	8.99	7.75
1905–10	1900s	65.90	0.75	8.10	18.36
West Africa					
1817–36	1820s/30s	131.00	5.30	18.70	17.60
1837–46	1840s				
	1850s				
1859–63	1860s	34.87	2.99	3.64	9.27
1869–73	1870s	208.40	9.91	13.20	25.75
1879–84	1880s	135.70	2.91	8.98	13.69
1890–99	1890s	41.90	4.10	41.90	0.90
1906–10	1900s	23.10	0.58	2.43	5.03

Sources: See Table 6.

Note: This table picks up on diseases labelled "diseases of the stomach and bowels" in 1817–1836, "diseases of the digestive system" in 1837–1846, "dysentery and diarrhea" in 1859–1863, "diseases of the digestive system" in 1869–1873 and 1879–1884, the sum of "dysentery" and "diseases of the digestive system" in 1890–1899 and 1905–1910.

Table 9   Malaria

Years	Standing for:	Per 1000 strength		Percentage of total	
		Admissions	Deaths	Admissions	Deaths
West Indies					
1817–36	1820s/30s	168.00	4.60	23.90	11.50
1837–46	1840s	58.30		7.59	
	1850s				
1859–63	1860s	86.60	1.80	9.66	8.94
1869–73	1870s	114.00	1.07	11.54	5.15
1879–84	1880s	133.50	1.83	12.55	12.15
1890–99	1890s	153.50	2.56	13.82	20.68
1905–10	1900s	120.20	0.00	14.82	0.00
West Africa					
1817–36	1820s/30s	54.00	2.40	7.70	8.00
1837–46	1840s				
	1850s				
1859–63	1860s	190.97	1.20	19.93	3.47
1869–73	1870s	500.16	7.24	31.68	18.81
1879–84	1880s	477.00	2.91	31.55	13.69
1890–99	1890s	933.40	6.01	54.12	33.56
1906–10	1900s	234.10	1.35	34.44	18.70

Sources: See Table 6.
Note: Based on data for "fevers" 1819–1836, for "paroxysmal fevers" for 1859–1863 through 1879–1884, and for "malaria" in 1890–1899 and 1905–1910.

NOTES

1 This body of research goes back at least to Curtin (1968) and comes down to Steckel and Jensen (1985: 34–35), which lists most of the relevant articles. See also Higman (1976).

2 These are principally found in the Great Britain Parliamentary Papers (PP), especially Alexander Tulloch and others, "Statistical Reports of Sickness, Invaliding, and Mortality among Troops in the West Indies," (PP, 1837–1838: XL (138)) and "Statistical Reports on Sickness, Mortality, and Invaliding among Troops in Western Africa, Cape of Good Hope, and Mauritius" (PP, 1840: XXX [C.228]), and in the reports of the Army Medical Service published annually from 1859 onward. That series also appeared in PP.

3 The Windward and Leeward Command is taken as the most reliable West Indian sample at this period because it was the largest, and because it included a diversity of West Indian conditions.

4 Percentage of deaths in the "Febrile group" death at sample time periods.

	1859–1863	1868–1873	1879–1884	1890–1899
Continued	29	39	0	45
Yellow	0	7	8	0
Paroxysmal	71	53	92	55

Great Britain Army Medical Service Reports (AMSR) reports for 1864: 65; 1874: 77–78; 1885: 203; 1900: 289.

5 These decreases of 97% for the West Indies and 70% for West Africa compare with an equivalent drop of 84% for British troops serving in Britain itself, 95% for European troops serving in the West Indies, and 99% for British troops serving in British West Africa (PP, 1837–1838, XL [138]; PP. 1840, XXX (C. 228); AMSR for 1910 through 1914).

6 McKeown (1976) was succeeded by a great variety of commentary that can be found summarized in Fogel (1984). It was also the central focus of the Fall 1983 issue of the Journal of Interdisciplinary History.

7 Deaths from malaria were 17.14 per thousand for these years, out of a total death rate for European non-coms of 40 thousand (AMSR for 1900:291).

8 This is from AMSR annual series for 1910 through 1914, data complete to July 31, 1914.

9 It is impossible to assign cause here, as it could be done for earlier times. After 1910, the Royal Army Medical Corps stopped reporting cause-of-death for non-European troops. An extensive search in the Public Record Office and other British collections failed to turn up manuscript reports that might fill the gap.

REFERENCES

Aufderheide, A. C., J. L. Angel, J. O. Kelley, A. C. Outlaw, M. A. Outlaw, G. Rapp, Jr., and L. E. Wittmers (1985) "Lead in Bone III. Prediction of Social Correlates From Skeletal Lead Content in Four Colonial

American Populations (Catoctin Furnace, College Landing, Governor's Land, and Irene Mound)." American Journal of Physical Anthropology 66: 353–361. •

Bruce-Chwatt, L. J. (1980) Essential Malariology. London: England. ¢

Burnet, Sir M. and D. O. White (1972) Natural History of Infectious Disease. 4th ed. Cambridge, England.

Curtin, P. D. (1968) "The Epidemiology of the Slave Trade." The Political Science Quarterly 83: 190–216.

——— (1969) The Atlantic Slave Trade: A Census. Madison, WI.

Fogel, R. F. (1984) Nutrition and the Decline of Mortality since 1700: Some Preliminary Findings. Cambridge MA: National Bureau of Economic Research, Working Paper 1402.

Great Britain Army Medical Service Reports [AMSR] (1840, 1859, 1860, 1861, 1862, 1864, 1871, 1872, 1873, 1874, 1880, 1885, 1890, 1900, 1909, 1911, 1914) London, England.

Great Britain Parliamentary Papers [PP] (1837–1838, 1840) 2 volumes. London, England.

Handler, J., A. C. Aufderheide, R. S. Corruccini, E. M. Brandon, and L. E. Wittmers, Jr. (1986) "Lead Contact and Poisoning in Barbados Slaves: Historical, Chemical, and Biological Evidence." Social Science History 10: 399–425.

Higman, B. W. (1976) Slave Population and Economy in Jamaica, 1807–1834. Cambridge, England.

Kiple, K. F. (1984) The Caribbean Slave: A Biological History. New York, NY.

——— and V. Kiple (1980) "The African Connection: Race, Disease and Racism" Phylon 41:211–222. •

McKeown, T. (1976) The Modern Rise of Population. New York, NY.

Packard, R. (1983) "White Plague, Black Labor: Industrialization and Tuberculosis in Southern Africa, 1850–1960." Unpublished paper presented at African Studies Association. Boston, MA (10 December).

Rosenberg, C. E. (1979) "Florence Nightingale on Contagion: The Hospital as a Moral Universe," in C. E. Rosenberg (ed.) Healing and History: Essays for Charles Rosen. London and New York.

Smith, D. C. (1976) "Quinine and Fever: The Development of the Effective Dosage." Journal of the History of Medicine (July): 343–367.

Steckel, R. and R. Jensen (1985) Determinants of Slave and Crew Mortality in the Atlantic Slave Trade, Cambridge, MA, National Bureau of Economic Research, Working Paper no. 1540.

Lead Contact and Poisoning in Barbados Slaves: Historical, Chemical, and Biological Evidence

JEROME S. HANDLER, ARTHUR C. AUFDERHEIDE,

ROBERT S. CORRUCCINI, ELIZABETH M. BRANDON,

AND LORENTZ E. WITTMERS, JR.

LEAD CONTACT AND lead poisoning have received scant attention in discussions of early West Indian societies but are potentially important issues in considering the health and medical problems of blacks. Although our discussion focuses on Barbados, the West Indian historical literature strongly suggests that our general findings are applicable to other Caribbean areas and have implications for understanding some of the disabilities of early white populations as well. In this paper we also seek to illustrate how bioanthropological and chemical analyses of slave skeletal remains and historical data can complement one another in defining and investigating various dimensions of slave life.

Jerome S. Handler and Robert S. Corruccini are professors, and Elizabeth M. Brandon a Ph.D. student, in the department of anthropology, Southern Illinois University, Carbondale. Arthur C. Aufderheide is Professor and Head, Department of Pathology, and Lorentz E. Wittmers, Jr. Associate Professor, Department of Physiology—both in the School of Medicine, University of Minnesota, Duluth.

Archaeological research in Barbados, funded by the National Science Foundation and the Wenner-Gren Foundation for Anthropological Research, was done in collaboration with Frederick W. Lange. Bioanthropological analyses of skeletal materials was partially supported by Southern Illinois University's Office of Research and Development; support for the chemical analyses was provided by the St. Luke's Foundation (Duluth), Minnesota Medical Foundation (Minneapolis), the Archaeometry Laboratory (University of Minnesota, Duluth), and the Center for Ancient Studies (University of Minnesota, Minneapolis). Some of the historical research was conducted

Modern studies treating medical issues in West Indian slave societies have barely discussed lead poisoning in general or its relation to slave morbidity in particular. Although some works state or imply that slaves were affected by lead poisoning, this is usually mentioned only briefly while other studies of British Caribbean slavery do not report lead poisoning at all when discussing slave diseases and health problems (Bridenbaugh and Bridenbaugh, 1972: 193–194; Craton, 1978: 125; Dunn, 1972: 217, 306; Kiple, 1984: 100; Sheridan, 1985: 200).

Various symptoms caused by lead absorption which would be diagnosed specifically today were unrecognized by early West Indian physicians and were undoubtedly hidden in their discussions of other slave diseases. It is clear, however, that a form of lead poisoning, the so-called "dry bellyache," which involved extremely painful intestinal cramps, was widespread in the West Indies during the seventeenth century and for much of the eighteenth. Called "dry" because the cramps were not accompanied by diarrhea but rather by severe constipation, the disease affected whites as well as blacks. It was also common in the British mainland colonies (e.g., Grainger, 1764: 32; Hillary, 1766: 182; Moseley, 1787: 525–540; Salmon, 1693: 854; Aronson, 1983: 38; Guinee, 1972: 283; Eisinger, 1982: 282; Wedeen, 1984: 43).[1]

Most early West Indian general medical works that mention or discuss the dry bellyache almost universally imply—and sometimes explicitly state—that they are referring only to whites (e.g., Hillary, 1766: 182–200; Hunter, 1785; Quier, 1773; Towne, 1726: 87–

---

while Handler held a summer fellowship at the John Carter Brown Library (Brown University) and a mini-sabbatical for research from the Office of Research and Development at Southern Illinois University. Briefer versions of this paper were given at the Society for Caribbean Studies conference (London, July 1985), the meeting of the Social Science History Association (Chicago, November 1985), and at the Workshop in Caribbean Ethnohistory and Historical Archaeology, sponsored by the Program in Atlantic History, Culture and Society, Johns Hopkins University (February 1986).

We are grateful to Malcolm Scott and his collaborators, D. R. Chettle and L. J. Somervalle, for making available to us their unpublished data relating bone lead levels to blood lead levels; and to John Gilmore, Kenneth Kiple, Richard Sheridan, and, particularly, Stanley M. Aronson and Richard Wedeen for their comments and advice on earlier versions of this paper.

98; Trapham, 1679: 129–130; Tryon, 1684: 58–60; Warren, 1740: 32–33; Williamson, 1817: 1: 243–245; 2: 20; Wright, 1828: 232). Although slaves are very rarely mentioned, some sources, especially those specifically concerned with slave medical issues, indicate that they were also victims (Cadwalader, 1745: 45; Clark, 1797: 118; Collins, 1811: 232; Dancer, 1801: 103; Grainger, 1764: 34; Hillary, 1766: 182; Moseley, 1787: 525–540; Sloane, 1707: 1: cxix, cxx; Thomson, 1820: 42).

For Barbados specifically, all references to dry bellyache are to whites; blacks are not mentioned. However, inferential historical evidence indicates that blacks also suffered from the disease and were thus subject to lead contamination (see below). The nature and degree of such contamination is not ascertainable from this evidence; it only suggests that lead poisoning existed. This qualitative picture is independently supported and quantified by bioanthropological data which provide a more concrete perspective on lead contact and lead intoxication; they also serve as objective checks on the historical sources.

PHYSICAL EVIDENCE AND SKELETAL LEAD CONTENT ANALYSIS

Bioanthropological data derive from an analysis of Barbados slave physical remains, part of a skeleton group archaeologically excavated from a slave cemetery at Newton plantation during the early 1970s. During the slave era, Newton typified medium to large-scale Barbados sugar plantations. Although only partially excavated, the cemetery yielded the remains of 104 individuals interred from about 1660 to 1820. As of this writing, the Newton collection constitutes the largest and earliest excavated group of African and African-descended slave remains yet reported from the Caribbean or mainland North America (Handler and Lange, 1978, 1979).

Over the past several years, analyses of the Newton skeletons, particularly the teeth, have yielded information on demographic, pathological, and sociocultural topics. The physical data, when combined with historical information, have enhanced our understanding of the lifeways of Barbados slaves and of the material conditions of their lives; they have also demonstrated the contributions and potential value of physical anthropology and archaeology in dealing with sparsely documented issues relating to Caribbean slave life (see Corruccini and Handler, 1980; Corruccini et al., 1982, 1985, n.d. a, n.d. b; Handler et al., 1982; Handler and Corruccini, 1983, 1986). These earlier analyses of the Newton remains are now extended to issues surrounding lead intoxication.

Lead products in historical and modern societies have exposed humans to lead quantities that exceed the body's ability to excrete this lead, thus resulting in body lead accumulation. The blood rapidly distributes the absorbed lead and selectively stores it in certain tissues and organs; about 10% of it is ultimately deposited in soft tissues (e.g., brain, liver), many of which are vulnerable to lead's toxic effects. If there is relatively limited exposure to lead and its absorption is not great, the lead is usually eliminated by the kidneys, leaving very little of it in such tissues as bone. On the other hand, with continued absorption the excretion threshold is exceeded, and lead circulating in the blood will then damage vulnerable tissues as well as continue to accumulate in bone. The lead deposited in bone tends to be biologically inert (though slow release with urinary excretion of this lead over a long period of time may damage the kidneys) but may provide some notion of the individual's cumulative lead absorption in the years preceding death.

A trace mineral analysis method, using atomic absorption spectroscopy and developed to measure skeletal lead content, had been successfully applied to several black and white North American colonial populations before its application to the Barbados sample (Aufderheide et al., 1981, 1985; for a technical description of this method see Wittmers et al., 1981).

The analyses of Newton's slaves, based on the skeletal tissue of 48 individuals (from whom a total of 52 samples were removed), yielded a mean bone lead content of close to 118 ppm (parts per million, or micrograms of lead per gram of bone ash). This lead concentration is three to four times that of mainland colonial slave samples and is comparable to mainland colonial whites with known lead exposure (Aufderheide et al., 1981, 1985). This concentration range is also comparable to bone specimens derived from putatively lead-poisoned Romans (Mackie et al., 1975; Waldron et al., 1976). No other New World bone specimen sample demonstrates such a wide range of lead concentration values, from zero to more than 400 ppm. The 95% confidence limits of this mean lead content are from 90.5 to 144.7 ppm. Eighty-one percent of the 21 individuals who died after an estimated age of 30 (when appreciable lead could have accumulated from constant exposure sources) have lead content above 100 ppm.[2]

In order to evaluate possible relationships between bone lead content and physical or cultural traits, several statistical tests were conducted. Females showed a higher lead value than males, but this statistical difference may be due to sampling variation and error in sex assignment to poorly preserved skeletons. However, the *variation* in lead content in females is higher than in males. This may reflect greater variation in occupational exposure to environmental lead, as might have occurred among domestic servants as contrasted to fieldworking female slaves. For the Clifts plantation in Virginia, for example, investigators assumed that some female slaves were household servants in order to explain their higher lead values (Aufderheide et al., 1981). Correlation is significant between age at death and lead concentration. The trend is suggested by the increased lead levels by decade of life: age 10–19, 58 ppm; age 20–29, 110 ppm; age 30–39, 112 ppm; age 40–49, 136 ppm; age 50–59, 158 ppm. The positive lead content correlations with age support the hypothesis that lead accumulation was a direct consequence of the length of time a slave was resident in Barbados.

Clinical Implications of Skeletal Lead Content

Information about the quantity of lead in body tissue relative to clinical symptoms of lead poisoning in living populations depends on the literature of modern toxicologic experience (Mahaffey, 1977). Although the amount of lead to which an organ is exposed determines the degree of the organ's impairment and the intensity of the resulting symptoms, in living persons it is not feasible to biopsy bone, brain, or other vital organs to measure their lead content. Thus, except for the occasional use of lead concentration in deciduous teeth and the recent practice of measuring urinary lead excretion after administering a chelating agent (a chemical compound that binds with certain metals causing them to be excreted in the urine), the clinical literature of lead poisoning relates symptoms to the lead level in blood—a much more accessible material.

Until recently measuring both the blood and the bone lead content for the same individual has been difficult because of problems in obtaining a bone sample for chemical analysis in a living person. This difficulty has been overcome by an x-ray fluorescent method which measures bone lead in live individuals whose blood lead level was measured simultaneously. Since modern medical experience demonstrates a rough but useful correlation between blood lead concentration and at least certain lead poisoning symptoms (Hernberg, 1980), it becomes possible to predict symptoms of lead toxicity that would have been expected in Newton's living slave population. The x-ray fluorescent method provides a small but useful body of relevant data (Ahlgren et al., 1980; Christofferson et al., 1984; Eastwell et al., 1983; Scott, 1985).

Through regression analysis of such data, using the individual's age (ascertained from the skeletal remains) as the years of lead exposure, the mean blood level for each Newton slave was estimated from the measured bone lead concentration. These derived values were then arranged into five groups of blood lead concentration ranges; such groupings have been found clinically useful in establishing the presence or severity of some of the symptoms or signs of lead toxicity (Hernberg, 1980).

Nearly three-fourths of Newton's slaves appear to fall in a range wherein no or only mild symptoms of lead toxicity might have emerged, resulting in little, if any, impairment of their daily activities (Table 1). However, a significant fraction of those falling in the "moderate" and "severe" groups would be expected to have suffered from dry bellyache at some time; those in the higher ranges of these groups were probably affected severely and frequently enough to have their work and social activities significantly

Table 1   Frequencies arranged in five groups based on
calculated blood lead values for Newton slave skeletons*

Calculated mean blood lead**	Expected severity of symptoms	Slaves	
		Number	Percent
0–39	None	17	35
40–79	Mild	18	38
80–119	Moderate	6	13
120–199	Severe	4	8
Over 200	Very severe	3	6

* Average values were used for twice-sampled specimens.
** Micrograms of lead per deciliter of blood.

impaired, possibly with some peripheral nerve defects. At least some in the "very severe" group may well have died of brain toxicity with convulsions and terminal coma.

Lead alters many of the body's chemical systems and ultimately can impair most organs. Modern medicine recognizes a variety of clinical symptoms and signs of lead poisoning. For purposes of this paper, however, we are particularly interested in those symptoms or signs which are sufficiently overt that they could have been observed in earlier periods and recorded in historical sources. The principal symptoms results from lead's effects on the intestinal tract, peripheral nerves, and brain (see Table 2 for a summary).

Intestinal tract: Mild lead poisoning produces appetite loss, nausea, and vomiting, but as lead levels increase the intestine is paralyzed (producing constipation) and then stimulated into painful contractions or abdominal cramps. Higher lead levels may induce spasms of the abdominal wall muscles, generating excruciating pain. Diarrhea is absent from this intestinal disease, hence the historical term "dry bellyache." The presence of intestinal symptoms correlates fairly well with blood lead levels (low calcium diets, probably common among Barbados slaves, enhance

Table 2   General relationship of blood lead level to severity of three signs or symptoms of lead intoxication

| Organ | Sign or symptom | Blood lead lev | | |
		0–39	40–79	80–119
Intestinal tract	Colic	None	Appetite loss; nausea	Vomiting; con stipation; coli
Nerves	Palsy	None	None	Weakness in e tensor muscle
Brain	Convulsion	None	None	Occasional

lead absorption from the intestinal tract, leading to higher blood and bone lead levels from a given ingested lead dose [Mahaffey et al., 1973; Barltrop and Khoo, 1975; Moore et al., 1978]).

Nerves: Lead slows electrical conduction, especially along nerves supplying the muscles that raise wrists and feet. This results in a weak grip in mildly impaired persons. Severely toxic conditions may cause incapacitating paralysis ("palsy") of such muscles, producing a complete inability to lift the wrist or even the foot. Varying degrees of sensory loss may accompany the paralysis, similar to the sensation of one's foot "falling asleep." Close correlation of nerve symptoms with blood lead levels is less well documented, although clinical muscle weakness or paralysis is usually evident only at higher values of lead content.

Brain: Children are much more susceptible than adults to the effects of lead toxicity on the brain. Even in children, however, considerable variation in these effects occurs at given blood levels, and predictions listed in Table 2 should be viewed as generalizations. Mildly affected adults or children may show mood or behavioral aberrancies or headaches. The most easily recognized symptoms are convulsions; in severe cases, they can become fre-

licrograms per deciliter

120–199	Over 200
Frequent severe colic	Colic with muscle spasm
Marked weakness or paralysis	Extensor muscle paralysis common
Common	Life threatening; coma

quent and prolonged, ultimately producing coma and death (lead encephalopathy).

Such symptoms or signs are among the more obvious and observable effects of lead poisoning, ones that often accompany historical accounts of dry bellyache (see below). But lead has other, albeit more subtle, toxic effects. For example, even relatively low blood lead levels can produce measurably impaired intellect and mental retardation in children, and lead's interference with hemoglobin formation causes anemia with its accompanying weakness, loss of energy, and shortness of breath. High blood pressure has also been related to lead as well as speech loss, deafness, blindness, visions, and insanity. Even after cessation of exposure, lead may be leached from the bone and excreted in the urine for many years, damaging the kidneys and resulting in fatal renal failure (Betts et al., 1973; Harlan et al., 1985; Lauwers et al., 1986; Needleman et al., 1979; Vermande-Van Eck and Meigs, 1960: 223; Zielhuis, 1975).

In laboratory animals, lead exposure has been shown to decrease fertility, increase stillbirths and miscarriages, cause disturbances in the menstrual cycle, reduce average birth weights and the survival rate of newborns, and produce weak and slowly developing offspring (e.g., Harris et al., 1979; Stowe and Goyer, 1971; Vermande-Van Eck and Meigs, 1960; Weller, 1915; Jacquet, 1977). Although Bell and Thomas (1980: 183), after reviewing the literature, conclude that lead's "full impact on human reproduction remains unresolved," Uzych (1985: 9, 16) has more recently observed that a widely accepted industrial view holds that maternal lead exposure in humans "may seriously jeopardize the health of the unborn child." In addition, he writes, a corpus of data "indicates that paternal lead exposure may adversely affect pregnancy outcome" and cause increases in miscarriages, stillbirths, and postnatal mortality; exposure to lead in males may also "cause decreased fertility . . . and be associated with chromosomal changes." In brief, although more data in this area are needed, available information suggests that human male exposure to lead "may be associated with significant reproductive-related harm."

In summary (cf. Table 1), the Newton skeletal lead content suggests that the plantation's living slave population had widespread and significant access to one or more lead sources. The evidence indicates they absorbed this lead in quantities great enough to produce some symptoms or signs of lead poisoning at some time during their lives in perhaps as many as one-third of them, severe enough to interfere with their usual activities at least intermittently in a smaller number, and to threaten or terminate life in a significant minority. Thus, the Newton skeletal lead concentrations are of such an order to expect that the plantation's slaves, as a population, regularly displayed manifestations of clinical lead poisoning ranging from mild to marked severity. This conclusion is independently and generally supported by the historical evidence which suggests the presence of dry bellyache in Barbados' wider slave population.

LEAD POISONING IN BARBADOS: HISTORICAL EVIDENCE

"Called . . . by the people of Barbadoes the dry Belly-Ach," wrote Dr. Richard Towne (1726: 87) in the 1720s, "the nervous colick . . . is so popular a disease . . . that it may very justly be reckoned as endemic . . . , most people there at one time or other having felt its cruelty"; the dry bellyache was the "most frequent and most fatal species" of a general category of diseases labelled "colicks," i.e., spasmodic abdominal pains. The earliest known direct reference to the disease occurs in 1660, when a colonist reported a "weakness and feebleness in all my lymbes, being the dreggs of a desperate disease which we call the Belly-ake" (quoted in Bridenbaugh and Bridenbaugh, 1972: 193). Thomas Tryon, who had lived in Barbados during the 1660s, also mentions this "most cruel disease" (1684: 58–59) which reached epidemic proportions by 1695, if not much earlier (Russell, 1695; Dunn [1972: 306] describes an incident in which the dry bellyache "even affected Barbados politics in 1684").

The dry bellyache was "so called from its affecting that part of the body with great costiveness [severe constipation] and pain" (Hughes, 1750: 34). With the first noticeable symptoms, Towne (1726: 88–90) reported, "the belly is seized with an intolerable piercing pain," and during the early phases, which might last a week or two, "the patient is on a perpetual rack, with scarce any remission or pause from pain. . . . The belly continues . . . obstinately costive, very little urine is made, the strength is greatly impaired"; and "the breath stinking very offensively," added

Hughes (1750: 34). Based on his experiences in Barbados, Towne (1726: 88) concluded "there is not in the whole compass of infirmities which flesh is heir to, any one that afflicts human nature in a more exquisite degree than this unmerciful torture." In short, the dry bellyache involved "excruciating torture of the bowels" (Collins, 1811: 232) and was considered, according to Dr. James Clark (a late eighteenth-century resident of Dominica), "the most painful of the diseases to which the inhabitants of the West Indies are liable. . . . The torments of those labouring under this disease are beyond conception, and excite the commiseration of all who attend them" (Clark, 1797: 115–116).

Dr. William Hillary (1766: 183–185), a well-known English physician who practiced in Barbados in the late 1740s and 1750s, provides a detailed and vivid description of dry bellyache (which, to some extent, is based on Towne's [1726: 88–90] earlier description):

> It generally seizes the patient with an acute pain at the pit of the stomach, which extends itself down with gripping pains to the bowels, which are soon after much distended with wind, with frequent reachings to vomit. . . . The belly usually continues most obstinately costive and the patient discharges but little urine, and that often with pain and much difficulty. . . . The extreme parts of the body are often cold, and sometimes the violence of the pain causes cold clammy sweats, and faintings: their mind is generally much affected, and their spirits sunk very low . . . they become weak, and that weakness increases until those extreme parts [of the arms and legs] become paralytic, with a total loss of motion, though a benumbed sensation often remains. The subtle cause of this disease is sometimes carried . . . to the brain, and produces a stupor, or a delirium; and soon after the whole nervous system is so affected as to produce strong convulsions which too often are followed by death.

In one form or another the symptoms described by Hillary are also reported in other contemporary descriptions of the disease in Barbados, and are also commonly reported for other British mainland and Caribbean colonies (e.g., Hughes, 1750: 34; Cadwalader, 1745: 1–2; Clark, 1797: 115–119; Hunter, 1785; Wedeen, 1984: 24, 43. Eisinger [1982: 280] provides an effective modern description of "colica Pictonum," based on historical accounts).

As indicated above, although some West Indian sources mention black victims of dry bellyache, blacks are not mentioned in the Barbados sources. Inferential historical evidence, however, suggests that slaves suffered from the disease. This evidence derives from the prevalence of dry bellyache reported for the island during the seventeenth and eighteenth centuries and the facts that no medical accounts explicitly exclude blacks and few specifically mention the race of patients. Moreover, the knowledgeable Griffith Hughes (1750: 34), writing of Barbados in the 1730s and 1740s, noted that the principal victims of dry bellyache were rum distillers, sugar boilers, and plantation overseers; at the time, distillers were generally poor whites, but slaves were also distillers and they also constituted the majority of the sugar boilers (Bennett, 1958: 12; Dickson, 1789: 40–41; Drax, 1755: 47–48; Ligon, 1657: 90–91; Oldmixon, 1741; 2: 154).

Inferential historical evidence, then, and solid physical evidence from the Newton skeletons mutually support one another in pointing to lead poisoning as a major pathology among Barbados slaves.

Possible Sources of Lead in the Newton Skeletons

The possibility of environmental contamination of archaeological bones always needs to be considered in a skeletal mineral study; however, we can establish no likely factors to suggest post-mortem contamination of the Newton skeletons. All evidence indicates that the bone lead was deposited during the lifetimes of the individuals concerned. What, then, is the most likely source (or sources) of lead in Newton's burials?

Although they focus on white populations, modern historical studies of lead contamination and poisoning in the North American colonies and England offer some clues. Lead could have contaminated a fairly long list of material products such as flour, whitened bread, snuff, hair dyes, certain cosmetics, house paints, glass, tea, pepper and various medicaments, including opiates, which Barbados imported. Although some of these items may have occasionally been used by Barbados slaves, none (with the possible exception of medicines administered by plantation doctors) played a significant role in slave life (e.g., Aronson, 1983:

39–40; McCord, 1954b: 80, 1954c: 123; Wedeen, 1984: 50, 60, 61, 174, 175; Towne, 1726: 120; Handler and Lange, 1978: 291).[3]

Another category of goods which may have affected slaves includes various foods and beverages that were contaminated by pewter and lead-glazed vessels used for storage, preparation, or serving. In eighteenth-century England, for example, lead-contaminated cider that was stored in lead-glazed vessels, and a variety of other liquids, including wine, could also absorb lead when made or stored in lead-glazed earthenware or other lead-containing vessels such as pewter. Cider and wine were regular English exports to Barbados, as were "leaden ware" and pewter. Slaves, however, usually did not consume such beverages although they may have had occasional access to them. In addition, Barbadian whites used pewter, and such pewter items as "dishes," "pans," "spoons," "flasks," "water plates," "measures," and "pots" of various sizes were found in seventeenth- and eighteenth-century middle and upper socioeconomic level households; the 1781 effects of a coppersmith included 1,038 pounds of "new lead" and 1,304 pounds of "old pewter," also suggesting the extent of lead and pewter usage. However, there is no evidence that such items functioned to any degree in slave households or domestic life (Aronson, 1983: 39–40; Guinee, 1972: 284; McCord, 1953b: 573, 576; Waldron, 1969: 75; Wedeen, 1984: 44, 66; Frere, 1768: 120–121; Oldmixon, 1708; 2: 154–162; Ogilby, 1670: 380. Also, household inventories: see, for example, Recopied Deeds Books, RB 3/5: 96, 374, 451; 3/24: 459; 3/37: 104; and Inventories, Boxes 1780–1786, 1787–1793: passim, Barbados Department of Archives).

As in the North American mainland colonies, Barbadians also could have had their water supplies contaminated by lead drains and household gutters. Lacking major rivers and with an irregular distribution of surface springs, islanders largely depended on rainwater. Whites sometimes excavated wells to tap underground springs or streams, but they commonly used cisterns, usually built adjacent to the plantation owner's or manager's house, which collected the rain that funneled through roof gutters. These gutters were of lead, and fragments of them can still be found at some old plantation houses today. Although domestic slaves may have had some access to the rainwater stored in cisterns, most plantation slaves were compelled to use open ponds for their water supplies (Aronson, 1983: 39; Handler and Lange, 1978: 299–300).

Historical sources indicate that Barbados slaves used earthenware in their households. Some of this pottery, either locally made or imported, may have been lead glazed, but no archaeological or historical evidence suggests the extent of its usage. Moreover, despite their use of pottery, the slaves' most common household items were made from organic materials such as calabashes and gourds. Thus, although lead-glazed pottery as a possible contaminant of Newton's skeletons cannot be discounted, its role remains problematical (Handler, 1963a, 1963b; Handler and Lange, 1978: 136–142).

Based on presently available evidence, *rum* appears to be the most likely *major* source (though probably not the only one) of lead contamination among Newton's slaves and, by extension, among Barbados slaves in general.

Abundant evidence exists that consumption of lead-contaminated alcoholic beverages in general can result in lead poisoning, and modern historical studies also suggest that lead poisoning resulting from alcohol consumption was quite common in England, North America, and the British West Indies during the eighteenth century. In particular, rum—much of it "grossly contaminated . . . whether . . . distilled in the West Indies or in New England"—was a major contributor to lead poisoning, a common disorder among North American colonials (McCord, 1953a: 393; cf. 1954c; Aronson, 1983; Eisinger, 1982; Waldron, 1969; Wedeen, 1984: 40, 45, 46, 112).

In the 1670s, Dr. Thomas Trapham (1679: 133) observed similarities in the symptoms of cattle exposed to lead fumes in Derbyshire, England, and those appearing in Jamaican victims of dry bellyache. However, he made no explicit connection between the disease and lead poisoning, and the symptoms of dry bellyache were not established as lead poisoning in the medical literature until the 1760s. Although starting at least a century earlier, West Indian writers on the disease recognized some connection between it and rum, not until the late eighteenth century, not many years after the link between dry bellyache and lead poisoning was made, was the role of rum in producing the disease also identified (Aronson, 1983: 39; McCord, 1953a: 393–396, 399; Wedeen, 1984:

34, 40, 42, 45, 47; Hillary, 1766: 182; Towne, 1726: 89–90; Tryon, 1684: 59–60; cf. Sloane, 1707; I: cv, cviii, cxix; Hughes, 1750: 34, 36).

By the late eighteenth century most physicians writing about the West Indies came to accept the linkage between dry bellyache, on the one hand, and rum and lead, on the other. Although some continued to deny that contaminated rum was a major cause of the disease (Moseley, 1787: 530–531; Dancer, 1801: 103), the number of sceptics gradually decreased, and modern medical history literature agrees that the rum was contaminated by lead used in distillation machinery, particularly the "worms" and "still heads" (e.g., Eisinger, 1982: 282; Guinee, 1972: 284; McCord, 1953a: 393, 394, 395, 399; Weeden, 1984: 42).

Distillation machinery involves three major components: a *boiler* (or *still body*) for heating the liquid; a *condensor* which cools the vapor and turns it into liquid again; and a *receiver,* a vessel which collects the distilled liquid. The "worm" was the contemporary name for the condensor, a long spiral tubing; the "still head" (or "still neck") was the boiler part that prevented the liquid's accidental boiling over. England's exports to the West Indies in general, it should be stressed, included large quantities of "boylers, stills, and other useful vessels of copper, lead, and pewter," and until the late eighteenth or early nineteenth centuries West Indian plantation distilleries used copper stills, usually outfitted with pewter or lead "worms" and "still heads" (Thomas, 1690: 11; Miller, 1815: 64; Porter, 1830: 94, 204–206; Hunter, 1785: 235–236; Edwards, 1810; 3: 52; Clark, 1797: 124; Moseley, 1787: 530–531).

Early Barbados inventories of plantation distillery equipment frequently mention "stills and worms" and sometimes specify the material of their manufacture. A 1660 inventory, for example, notes "four copper stills and heads . . . [and] four pewter worms"; the "worm being leaded," specifies a 1685 inventory. One in 1789 mentions 1,327 pounds of "old pewter worms"; in the same year another includes "5 leaden worm moulds." Distilleries also contained "cisterns of working liquor" and "receiving cisterns" that could be iron, or lined with, or made of, lead. A 1746 inventory also lists a "leaden water pump" in the distillery, suggesting what may have been a more widespread pattern (Recopied Deeds Books, RB 3/4: 186, 702; 3/5: 198, 614–615, 879; 3/22: 491–

492, 505–506; 3/27: 196; 3/37: 104; Inventories, Boxes 1780–1786, 1787–1793: Hackett, Taylor, Byrrowes; Barbados Department of Archives; Belgrove, 1755: 24–25, 29; Drax, 1755: 78–79).

Lead dissolves fairly easily, particularly in acid solutions which characterize fermentation products. Alcohol in general can not only dissolve substances but also can effectively dissolve lead. Heat facilitates the process. Since distillation involves heating a liquid, when lead distillation equipment is used (or even copper equipment soldered with lead) the lead is particularly vulnerable to being leached by the acidic fermented solution from the equipment into the liquid (e.g., Eisinger, 1982; McCord, 1954a; Waldron, 1969; cf. Hunter, 1785). These general comments are particularly applicable to rum distillation as it was practiced in colonial America and the early West Indies.[4]

Other aspects of West Indian sugar technology also probably contributed to lead contamination. Dr. John Hunter of Jamaica observed (1785: 236): "In the process of making sugar, the juice of the canes comes frequently in contact with lead." Windmill rollers could be "plated of lead," as a Barbados plantation inventory recorded, and the cane juice was first collected in a lead-lined cistern, or "leaden bed" under the rollers, from which it flowed through a lead pipe, an open lead gutter, or a lead-lined wooden gutter, "exposed to the action of the open air, which is known to corrode lead in some degree," to the boiling house (Hunter, 1785: 236; see also, Edwards, 1810; 3: 38, 40; Miller, 1815: 61; Sheridan 1973: 114–115; and plantation inventories in Recopied Deeds Books, RB 3/4: 186, 702; 3/5: 615–616; 3/22: 505–506; 3/25: 390; Inventories, Boxes 1780–1787, 1787–1793: passim, Barbados Department of Archives).

The boiling house could also contain a "leaden cistern to receive liquor from the mill" and a "leaden gutter" could convey the liquid to the first of the "coppers." Although the large cauldrons, variously called "boilers" or "coppers"—in which the juice was boiled and crystallized—were of copper, they were often lined or "lay'd" with lead; the "coppers" themselves could be set in lead-covered beds. For example, in the late seventeenth century, Henry Drax, a Barbados planter, instructed his manager that in preparing for sugar manufacture, the boiling-house coppers should be "in good repair, and well faced with lead, which must be very thick"; "all the coppers and leaden beds," he stressed, "must be scowered and washed clean." The crystallized sugar, removed from the last and smallest "copper"—the "tayche"—would be placed to cool in a wood or metal vat, which may have used lead, and the residue of sugar crystallization to be used in rum making was conveyed by lead gutters to another reservoir at the still (Drax, 1755: 75–76; Recopied Deeds Books, RB 3/5: 594, 615–616; 3/22: 505–506; 3/25: 390; 3/37: 104, Barbados Department of Archives; Hunter, 1785: 236; Miller, 1815: 62; Oldmixon, 1708; 2: 152; Hartley 1949: 68–69).

Jamaicans took lead from old worms, combining it with tin to make solder (Hunter, 1785: 240); this custom probably also existed elsewhere in the West Indies. In any case, Barbados plantations apparently commonly used lead solder to repair "boilers" as well as other sugar and rum making equipment. In the mid-eighteenth century a Barbados planter advised that the "metals and utensils" required for a 500 acre plantation should include "10,000 lb. of lead . . . per solder," and early nineteenth-century records of Drax Hall, one of the island's oldest sugar plantations, show repair expenditures for "leading 3 racking coppers," "leading and soldering 5 tayches," "lead making and soldering round the top of a skipping gutter," and "lead soldering round the top of 3 scumming cisterns"; in fact, in 1818 the plantation purchased several "sheets [of] milled lead, 16 ft. by 6 ft." There is every reason to believe that Drax Hall reflected the practices of other Barbadian plantations in the same and earlier periods (Belgrove, 1755: 37–38; Records of Drax Hall, Invoices and Receipts, 1818–1831, Z9/3/1, Z9/3/2, Barbados Department of Archives).

RUM IN BARBADOS SLAVE LIFE

"There is more rum made in Barbadoes," an island resident enthusiastically proclaimed in 1710, "than all the sugar plantations in the universe" (Walduck, 1710). Most plantations had distilleries, and from about the mid-seventeenth century slaves (and whites) became heavy rum consumers. "The blacks, both men and women, are very fond of rum," Pinckard (1806; 1: 205) observed in 1796. His observation was echoed in earlier as well as later years by other commentators on this "noble intoxicating liquor which the Negroes as well as white servants put too much delight in" and which "servants and slaves . . . drink in great abundance"

(Thomas, 1690: 17; Ogilby 1670: 380; see also, Anonymous, 1810: 42; Hall, 1924: 13; Hughes, 1750: 36; Hendy, 1833: 34–35). Slavemasters complained about "the excessive use of strong liquor," and although two early laws were designed to curtail slave drinking activities and their access to rum and other alcoholic beverages, the laws had limited impact (Society for the Improvement of Plantership, 1811: 128; Hall, 1764: 131; Moore, 1801: 239; Oldmixon, 1741; 2: 52).

Slaves consumed rum in a number of religious and recreational contexts. In addition, although masters often frowned on rum drinking, especially in social situations they could not easily control, it became a common practice for plantations to allocate small portions of rum (or rum mixed with water) and molasses as part of regular food rations, as special treats, in damp or chilly weather, or even as medicaments (Barbados Assembly, 1818: 42, 43, 47; Barbados Council, 1824: 106, 113; Dickson, 1789: 13; Drax, 1755: 67; Gibbes, 1797: 7; Holder, 1788: 22; Jordan, 1824: 7; Ligon, 1657: 51; Parry, 1789: 14).

In their consumption of rum, slaves (and poor whites) tended to drink "low-wine," the product of the first distillation in the rum-making process and "so strong a spirit" it was easily cumbustible (Ligon, 1657: 92–93; cf. Edwards, 1810; 3: 55; Miller, 1815: 65). "Low-wine" or "new rum" was observed to have particularly noxious effects, a number of West Indian writers in Barbados and elsewhere considering it to have been a prime cause of the dry bellyache. Hughes (1750: 34, 36), for example, observed how the disease's main victims were those who "immoderately" drank "new hot rum," as well as "very strong punch made exceedingly strong with new rum," and Clark (1797: 118, 125) wrote of Dominica that only the "lower orders" of whites as well as blacks who could not "afford to drink old rum or wine" acquired the disease. Dr. John Hunter (1785: 240, 243–247), a British Army physician stationed in Jamaica in the early 1780s, made comparable observations, noting that rum was often carried directly from the distillery to the market without ageing. He argued that aged rum "loses its noxious qualities in one year" and that a major reason why dry bellyache was decreasing in Jamaica at his writing was that the rum was now "almost always of a good age" (cf Grainger, 1764: 34; Hillary, 1766: 182; Wright, 1828: 232).[5]

In the mid-eighteenth century, Hughes (1750: 34) remarked that in Barbados the dry bellyache "was formerly much more frequent and fatal than it hath been of late." In the only other later reference to the disease on the island, a British visitor—a naturalist—in the 1780s (who appears to have derived his information from knowledgeable sources) recorded that "the dry belly ach is more prevalent in Barbados than in the other islands" (Anderson, 1785). Sources for other West Indian areas seem to lack discussions of dry bellyache after the late 1700s, or explicitly report it as "much less frequent than formerly" (Dancer, 1801: 102; also, Clark, 1797: 124; Hunter, 1785: 240; Lempriere, 1799; 1: 45; Moseley, 1787: 529–530, 539; Quier, 1773; Williamson, 1817; 1: 243; Wright, 1828: 232). By the late eighteenth century, the dry bellyache had also diminished in the mainland colonies (Eisinger, 1982: 280, 282, Guinee, 1972: 283, 284; McCord, 1953a: 393, 398; Wedeen, 1984: 41–42, 43, 47, 59). Thus, there is a consistency in the wider evidence from British America which suggests that, as on the mainland and elsewhere in the West Indies, the dry bellyache had significantly abated in Barbados by the late eighteenth century, although it still may have been more common there than elsewhere in the West Indies.

Although the factors responsible for this decrease are uncertain, changes in rum distilling technology were probably significant. As the knowledge of lead's poisonous effects spread in the late 1700s, lead was increasingly eliminated from distilling machinery and replaced by tin (Hunter, 1785: 239–240; Clark, 1797: 124), and Guinee's (1972: 284) observation for the mainland is undoubtedly also broadly applicable to the West Indies: "The gradual disappearance of lead colic was largely due to cultural, economic and technologic changes in society without significant intervention by the medical profession."

SUMMARY AND CONCLUSIONS

As is the case today, rum and rum-based drinks were fundamental to the fabric of Barbadian life several centuries ago; blacks and whites were frequent consumers. It is also quite likely that rum was a *primary* contributor to the dry bellyache, and that, indeed, as in the mainland colonies, "there was a demon in the rum" (McCord, 1953a: 393).

Until very recently Barbados' lower classes principally consumed non-aged white rum. This habit, born of economic reasons, continued a practice established during the period of slavery when slaves and poor whites largely drank "new rum." Even though "new rum" was particularly toxic, if contemporary observers can be believed, in earlier periods all rum was distilled with lead equipment, and consumers of all socioeconomic levels and racial groups were thus vulnerable to lead contamination.

Historical evidence indicates that both slaves and whites contracted dry bellyache. However, this evidence is insufficient to determine which group was the greater victim. Whites of all class levels seem to have had greater access to alcoholic beverages and other ingested lead than slaves—they even may have had a greater incidence of the dry bellyache. We cannot assert this with certainty because West Indian historical sources, with one exception,[6] omit comparative racial statements and we have no white skeletal materials for analysis. However, the physical evidence from Barbados suggests that lead contamination in the West Indies may have been more extensive among slaves (and whites?) than the historical sources themselves report.

Although we lack white skeletal remains, historical evidence suggests that white lead absorption would not have been less than that of slaves, and was probably greater. In any case, the lead toxicity slaves experienced undoubtedly had a variety of implications for their general health that were unrecognized by contemporary doctors—and hence have not been investigated by modern scholars. If, indeed, we are dealing with a population in general that suffered lead poisoning to some degree this may help to understand and amplify other areas of slave (and white) behavior and pathology that are superficially reported or not reported at all in the historical sources.

In this paper we have argued that the health implications of lead intoxication in Newton slaves and, by extension, Barbados slaves in general, were great enough to have had substantial social, behavioral, and economic effects generally unappreciated by modern scholarship. Moreover, the Barbados evidence, in conjunction with historical evidence from elsewhere, suggests that a similar pattern of pathology also existed in other rum-producing West Indian islands. Evidence of this pattern is present in historical accounts which discuss the dry bellyache (principally its intestinal symptoms), but the evidence is so widely scattered that its significance becomes apparent only when ferreted out and accumulated. The chemical bone lead analysis confirms suggestions in the historical literature concerning lead poisoning in slaves; it also provides quantitation to this evidence and identifies lead as the probable etiology of numerous other symptoms and causes of death unrecognized by early medical practitioners and later historians who relied on their writings. In brief: A previously unappreciated epidemic of lead poisoning in early West Indian slave societies.

NOTES

1 Seventeenth- and eighteenth-century English language medical literature uses the term "dry bellyache" (which seems to have been coined in the West Indies) synonymously with "dry gripes" (apparently mainly employed in the mainland colonies, where it was also called the "West Indian dry gripes"), "colica Pictonum," "lead colic," "nervous colic," and "Devonshire colic." Although "dry bellyache" was not the only term used in the West Indies (nor was its usage confined to the West Indies), it appears to have been the most common West Indian term and apparently was employed more in the West Indies than elsewhere (see, for example, Cadwalader, 1745: 1–2; Collins, 1811: 232; Clark, 1797: 124; Dancer, 1801: 103; Grainger, 1764: 32, 34; Hillary, 1766: 182; Hunter, 1785; Lempriere, 1799; 1: 45; Moseley, 1787: 525–540; Towne, 1726: 87; Thomson, 1820: 42; Warren, 1740: 32–33; cf. Eisinger, 1982: 281 and primary sources quoted in Wedeen, 1984: 24–25, 41, 43, 47, 48; Aronson, 1983: 38, 39; and Guinee, 1972).

2 Elsewhere we detail our statistical procedures and present our raw data; we elaborate the test results with respect to bone lead content and demographic characteristics as well as to several sociocultural features. We also discuss the archaeological implications of these results with respect to various dimensions of slave life and the wider problem of the retention, modification, or loss of African customs in the New World (see Corruccini et al., n.d. a).

3 James Clark (1797: 124, 125) of Dominica provides unique information in reporting that dry bellyache's victims included those living in "newly painted houses, or . . . employed in painting with white lead. . . . It has been observed that all house-painters have the disease more or less in the West Indies." It is known that some of Barbados' free blacks were housepainters, and although the island's slave houses were probably unpainted, as with free blacks some slaves were probably housepainters during the eighteenth century (Handler, 1974: 122–124). Slaves valued tobacco. Although archaeological and historical evidence indicates they only used it in cigars and pipes (Handler and Lange, 1978: 133–134),

they may have occasionally consumed snuff, a suggestion made by John Gilmore (pers. comm.).

4 As early as 1723, a Massachusetts law recognized that "strong liquors and spirits that are distilled thro' leaden heads or pipes, are . . . unwholesome and hurtful"; it prohibited the use of "leaden heads or worms" and forbade their manufacture from "coarse and bare pewter, or . . . any mixture of lead" (Massachusetts, 1742: 240–241).

5 Alone among West Indian writers on the subject, Dr. John Quier (1773) who, by his writing in 1773 had practiced for six years in Jamaica, reported that although blacks "in general use great quantities of the newest and vilest rum," he never "saw or heard" of any black with dry bellyache; moreover, all persons he ever encountered with the disease were "people of the better sort."

6 Dr. James Grainger (1764: 34), a resident of the West Indies, mostly St. Kitts, from late 1759 to 1766, observed that blacks "are oftener tormented with the dry Belly Ach than the whites."

REFERENCES

Ahlgren, L., B. Haeger-Aronsen, S. Mattsson, and A. Schütz (1980) "In-Vivo Determination of Lead in the Skeleton After Occupational Exposure to Lead." British Journal of Industrial Medicine 37: 109–113.

Anderson, A. (1785) "Barbados." Ms. 610. Linnean Society of London.

Anonymous (1810) Authentic History of the English West Indies. London.

Aronson, S. M. (1983) "Lead and the Demon Rum in Colonial America." Rhode Island Medical Journal 66: 37–40.

Aufderheide, A. C., F. D. Neiman, L. E. Wittmers, and G. Rapp (1981) "Lead in Bone II: Skeletal-Lead Content as an Indicator of Lifetime Lead Ingestion and the Social Correlates in an Archaeological Population." American Journal of Physical Anthropology 55: 285–291.

Aufderheide, A. C., J. L. Angel, J. O. Kelley, A. C. Outlaw, M. A. Outlaw, G. Rapp, and L. E. Wittmers (1985) "Lead in Bone III: Prediction of Social Correlates from Skeletal Lead Content in Four Colonial American Populations (Catoctin Furnace, College Landing, Governor's Land, and Irene Mound)." American Journal of Physical Anthropology 66: 353–361.

Barbados Assembly (1818) The Report from a Select Committee of the House of Assembly, Appointed to Inquire into the Origin, Causes, and Progress of the Late Insurrection. Barbados.

Barbados Council (1824) A Report of a Committee of the Council of Barbadoes, Appointed to Inquire into the Actual Condition of the Slaves in this Island. London.

Barbados Department of Archives (various dates) Recopied Deeds Books; Inventories, Boxes: Hackett, Taylor, Byrrowes, and Records of Drax Hall.

Barltrop, D. and H. E. Khoo (1975) "Nutritional Determinants of Lead Absorption," in D. Hemphill (ed.) Trace Substances in Environmental Health IX. Columbia: University of Missouri: 369–376.

162   JEROME S. HANDLER ET AL.

Bellgrove, W. (1755) A Treatise Upon Husbandry or Planting. Boston.

Bell, J. U. and J. A. Thomas (1980) "Effects of Lead on Mammalian Reproduction," in R. L. Singhal and J. A. Thomas (eds.) Lead Toxicity. Baltimore and Munich: Urban and Schwarzenberg: 169–185.

Bennett, J. H. (1958) Bondsmen and Bishops: Slavery and Apprenticeship on the Codrington Plantations of Barbados, 1710–1838. University of California Publications in History 62. Berkeley and Los Angeles.

Betts, P. R., R. Astley, and D. N. Raine (1973) "Lead Intoxication in Children in Birmingham." British Medical Journal 1: 402–406.

Bridenbaugh, C. and R. Bridenbaugh (1972) No Peace Beyond the Line. New York: Oxford University Press.

Cadwalader, T. (1745) An Essay on the West-India Dry-Gripes. Philadelphia.

Christoffersson, J. O., A. Schütz, L. Ahlgren, B. Haeger–Aronsen, S. Mattsson, and S. Skerfving (1984) "Lead in Finger-Bone Analyzed in Vivo in Active and Retired Lead Workers." American Journal of Industrial Medicine 6: 447–457.

Clark, J. (1797) A Treatise on the Yellow Fever, as it Appeared in the Island of Dominica . . . to which are Added Observations on . . . Some Other West Indian diseases. London.

Collins, Dr. (1811) Practical Rules for the Management and Medical Treatment of Negro Slaves, in the Sugar Colonies. London. (1st ed. 1803).

Corruccini, R. S., A. C. Aufderheide, and J. S. Handler, and L. E. Wittmers (n.d.a) "Patterning of Skeletal Lead Content in Barbados Slaves." Archaeometry. In press.

Corruccini, R. S. and J. S. Handler (1980) "Temporomandibular Joint Size Decrease in American Blacks: Evidence from Barbados." Journal of Dental Research 59: 1528. •

——— and K. P. Jacobi (1985) "Chronological Distribution of Enamel Hypoplasias and Weaning in a Caribbean Slave Population." Human Biology 57: 699–711.

Corruccini, R. S., K. P. Jacobi, J. S. Handler, and A. C. Aufderheide (n.d.b) "Implications of Tooth Root Hypercementosis in a Barbados Slave Skeletal Collection." American Journal of Physical Anthropology. In press.

Corruccini, R. S., J. S. Handler, R. Mutaw, and F. W. Lange (1982) "Osteology of a Slave Burial Population from Barbados, West Indies." American Journal of Physical Anthropology 59: 443–459.

Craton, M. (1978) Searching for the Invisible Man. Cambridge: Harvard University Press.

Dancer, T. (1801) The Medical Assistant; or Jamaica Practice of Physic. Kingston, Jamaica.

Dickson, W. (1789) Letters on Slavery. London.

Drax, H. (1755) "Instructions for the Management of Drax-Hall and the Irish-Hope Plantations [ca. 1670]," in W. Belgrove (ed.) A Treatise Upon Husbandry or Planting. Boston: 51–86.

Dunn, R. S. (1972) Sugar and Slaves: The Rise of the Planter Class in the

English West Indies, 1624–1713. Chapel Hill: University of North Carolina Press.

Eastwell, H. D., B. J. Thomas, and B. W. Thomas (1983) "Skeletal Lead Burden in Aborigine Petrol Sniffers." Letter to the Editor, The Lancet 2: 524–525.

Edwards, B. (1810) The History, Civil and Commercial, of the British Colonies in the West Indies. 3 vols. Philadelphia.

Eisinger, J. (1982) "Lead Wine: Eberhard Gockel and the Colica Pictonum." Medical History 26: 279–302.

Frere, H. (1768) A Short History of Barbados From its First Discovery and Settlement to the End of the Year 1767. London.

Gibbes, P. (1797) Instructions for the Treatment of Negroes, Etc. Etc. Etc. London.

Grainger, J. (1764) An Essay on the More Common West India Diseases. London.

Guinee, V. F. (1972) "Lead Poisoning." The American Journal of Medicine 52 (3): 283–288.

Hall, R. (1764) Acts, Passed in the Island of Barbados. London.

——— (1924) A General Account of the First Settlement and of the Trade and Constitution of the Island of Barbados, Written in the Year 1755. E. M. Shilstone (ed.) Barbados.

Handler, J. S. (1963a) "Pottery Making in Rural Barbados." Southwestern Journal of Anthropology 19: 314–334.

——— (1963b) "A Historical Sketch of Pottery Manufacture in Barbados." Journal of the Barbados Museum and Historical Society 30: 129–153.

——— (1974) The Unappropriated People: Freedmen in the Slave Society of Barbados. Baltimore: Johns Hopkins University Press.

Handler, J. S. and R. S. Corruccini (1983) "Plantation Slave Life in Barbados: A Physical Anthropological Analysis." Journal of Interdisciplinary History 14: 65–90.

——— (1986) "Weaning Among West Indian Slaves: Historical and Bioanthropological Evidence from Barbados." William and Mary Quarterly 43: 111–117.

Handler, J. S. and F. W. Lange (1978) Plantation Slavery in Barbados: An Archaeological and Historical Investigation. Cambridge: Harvard University Press.

——— (1979) "Plantation Slavery on Barbados, West Indies." Archaeology 32: 45–52.

Handler, J. S., R. S. Corruccini, and R. J. Mutaw (1982) "Tooth Mutilation in the Caribbean: Evidence from a Slave Burial Population in Barbados." Journal of Human Evolution 11: 297–313.

Harlan, W. R., J. R. Landis, R. L. Schmouder, N. G. Goldstein, and L. C. Harlan (1985) "Blood Lead and Blood Pressure. Relationship in the Adolescent and Adult U.S. Population." Journal of the American Medical Association 253: 530–534.

Harris, W. A., T. E. Harden and E. B. Dawson (1979) "Apparent Effect of Ascorbic Acid Medication on Semen Metal Levels." Fertility and Sterility 32: 455–459.

Hartley, H. M. (1949) "Of the Produce of the Plantations," in F. J. Kling-
berg (ed.) Codrington Chronicle: An Experiment in Anglican Altruism
on a Barbados Plantation, 1710–1834. University of California Publications in History 37: 63–84. Berkeley and Los Angeles.

Hendy, T. W. B. (1833) An Attempt to Prove the Fallacy of Inflicting Cor-
poral Punishment to Prevent or to Lessen the Commission of Crime.
Barbados.

Hernberg, S. (1980) "Biochemical and Clinical Effects and Responses as Indicated by Blood Concentration," in R. L. Singhal and J. A. Thomas
(eds.) Lead Toxicity. Baltimore and Munich: Urban and Schwarzenberg: 367–399.

Hillary, W. (1766) Observations on the Changes of the Air and the Concomitant Epidemical Diseases in the Island of Barbadoes. London. (1st
ed. 1759).

Holder, H. E. (1788) A Short Essay on the Subject of Negro Slavery, with
Particular Reference to the Island of Barbados. London.

Hughes, G. (1750) The Natural History of Barbados. London.

Hunter, J. (1785) "Some Experiments Made upon Rum, in Order to Ascer-
tain the Cause of the Colic, Frequent Among the Soldiers in . . .
Jamaica, in the Years 1781 and 1782." Medical Transactions, Published
by the College of Physicians in London 3: 227–249.

Jacquet, P. (1977) "Early Embryonic Development in Lead-Intoxicated
Mice." Archives of Pathology and Laboratory Medicine 101: 641–643.

Jordan, J. W. (1824) An Account of the Management of Certain Estates in
the Island of Barbados. London.

Kiple, K. F. (1984) The Caribbean Slave: A Biological History. Cambridge:
Cambridge University Press.

Lauwers, M. C., R. C. Hauspie, C. Susanne, and J. Verheyden (1986)
"Comparison of Biometric Data of Children with High and Low Levels
of Lead in the Blood." American Journal of Physical Anthropology 69:
107–116.

Lempriere, W. (1799) Practical Observations on the Diseases of the Army
in Jamaica . . . between the Years 1792 and 1797. 2 vols. London.

Ligon, R. (1657) A True and Exact History of the Island of Barbados.
London.

McCord, C. (1953a) "Lead and Lead Poisoning in Early America: Benjamin
Franklin and Lead Poisoning." Industrial Medicine and Surgery 22:
392–399.

——— (1953b) "Lead and Lead Poisoning in Early America: The Pewter
Era." Industrial Medicine and Surgery 22: 573–577.

——— (1954a) "Lead and Lead Poisoning in Early America: The Lead
Pipe Period." Industrial Medicine and Surgery 23: 27–31.

——— (1954b) "Lead and Lead Poisoning in Early America: Lead Compounds." Industrial Medicine and Surgery 23: 75–80.

——— (1954c) "Lead and Lead Poisoning in Early America: Clinical Lead
Poisoning in the Colonies." Industrial Medicine and Surgery 23: 120–
125.

Mackie, A., A. Townshend, and H. A. Waldron (1975) "Lead Concentratrations in Bones from Roman York." Journal of Archaeological Science 2: 235–237.

Mahaffey, K. R. (1977) "Relation Between Quantities of Lead Ingested and Health Effects of Lead in Humans." Pediatrics 59: 448–456. ,

Mahaffey, K. R., R. A. Goyer, and J. K. Haseman (1973) "Dose Response to Lead Ingestion in Rats Fed Low Dietary Calcium." Journal of Laboratory Clinical Medicine 82: 92–101.

Massachusetts (1742) Acts and Laws of His Majesty's Province of the Massachusetts-Bay in New-England. Boston.

Miller, G., Jr. (1815) The Traveller's Guide to Madeira and the West Indies. Haddington, Eng.

Moore, S. (1801) The Public Acts in Force; Passed by the Legislature of Barbados. London.

Moore, M. R., P. A. Meredith, B. C. Campbell, A. Goldberg, and A. Baird (1978) "The Effect of Calcium Glycerophosphate on Industrial and Experimental Lead Absorption." Drugs Under Experimental Clinical Research 4: 17–24.

Moseley, B. (1787) A Treatise on Tropical Diseases, on Military Operations, and on the Climate of the West Indies. London.

Needleman, H. L., C. Gunnoe, A. Leviton, R. Reed, H. Peresie, C. Maher, and P. Barrett (1979) "Deficits in Psychological and Classroom Performance of Children with Elevated Dentine Lead Levels." New England Journal of Medicine 300: 689–694.

Ogilby, J. (1670) America: Being the Latest and Most Accurate Description of the New World. London.

Oldmixon, J. (1708) The British Empire in America. 2 vols. London.

——— (1741) The British Empire in America. 2 vols. London.

Parry, D. (1789) "Extract of a Letter from Governor Parry to the Right Honourable Lord Sydney, August 18, 1788." British House of Commons Parliamentary Papers 26: 13–24. London.

Pinckard, G. (1806) Notes on the West Indies. 3 vols. London.

Porter, G. (1830) The Nature and Properties of the Sugarcane. London.

Quier, J. (1773) "Letter VI. Account of the Bilious Cholic, Called the Dry Belly-Ache," in D. Monro (ed.) Letters and Essays on the Small-Pox and Inoculation, the Measles, the Dry Belly-Ache . . . of the West Indies. London, 1778: 150–194.

Russell, F. (1695) "Letter to Lords of Trade and Plantations, 23 March," in Calendar of State Papers, Colonial Series: America and West Indies 1693–1696: 445. London.

Salmon, W. (1693) Seplasium. The Compleat English Physician. London.

Scott, M. (1985) Unpublished Data. Department of Medical Physics, University of Birmingham, England.

Sheridan, R. (1973) Sugar and Slavery: An Economic History of the British West Indies, 1623–1775. Baltimore: Johns Hopkins University Press.

——— (1985) Doctors and Slaves: A Medical and Demographic History of Slavery in the British West Indies, 1680–1834. Cambridge: Cambridge University Press.

Sloane, H. (1707) A Voyage to the Islands Madera, Barbados, Nievis, S. Christophers and Jamaica. London.

Society for the Improvement of Plantership in the Island of Barbados (1811) Minutes. Liverpool.

Stowe, H. D. and R. A. Goyer (1971) "The Reproductive Ability and Progeny of F_1 Lead-Toxic Rats." Fertility and Sterility 22: 755–760.

Thomas, D. (1690) An Historical Account of the Rise and Growth of the West India Colonies. London.

Thomson, J. (1820) A Treatise on the Diseases of the Negroes as They Occur in the Island of Jamaica. Jamaica.

Towne, R. (1726) A Treatise of the Diseases Most Frequent in the West Indies. London.

Trapham, T. (1679) A Discourse on the State of Health in the Island of Jamaica. London.

Tryon, T. (1684) Friendly Advice to the Gentlemen Planters of the East and West Indies. London.

Uzych, L. (1985) "Teratogenesis and Mutagenesis Associated with the Exposure of Human Males to Lead: A Review." The Yale Journal of Biology and Medicine 58: 9–17.

Vermande-Van Eck, G. J. and J. W. Meigs (1960) "Changes in the Ovary of the Rhesus Monkey After Chronic Lead Intoxification." Fertility and Sterility 11: 223–234.

Waldron, H. A. (1969) "James Hardy and the Devonshire Colic." Medical History 13: 74–81.

Waldron, H. A., A. Mackie, and A. Townshend (1976) The Lead Content of Some Romano-British Bones. Archaeometry 18: 221–227.

Walduck, J. (1710) "Letter to J. Petiver." Sloane Manuscripts 2302. British Library.

Warren, H. (1740) A Treatise Concerning the Malignant Fever in Barbados and the Neighboring Islands. London.

Wedeen, R. P. (1984) Poison in the Pot: The Legacy of Lead. Carbondale: Southern Illinois University Press.

Weller, C. V. (1915) "The Blastophthoric Effect of Chronic Lead Poisoning." Journal of Medical Research 33: 271–293.

Williamson, J. (1817) Medical and Miscellaneous Observations Relative to the West India islands. 2 vols. Edinburgh.

Wittmers, L. E., Jr., A. Alich, and A. C. Aufderheide (1981) "Lead in Bone I: Direct Analysis for Lead in Milligram Quantities of Bone Ash by Graphite Furnace Atomic Absorption Spectroscopy." American Journal of Clinical Pathology 75: 80–85.

Wright, W. (1828) Memoirs of the late William Wright. Edinburgh.

Zielhuis, R. L. (1975) "Dose-Response Relationships for Inorganic Lead: I. Biochemical and Hematological Responses." International Archives of Occupational Health 35: 1.

The Black Saturnalia and Relief Induced Agonism

ROBERT DIRKS

RELIEF INDUCED AGONISM is not a textbook disease. The World War II Minnesota starvation experiments produced the first and to my knowledge only clinical observations of its symptoms, hyperirritability and querulousness upon refeeding following a protracted period of semistarvation (Keys et al., 1950: 917–918). The mechanisms involved in this reaction are a mystery and remain uninvestigated. I suspect the reason why relief induced agonism receives little attention has to do with its limited epidemiology. It is in fact a highly transient stress response most visible only among the very poor and then usually only amidst the most dire famine conditions. The disease causes complaints, exigent behaviors, and disrupts relief operations, but under such emergency circumstances problems are everywhere, and, overall, relief induced agonism counts as a relatively minor source, at least from the perspective of government and medicine.

From the standpoint of ethnology and history, however, relief induced agonism appears to have major importance. Perhaps I should say "classical importance" because judging from the results of my research it represents the key to solving the long-stand-

Robert Dirks is an associate professor of anthropology at Illinois State University.

Financial support for various aspects of this research has come from the National Endowment for the Humanities, the Illinois State Board of Regents, and the Graduate School of Illinois State University. My thanks to Deborah Dirks for her help in coding data.

ing question of the origin and incidence of annual rituals of conflict. Sir James Frazer, who grappled with this problem in *The
Golden Bough* (1911–1915), characterized such rites as "annual
periods of license" wherein, amidst outpourings of mirth and
jollity, "darker passions find a vent." In what follows, I recount
how research bearing on the ethnohistory of the Black Saturnalia,
the tumultuous annual revels of British West Indian slaves, led me
to associate relief induced agonism with such events. I go on to
discuss the theoretical basis for making this connection and to describe the manner in which propositions derived from this theory
were tested. I conclude by sketching a cultural evolutionary interpretation of the Black Saturnalia, suggesting how such a great
complex of celebration and symbolic expression can arise from
the seeds of physiological stress and assume its own historically
specific meanings and motivations.

THE BLACK SATURNALIA

My first encounter with the Black Saturnalia—or, more properly,
a rather tame, Christian descendant of one of its component rites—
came on the island of Tortola in the predawn hours of Christmas,
1969, when I was awakened by a troupe of black villagers caroling
outside my door. Although I did not realize it at the time, such
early morning visits extended far back into British West Indian
history to a time when slaves sallied forth before sunrise to bid
holiday greetings to plantation managers and staff. This I learned
a couple of years later after becoming seriously interested in the
ethnohistory of the region.

What stimulated this interest was the belief that the cultural
ecological perspective I had brought to the study of modern island
life held great promise for a better understanding of slave culture.
Black populations of the British sugar colonies for the most part
had existed in a state of sustained natural decrease. They were
from a Darwinian perspective chronic failures artifically sustained
by forced immigration. How did this dismal situation affect culture? With an approach guided by this question and attentive to
physical survival and the economies of interaction, I envisioned
making an advance over the then prevailing psychological interpretations of slave ethnohistory.

The Black Saturnalia captured my attention from the very beginning of this work. Here was a complex of expressive culture constituting the ritual centerpiece of the plantation community. Such events have always attracted anthropological attention because they typically distill in symbolic forms culturally salient meanings. The Black Saturnalia offered exciting potential in that light alone. But, in addition, research in the early 1970s was just beginning to demonstrate the ecological sensitivities of ritual performance and how it played an active role in regulating community relations. Given my ecological agenda and because slave ritual life was virtually unstudied from my angle, I applied for and was granted funds to make a study of the Black Saturnalia and find out what could be learned about slave culture through the window of collective representation.

I found a fairly rich body of descriptive material, especially for early nineteenth-century Jamaica. By then the Saturnalia was in full flower. It began on the 24th of December when at noon overseers dismissed their laborers and suspended virtually all efforts to enforce the rules and routines that usually governed plantation life. Work came to an abrupt halt, even the legions of domestics abandoning their posts and leaving masters and mistresses to fend for themselves.

Once work ceased, the slaves hurried to their gardens to gather foodstuffs for holiday feasting. Many hastened from there to nearby markets carrying baskets of produce, planning to return with some new article of clothing to complete a holiday outfit. Masters assisted efforts to lay in stocks by handing out extra cereal rations, salt fish, and fresh meat. Liberal quantities of rum were also dispensed to sustain the monumental drinking sprees a good celebration required.

Plantation workers heralded Christmas Day by first paying respects to owners and overseers. The slaves came to the great house, performed various dances, and then saluted the residents with long speeches full of good wishes. Planters responded by passing out gifts, usually items of clothing. Besides presents, slaves expected entertainments. Accordingly, whites opened the doors of their residences to regale their visitors with choice foods and drinks. There was also music, and when it began the gentlemen of the estate unabashedly took common field hands as their dancing partners. The merriment usually became rather boisterous as the punch took effect with the slaves seizing the opportunity to lampoon their masters with satirical philippics and to communicate a little free advice. In due course, the gathering concluded and the slaves returned to their own quarters to dance through the night.

Sometimes activities at the great house did not conclude so promptly. Rather than a visit of a few hours the residence might be "appropriated" for a more lengthy stay. Record of one such occupation told of a two-day party in which various Africans gravitated to different corners of the house to play their own tribal rhythms while Creole slaves settled in the center of the main hall enjoying the music of their own fifes and drums. This created a disharmonious racket amplified by each group trying to outdo the others by having the loudest, merriest celebration of all.

The excitement continued on the day after Christmas whether the great house was taken over or not. Because slaves were perfectly free to come and go as they pleased, many proceeded to nearby towns to stroll through marketplaces filled with gaily decorated booths, displaying assortments of fine food and apparel. At this point, if not on Christmas day itself, drums might be heard announcing the arrival of John Canoe (or Jonkunno), an entertainer whose escapades constituted a major holiday event. John Canoes were masked characters impersonated by especially robust men. As described by Edward Long in 1774, they wore grotesque masks, carried wooden swords, and were followed about by choruses of intoxicated women. John Canoes roamed entire neighborhoods, stopping at every master's door to dance with terrific agility and violence. Householders customarily paid off this menacing visitor with a few small coins to which he responded with another brief interlude of dance. With upraised sword or, during later periods, some other terrific device, the character then continued on to find another audience and enact the same ritual sequence— ethologically: threat, appeasement, stayed threat.[1]

Actor-Boy was another traditional figure. Actor-Boys went around in troupes during the holidays wearing white masks, gowns, and fantastic headgear, escorted by a band of fifes and drums. Whenever a party came upon an audience from whom they could expect a few coins, they dramatized a scene, perhaps from Shakespeare's *Richard III* or a Pizarro play. Their performances in any case always involved portrayals of combat, death, and resurrection, though latter-day versions became costume shows in which participants vied for the favor of white gentlemen while keeping slave audiences at a distance with a cowhide whip. Disappointed contestants occasionally sustained the theme of violence further by assaulting the winner.

Complementing these male mummeries were parades of women organized into "sets." These gained prominence in the closing years of the eighteenth century, at first appearing only at Christmas but later enlivening New Year's celebrations along with John Canoes and Actor-Boys. The sets' pageants contained a powerful note of rivalry. In various locales women divided into factions, the Reds and the Blues. Every year each side contested with the other for superiority, trying to outshine its counterpart in beauty, grace, costume, and song. Again, a central theme appears to have been winning favor in the eyes of whites, and the Set-Girls, as they were called, could take this very seriously. Sometimes in the streets tensions ran so high that when Red and Blue met, a general melee ensued.

There were other groups and other events that became part of Jamaica's holiday revelries over the years, but always the climax was a final round of dancing and feasting. On New Year's Day it was more of the same, but the next morning came an abrupt retransformation: no sooner did the festivities end than all returned to their familiar chores.

Beyond Jamaica, events were never so lavishly developed or, perhaps, never so richly documented. Whatever the case, gay, licentious, and fierce celebrations were universal in nearly every sugar colony (Barbados being a prominent exception). Visitations to the great house are documented for Antigua, St. Kitts, St. Vincent, and Trinidad. Literary and oral histories tell of various mummeries on Nevis, St. Kitts, St. Vincent, and the Virgin Islands. Parading about in fancy dress is described for Dominica, Guiana, St. Kitts, and Tortola. The Saturnalia in these places may never have achieved the degree of spectacle seen on Jamaica, but it still managed to convey to white onlookers the same impression of impudent vitality. Indeed, against the background of the otherwise regimented, lockstep order of the plantation, the Christmas holidays appeared as nothing short of a "ferocious riot."

CONCURRENT EVENTS

Insurrections and Assassinations

The ferocious riot was not always ritualized. During the course of my research, I accumulated references to 70 slave uprisings. Occurring between 1649 and 1833, these included large-scale insurrections that engulfed entire islands as well as small-scale bloodlettings limited to single estates. Some were carefully planned, others apparently spontaneous. Actually, a number of them never took place because of premature discovery. Some of these may have been spurious, a product of planter paranoia, but I excluded patently doubtful cases.

Thirty-seven of the incidents included in my list can be dated to the month.[2] December is far and away the peak month, 35% of the attacks having taken place or having been scheduled to take place then. This clustering, assuming an equal chance for such incidents to be reported for any month, is far beyond what one would expect ($D = .583$, two-tailed $p = .001$). In Michael Craton's (1982: 335–339) listing of plots and uprisings one finds the same peaking about December tailing off into January, again a far cry from uniform distribution with low probability of it being due to chance ($D = .523$, two-tailed $p = .003$).

Because the Black Saturnalia occurred at precisely that juncture when uprisings were most likely, I immediately began looking at it as an example of what Max Gluckman (1954) called "ritualized rebellion," a symbolic enactment of what otherwise might take place in earnest. Gluckman studied such events among the Swazi, Zulu, and other Southeast African tribes where he perceived sociological, psychological, and biological involvements and a need for full explanation to draw upon interdisciplinary expertise. Gluckman, a social anthropologist, did not delve into the biology he believed at work; what struck me as most important at the time were the sociological, ecological, and nutritional parallels between his Southeast African cases and the situation in the British sugar colonies.

As for the sociology, the cornerstone of Gluckman's thinking was his structural-functional insight: the kingship rites of Southeast African tribes represented rebellion because rebellion was structured into the very political systems embracing them. Dissatisfactions with the king built more rapidly than the actual forces of rebellion. As a result, a surrogate outlet, a formal channel for venting discontent, was found. The political structure of plantation communities by no means resembled in any detail that of the Swazi or Zulu kingdoms, but it seemed plain enough that what planters called "the government of the cowskin" (compliance exacted by the cowhide whip) did not engender political repose.

Ecological Pulse and Seasonal Hunger

Gluckman saw it as no chance happening that rituals of rebellion coincided with seasonal change and a concomitant turnabout in nutritional status. The ripening of the first fruits of the year and the onset of harvest set into motion disruptive forces nearly everywhere in the region. Most tribes experienced an annual spell of semistarvation. While the so-called hungry months lasted, inanition placed a damper on social activities. But, as soon as there was more to eat, people embarked on an intense round of convivial events. At the same time they returned to unfriendly pursuits such as intracommunity quarreling and war. As Gluckman saw it, without a seasonal flux in food energy, without alternating periods of hunger and satiety, there would be no rituals of rebellion. The case of the Lozi, a group culturally not unlike Swazi or Zulu, but without annual episodes of starvation and without any apparent inclination ritually to malign their ruler, persuaded Gluckman that the institution of rituals of rebellion depended as much on a hunger season as on any particular type of political order.

I was not many weeks into my research before I discovered that most of the islands were subject to an ecological pulse affecting the intake of food energy. As many contemporary accounts noted, during the months leading up to December the slaves were in a difficult situation nutritionally (see Dirks, 1987: 77–80). About June, the beginning of the rainy season, the difficult, physically taxing work of preparing and planting the cane fields got under way. Food stores often ran low as this work progressed, and despite the practice of planters distributing high-calorie supplements to their predials, the stress showed. Those in the fields became visibly wasted. The slaves themselves spoke of the period as the "hungry months." To compound their difficulties intestinal disease at this time of the year was rampant. Then a sudden turnabout transpired: about the beginning of December local subsistence crops began to fruit. The crop of cane began to ripen, and on top of that the hurricane season came to an end making for safe passage to the colonies. At this point hundreds of vessels laden with corn, beans, and other provisions began to arrive from overseas replenishing storehouses with commodities many of the plantations depended upon for slaves' rations. Couple this with the fact that December was a relatively light month for estate labor and the fact that planters distributed large quantities of dry provisions and meats as holiday bonuses, and one is confronted with a set of coincidences that explain the astonishing physical transformation observers witnessed. Accounts tell of an almost instantaneous improvement in the appearance of predial slaves. Equally dramatic was their change in behavior, the torpid pace of the preceding months suddenly giving way to a new vitality. By Christmas the slaves seemed suddenly to be a people "recreated and renewed." Clearly, this recreation and renewal depended in large measure on the drastic upsurge in food availability.

Planters' Attitudes

Although the conditions Gluckman saw as necessary for rituals of rebellion to occur existed in the sugar colonies, what prevented me from interpreting the Black Saturnalia solely in terms of his theory was its demand for a cultural unity that clearly did not exist in plantation communities. Among the Swazi and Zulu, ruler and ruled shared a worldview. The king's subjects felt growing dissatisfaction with the person in power, but not for a moment did they express dissatisfaction with the system, with monarchy itself. Nothing in daily life suggested disrespect for kingship. There were rebels but no revolutionaries. The overt purpose of the ritualized malignings of the king was to purify him. The ruler himself agreed this was necessary. Hence, the rituals of rebellion of Southeast Africa did more than represent the divisive side of politics. The rites allowed king, princes, and commoners—ruler, rivals, and potential rebels—to gather about the throne in a common cause. Ritualized rebellion, as Gluckman explained, was in the final analysis an act of unity.

I saw as most improbable an interpretation of the Black Saturnalia that would resolve to a statement of solidarity between planter and slave. But, more importantly, the documentary evidence plainly indicated that the planters, unlike Southeast African monarchs, were not enthusiastic endorsers of the event. They participated because they felt they had to and not because they thought it a fine tradition.

The planters dreaded Christmas. As the holidays drew near, the slaves grew increasingly impertinent and theft more blatant. Whites took steps to insure their own safety and to protect their properties. Those living in towns hurried to their estates while the militia mobilized to stand guard. Another worry was the timely arrival of the first fleets of December and their cargoes of salt provisions because not issuing extra allowances at Christmas was known to spark destructive rampages. On the other hand, prohibiting celebration altogether was out of the question. Veteran planters advised newcomers not to interfere as it would surely cause trouble. On Antigua a planter was killed for denying his slaves leave to celebrate (Dirks, 1987: 168–170).

All told, the historical record suggested to me a kind of automatic, reflexive dynamic. Slave unrest intensified about the time of Christmas in synchrony with an upsurge in food energy intake. Planters recognized the sudden animation and aggressiveness, saw it as dangerous, and knew any untoward action could spell trouble. Hence, they found it more expedient and less costly to indulge their slaves in what they hoped would be harmless frivolities.

ECOLOGICAL AND PSYCHOLOGICAL DYNAMICS

Food Intake, Behavior, and Social Organization

As for the underlying dynamics, my first model drew heavily on research relating levels of food intake to behavior and social organization (see Dirks, 1975; 1978; 1979b). To acquire a firm grasp on how the annual pulse of starvation and plenty must have affected slave behavior, I researched the literature for accounts of famine, hunger seasons, and their relief. This work eventually led to publication of a major synthesis, describing transculturally the social responses to serious food shortage (Dirks, 1980). The study confirmed that beyond a certain level of severity starvation has an atomizing effect on society. This effect can be traced to an array of energy-sparing adjustments beginning at the cellular level. At the level of the organism reductions in energy expenditure far exceed what would be expected from loss of physical mass alone, owing in large part to curtailed activity. These curtailments include social interactions, particularly those not of immediate relevance to food acquisition; hence, the atrophy of noninstrumental relations and the increasing isolation of households and individuals under famine conditions.

Among societies that suffer annual hunger, cultural patterns exist to immediately adjust social life to physical and behavioral conditions. With the onset of the hunger months traditional moratoriums curtail visiting, hospitality, and costly ceremony. People remain at home doing only what is absolutely essential. In this way entire communities slip into an energy-saving posture as a matter of course, avoiding undue physical and psychological stress. With the return to more adequate nourishment, social life expands once more (Dirks, 1980). In effect, the intensity and extent of social life tracks the pulse of available energy, expanding and contracting in a manner Charles Laughlin and Ivan Brady (1978: 32–35) refer to as the "accordion effect."

In a volume dealing with the cultural evolutionary effects of food deprivation edited by Laughlin and Brady, I showed how the accordion effect could be seen operating in slave behavior (Dirks, 1978). Central to my contribution is the idea that planters and slaves could be viewed as ecological competitors. Culturally, they were defined as separate species. In actuality they occupied distinct, though overlapping, niches. This set the stage for competitive interactions issuing from the slave quarters most often in the form of what ecologists refer to as "scramble."

Visible in accounts of unrelenting theft and habitual dissimulation, scramble was an energetically low-cost approach to resource capture, requiring little or no coordination. It was thus well suited to a climate of hunger and social restriction. When, with the onset of December, behaviors were underwritten by a more liberal energy budget, spheres of interaction intensified and expanded, and slaves' competitive postures became more confrontational and contestive. I argue that slave insurrectionists implicitly recognized this and, even though whites were ready for trouble, repeatedly tried to capitalize on it. Outright violence aside, the transformation was ritually enacted in the agonistic behaviors and representations of the Saturnalia.

Social Psychological Stimulation

In addition to this ecological dynamic affecting planter-slave relations, I envisioned a complementary social psychology that would help explain the explosive quality of the Christmas holidays. My thinking here was influenced by observations made during the Minnesota experiment. Ancel Keys and his coworkers saw tensions arise from refeeding even in the absence of preexisting antagonism. The experimenters found that while their subjects were starving and emaciated, they were very tractable, but when the same individuals were given adequate food and began to recover their health and strength, they became irritable and difficult to manage. The situation became so tense the researchers likened it to that of an overheated boiler with uncertain safety valves (Keys et al., 1950: 917–918). Keys related this effect to field observations made in famine camps and among starving prisoners, and my own research turned up many more examples (Dirks, 1979c).

The Minnesota researchers explained their observations in terms of a sudden access to energy, but in addition proposed a cognitive explanation rooted in a frustrating disjunction between their subjects' expectations of a rapid return to normal and their actual slow progress toward recovery. Animal models of starvation made me question the necessity of this cognitive element. Experiments suggested that it was enhanced levels of interaction that accounted for hyperirritability and aggression rather than simply increased energy. I related this to the social atomism brought about by starvation and explained the aggressive excitation brought on at the conclusion of the hungry months in terms of a theoretical model developed by Bruce Welch (Dirks, 1979b: 99).

According to Welch (1965), the central nervous system exposed to a stable regime tends to synchronize and adjust to the prevailing level of stimulation. When that changes—when the mean level of environmental stimulation undergoes marked alteration, say, due to greatly increased intensity of interaction—these synchronies and adjustments become temporarily upset. Individuals become hyperexcitable. With slight breaks in a humdrum pattern the feeling is exhilarating. Extreme change arouses uneasy feelings. People experience tensions and anxieties. This is why intermissions in the midst of an otherwise confined or regimented life can usually be counted on to produce signs of stress and why places like liberty ports and military-leave towns have always been scenes of hard drinking and fighting. Thus, as my thinking about the Black Saturnalia developed, I was inclined to see it and the general unrest at the end of the hungry season as rooted in a dynamic of excitation and aggression, a dynamic originating in an ecological pulse affecting a drastic upsurge in the intake of food energy but triggered most directly by an increase in social interaction inserted into an otherwise confined, monotonous labor regime (see Dirks, 1975; 1978; 1979b).

RELIEF INDUCED AGONISM

Hypothetical Mechanisms

I saw problems with this model. Especially bothersome was evidence from my famine-related studies that irritability and unrest among previously starved individuals developed immediately and directly after refeeding. This suggested that an intervening social psychological dynamic, while perhaps operative, did not fully account for the agonistic response I saw at the root of the sugar colonies' December upheavals. The trouble was I could envision no mechanism by which food intake alone would engender hostile, aggressive behavior.

This changed as a consequence of a paper I presented at the 1976 annual meeting of the American Anthropological Association describing reactions to famine (Dirks, 1976). The paper included an account of the disturbances and fighting observed during the course of relief operations: shortly thereafter I received a letter from anthropologist Ralph Bolton. He suggested that the syndrome I reported could be a hypoglycemic effect. Subsequently, I published an account of what I labeled "relief induced agonism" and included in the article Bolton's hypothetical mechanisms (Dirks, 1979). One consideration was that a rapid uptake of fuel following prolonged starvation might produce the effect of temporarily lowering immediately available glucose below normal fasting levels thereby impairing brain functioning. A second possibility was that hypoglycemia itself might stimulate irritability, lowering the threshold for aggressive reaction to various stimuli. A third suggestion was that low blood sugar or rapid fluctuations in blood sugar levels could effect neural circuits and hormonal releases in a way that triggers offensive, refractory behaviors. Finally, if sluggish or otherwise impaired systems found that demanding, disruptive expression excited a short-term boost in glucose levels and imparted a sensation of well-being, then agonistic behavior would be reinforced.

Annual Unrest and Its Ritualization

Irrespective of the precise mechanism, the question I brought back to my thinking about the Black Saturnalia was whether a famine-related syndrome could apply to a situation of semistarvation and relief such as occurred at the conclusion of the hungry months in the sugar colonies. What persuaded me that it could was my discovery of John Robson's (1972: 1: 39–40) brief account of seasonal disturbances on East African sisal estates. Robson reported that unrest occurred annually at the end of that period of the year when diets were at their worst. He concluded that the turmoil could be attributed to malnutrition and advised nutritionists to be on the lookout for possible dietary causes for other recurrent episodes of this sort.

Robson saw subclinical pellagra as the specific malefactor in East Africa, but in light of the seasonal surges of fighting reported from elsewhere this seemed unconvincing. Rather what occurred to me was that Robson had seen the Keys' overheated boiler in a community setting, and as in the Minnesota experiment, it was bereft of good safety valves. Keys wrote of the absence of safety valves as an engineering design flaw in his experiment. It struck me that, if this was so, then the Black Saturnalia might be viewed as a triumph of human engineering. Not that the planters invented a safety valve but that they implicitly recognized one when they saw it. The Black Saturnalia and Gluckman's rituals of rebellion were, then, expressive events that had evolved to discharge agonistic emotion in culturally meaningful ways.

Here was a theory that lent itself to testing. It would require seeing the Black Saturnalia in worldwide perspective, setting forth propositions derived from the theory of progressive ritualization, and testing those propositions holoculturally. If they held for the class, then by inclusion a case would be made for the Saturnalia of the sugar colonies.

ANNUAL RITUALS OF CONFLICT

That the Black Saturnalia possessed the properties of a global class of events is not difficult to establish. Less than a decade after publication of Gluckman's essay on Southeast African rituals of rebellion, Edward Norbeck (1963), seeking to broaden the perspective on these rites, established that similar events existed beyond Southeast Africa. They were to be found throughout Africa's sub-Saharan regions. He also made clear that what Gluckman had called rituals of rebellion bore resemblance to other rites containing expressions of hostility. Gluckman had applied his label specifically to two kinds of ceremonies: those in which women behaved in aggressive ways toward men, and those in which subjects derided their king. Norbeck presented cases from a variety of cultures wherein men expressed ritualized antagonism toward women. He recounted descriptions of rites representing conflict between affinal kin, between community groups, and between individuals holding grievances against each other. Justifiably reluctant to extend Gluckman's designation, "rituals of rebellion," across such a big sphere of manifest meanings, Norbeck applied instead the cover term, "rituals of apparent conflict," or "rituals of conflict" for short, to this entire class of rites.

The Black Saturnalia can be viewed as a member of a subset of this class: seasonal or noncontingent events that contain episodes of ridicule, threat, assault, rivalry, or other contentions which, whether solemnly or playfully enacted, at other times are not prescribed, expected, or considered proper. I refer to this category, which includes a diverse assemblage of festivals, carnivals, political and religious ceremonies, and other yearly celebrations, as annual rituals of conflict.

HYPOTHESIS TESTS

With this category in mind, I deduced two hypotheses. The first bears on the global distribution: if annual rituals of conflict such as the Black Saturnalia are rooted in a physiological response set in motion by prolonged caloric hunger, then it follows that one ought to find a positive relationship between the worldwide incidence of seasonal hunger and the incidence of such rites. The second prediction bears on origin and development: if annual rituals of conflict originate in a generalized agonistic response, then the amplitude of this response ought to show a positive correlation with the presence of hunger seasons. This latter prediction follows from a principle of ritualization. It states in essence that as expression evolves from its source it progresses from raw behavior toward precise performance thereby losing amplitude. To put this in another way, ritual is first and foremost a communication device. As it develops, it tends to become more restrained, more polished or economical in its performance, and less and less a consummate activity. Over time secondary messages may develop and even replace the founding motive. Thus, highly evolved rites can go so far as to become entirely detached from their original environment, assuming as it were lives of their own. In such cases, the original emotion that compelled performance is likely to be reduced to some highly constrained, abstract representation in contrast to the stark, high-amplitude enactments typical of less highly evolved rites.[3]

Incidence

To test these propositions holoculturally, I turned to the Human Relations Area Files' (H.R.A.F.) probability Sample (Version A), a data base of 60 rural, nonindustrial societies selected to represent the universe of such societies worldwide (Naroll et al., 1976). Each group in the sample was evaluated for the presence of annual rituals of conflict using the definitions and procedures reported in Part I of the Appendix. Here let it simply be noted that the most frequently encountered examples of the rites in question were tournaments or other physical contests, sham battles, playful attacks on persons or their property, rude pranks, and customary interludes of ridicule or mockery. The incidence of such events among Probability Sample societies is indicated in table I, column III.

To test the assertion that annual rituals of conflict will be found in positive association with seasonal hunger also required studying the Probability Sample cases with an eye toward ascertaining adequacy of food supply throughout the year. For this purpose, I defined a hunger season as an annual interlude of weeks or months during which all or part of a population experiences a perceptible decline in nutritional status. A preliminary survey of sources es-

Table 1 Probability Sample, summary of rankings

Ia	IIb	IIIc	IVd	Ve	VIf
MP5	Amhara	2	3	2	2
AZ2	Andamans	1	2	.	1
O18	Aranda	1	2	.	1
FE12	Ashanti	2	2	1	2
SF5	Aymara	2	4	2	2
FO7	Azande	1	4	.	2
SO11	Bahia Brazil	2	1	2	2
FQ5	Bemba	2	4	3	1
NF6	Blackfoot	2	3	2	1
SP8	Bororo	1	4	.	.
SR8	Bush Negroes	1	1	.	1
SC7	Cagaba	1	2	.	.
RY2	Chukchee	2	2	2	1
ND8	Copper Eskimo	1	4	.	1
SB5	Cuna	1	1	.	2
FA16	Dogon	2	3	2	.
FK7	Ganda	1	3	.	2
AR5	Garo	2	3	1	2
SM4	Guarani	1	1	.	1
MS12	Hausa	2	4	2	2
ES10	Highland Scots	2	1	1	2
NT9	Hopi	1	1	.	2
OC6	Iban	1	3	.	1
OA19	Ifugao	2	3	2	2
NM9	Iroquois	2	3	2	1
MS14	Kanuri	2	4	2	.
OJ29	Kapauku	1	1	.	1
AR7	Khasi	2	3	2	.
NR10	Klamath	1	3	.	1
AA1	Korea	2	4	2	2
MA11	Kurd	1	2	.	2
EP4	Lapps	1	1	.	1
OQ6	Lau	1	2	.	2
FQ9	Lozi	1	3	.	2
FL12	Masai	1	1	.	1
S17	Mataco	2	4	3	.
NG6	Ojibwa	1	3	.	1
SH4	Ona	1	1	.	1
NQ18	Pawnee	2	1	2	1
FO4	Pygmie	1	1	.	1
AW42	Santal	2	4	2	2

Table 1   Probability Sample, summary of rankings (*continued*)

I[a]	II[b]	III[c]	IV[d]	V[e]	VI[f]
MT9	Senussi	1	2	.	1
EF6	Serbs	2	4	2	2
MW11	Shluh	2	3	2	2
AX4	Sinhalese	2	1	2	.
MO4	Somali	2	4	3	1
AD5	Taiwan Hokkien	2	1	1	2
NU33	Tarahumara	2	4	2	.
AO7	Thai	1	2	.	2
OT11	Tikopia	1	4	.	1
FF57	Tiv	1	3	.	1
NA12	Tlingit	1	2	.	1
OG11	Toradja	2	2	2	1
OL6	Trobriands	2	3	2	1
OR19	Truk	1	1	.	1
SQ19	Tucano	2	3	3	1
NV9	Tzeltal	2	4	1	2
MS30	Wolof	2	4	3	2
RV2	Yakut	2	4	1	.
SQ18	Yanoama	2	1	2	1

[a] H.R.A.F. Probability Sample societal codes
[b] names of societies
[c] presence or absence of annual rituals of conflict: 1 = annual rituals of conflict absent, 2 = annual rituals of conflict present
[d] annual food supply (for values see Appendix, Part 2)
[e] level of agonistic expression (for values see Appendix, Part 3); "." indicates cases without annual rituals of conflict
[f] level of cultural complexity (a compression of Murdock's and Provost's quartile ranks): "." indicates uncoded case, 1 = low, 2 = high.
The following cases coded by the author: Bahia, Blackfoot, Guarani, Highland Scots, Hopi, Iroquois, Lau, Ona, Senussi, Serbs, Shluh, Taiwan Hokkien, Tlingit, Tzeltal.

tablished that certain inferences would be necessary to operationalize this definition. Ethnographers rarely submit direct evidence or precise measures in support of their assertions regarding hunger. Consequently, it was allowed that evidence of seasonal hunger would include unelaborated statements, including those attributed to informants, declaring the existence of either seasonal food scarcity or starvation. In addition, reports of (1) an annual period of weight loss, (2) a seasonal decrease in the number of meals per day, (3) a seasonal switch in diet to "emergency" or supplementary foods, and (4) complaints of hunger voiced during particular times of the year were accepted as evidence.

The preliminary survey of ethnographic sources also made it clear that a hunger season cannot simply be said either to exist or not. True, in some instances one encounters unambiguous claims that scarcity occurs every year. However, when ethnographies mention scarcity, they more often portray some variability. Food supply may be more or less depleted during certain seasons, but even so not every year brings starvation. The coding rules presented in Part 2 of the Appendix were written to reflect this. Evaluation of Probability Sample cases against the informational requirements stipulated in the Appendix resulted in the codes indicated in table I, column IV.

As predicted, the relationship between hunger seasons and the incidence of annual rituals of conflict is positive (n = 60, tau-b = +.314, p < .005). Peoples whose annual cycles include periods of food scarcity and starvation are more likely than others to celebrate yearly rites containing some sort of agonistic expression. What is more, the sequence of events is revealing. In 75% of the societies determined to celebrate annual rituals of conflict, the celebration occurs during or immediately following a harvest (including the natural harvests of hunter-gatherers). Furthermore, in 75% of those cases in which conflict rites are associated with harvests, data show the harvest terminates a period of hunger.

Amplitude of Form

Let us turn now from the question of incidence to that of amplitude and the prediction that rites high on that score will tend to be found in environments most severely troubled by annual hunger. Here analysis begins with recognition that annual rituals of conflict worldwide vary greatly in mode of expression. In some cases, it is rhetorical; tensions and hostilities are represented by words alone instead of actions. In others, conflict sometimes receives violent enactment as in the case of the Black Saturnalia. These respective cases represent the extremes of amplitude in agonistic expression. In between, one finds rites in which contentions are portrayed in the form of athletic contests, sham battles, mock assaults, or other turbulent kinds of behavior short of any outright fighting. Thus, we have a scale of agonistic expression in annual rituals of conflict: (1) purely verbal or other abstract or vicarious displays of hostility, (2) ritual contests and other physical enactments of aggression unaccompanied by actual fighting, (3) naked conflict concurrent with or occasionally sparked by highly animated ritualized forms. These distinctions provide the basis for the ranking scheme presented in Part 3 of the Appendix. Part 3 also describes the coding procedures used to evaluate cases. Table 1, column V displays the results of these procedures.

Those results cross-tabulated against the codes for seasonal food supply reveal a postive correlation (n = 32, tau-b = +.296, p < .05); the greater their exposure to annual hunger the greater the amplitude of peoples' aggressive displays. This supports the hypothesis that the most unrefined examples of annual rituals of conflict, those that would appear to have evolutionary priority, are disproportionately found in those ecologies suspected of giving rise to relief induced agonism.

Cultural Complexity

Statistical associations never demonstrate causality. However, multiple associations consistent with the predictions of causal theory enhance its credibility. With this in mind, I tested the amplitude of agonistic expression in annual rituals of conflict against level of cultural complexity, a widely accepted measure of general evolution. If agonism is the founding emotion underlying annual rituals of conflict, then the most turbulent expressions of it ought to be found among societies that, for whatever reason, generally have retained autochthonous social and cultural forms.

This is a readily testable proposition. Murdock and Provost (1973) have ranked the Standard Cross-Cultural Sample by complexity using a combination of scales that measure population density, urbanism, social integration, and other key indicators of modern social development and cultural complexity. Thirty-seven of their cases appear in the Probability Sample. I rated another fourteen cases using their scales. The coded cases were then divided into two echelons, high complexity versus low complexity, the latter corresponding to the first and second quartile in Murdock's and Provost's ranking, the former to the third and fourth. These procedures yielded the discriminations given in table 1, column VI.

These data cross-tabulated against the way agonism is expressed (amplitude) reveal a decidedly negative association (n = 25, tau-b = −.446, p < .01), indicating that relatively complex societies tend toward more refined, less strife-filled enactments of conflict. Those societies that have retained relatively early forms overall also incline to retain in their annual rites expressions of agonism having relatively high amplitude. Thus, there appears another line of evidence supporting the theory that the form of annual rituals of conflict is affected by cultural evolution. That this works specifically on amplitude is indicated by the fact that complexity does nothing to actually suppress the incidence of rituals of conflict; indeed, level of complexity is positively related to their incidence (n = 51, tau-b = +.294, p = .02).

DISCUSSION

In light of the above findings, annual rituals of conflict would appear subject to an evolutionary process. Lines of evidence drawn from laboratory and clinical observations, behavioral reports from hunger-stricken field sites, and holocultural relationships linking annual rituals of conflict to seasonal hunger- and starvation-ending harvests suggest that the process begins from a biological baseline, an emotional, behavioral disturbance connected with refeeding in the wake of prolonged starvation. This affliction, relief induced agonism, clearly affects interactions and would appear to take on cultural form through repetition. At first the form might be somewhat ill-defined, consisting only of a certain periodicity. The end of the lean months becomes an interlude of unrest as Robson reported or a celebration period marred, as it were, by discord. Dancing and other activities occur in tandem with quarreling. Even this can come to possess, judging from certain of the Probability Sample cases, something of a ritualized character owing to its stereotypic, highly predictable occurrence.

Further evolution would lead to the genesis of a derivative, parallel form such as the sham battle. Actual fighting still can take place, if only sporadically at this stage, but concurrent ritualistic contests siphon off energies that otherwise might be discharged in earnest. Just as certain nonhuman species engage in ritual threat rather than in fighting in certain circumstances, so human aggression can apparently become at least partially channeled, allowing for the necessary emotional discharge while mitigating the potential for serious harm.

Full ritualization, apparently abetted by growing cultural complexity, reduces risk further. With conflict entirely formalized, satisfactions quite apart from the expression of a nutritionally sensitive emotional state can move to the fore and offer reason enough for celebration. Thus, as suggested in table 2, annual rituals of conflict, particularly those unaccompanied by violent activity, can become detached from hunger seasons, perhaps to assume economic or political functions alone. Their original impetus, relief induced agonism, may no longer be a compelling force. This liberation might come about by virtue of technical advances that improve the constancy of food supply or by migrations or borrowings that carry a rite beyond the confines of the starvation-troubled land where it originated. In any event, the potential for annual rituals of conflict to become separated from environments plagued by food scarcity is especially obvious in the case of purely rhetorical or vicarious rites.

These theoretical transformations accord well with what we know of the Black Saturnalia, particularly its best-documented component, John Canoe. Essentially a "threat" intended to elicit an "appeasement" (i.e., a gift) from onlookers, it appears to have been carried in prototypical form from West Africa to Jamaica as early as the seventeenth century. Later came costume changes and the appearance of a structure fashioned along the lines of another Old World folk rite, the Western European "house-visit."

Table 2 Distribution of agonistic activity against hunger
season among Probability Sample societies

	Hunger season			
	(1) Denied	(2) Not evident	(3) Occasional	(4) Annual
Agonism				
(A) None	10	8	6	4
(B) Verbal	2	1	1	2
(C) Contestive action	4	2	8	7
(D) Actual fighting	0	0	1	4

From these syncretistic roots, the colorful yet menacing character of the early nineteenth-century John Canoe blossomed (Dirks, 1979a; 1979b: 93–95).

Near the end of slavery, just as conditions were being improved, the celebration began to decline on Jamaica. With abolition former slaves left the plantations in droves to embark upon own-account agriculture. When Martha Beckwith (1929) described Jamaican rural culture, John Canoe survived as "Christmas sport" in remote communities. The rite clearly retained the character of conflict but without any apparent tendency to spark violent affrays. As seasonal want had been substantially mitigated by this time, this evolution toward a less volatile portrayal of agonism represented a step in the expected direction. Were one to chart it on table 2, the point of departure would be D4, the position in keeping with the nature and circumstances of the original saturnalia, with subsequent movement to point C3.

This movement would continue. In the 1950s John Canoe underwent a revival. A Kingston newspaper brought the tradition back to prominence by sponsoring a national competition, and to this day the contest goes on annually with troupes performing for prizes before large audiences. The event, as such, might still be seen as contestive. But given its reinterpretation—the fact that it has become largely a vicarious event—plus the absence of seasonal hunger, the John Canoe of today would be entered on table 2 at point B2, even further removed from its point of origin.

Still, one can glimpse the original connection between action and emotion. John Canoe today might not impart to a Jamaican audience anything overtly having to do with conflict, but nonetheless I find it revealing that spectators still feel that what goes on is somehow "wild and scary" (Bettleheim, 1979: 84). Spectators reported the same feelings nearly two hundred years ago, suggesting that this rite, despite changes in meaning, has successfully engaged the same emotions across immense temporal and cultural horizons (Dirks, 1987: 177–178).

CONCLUSIONS

Viewed in broad, theoretical perspective, the nonrandom coincidence between agonism ritually portrayed and the throb of a powerful ecological pulse affecting the intake of food energy appears consistent with the contention of theorists that ritual in general is rooted in stress (e.g., Chapple, 1970: 295–296). The particular stress my research implicates may be poorly understood in terms of its underlying mechanisms, but as it stands no other phenomenon can account for the worldwide tendency of annual rituals of conflict to occur immediately following the ebb point in annual food energy pulses. Mechanisms quite different from those suggested by Bolton (personal communication) may be involved, possibly a psychodynamic along the lines suggested by Welch. In any case, it is very doubtful that origin and incidence of annual rites of conflict can be laid *solely* at the door of cultural factors with biology ruled out.

This is not to deny the relevance of culture. Political structure and organization appear especially pertinent. In testing Gluckman's thinking, my research uncovered a fairly strong, positive relationship between the range of community decision-making and the celebration of rites of conflict (n = 26, tau-b = +.330, p < .05). In other words, societies that accord relatively little opportunity for individuals to make decisions are disproportionately given to ritualized representations of discontent. In addition, societies in which powerful formal sanctions are available to enforce decisions are more apt to celebrate annual rituals of conflict than those in which sanctioning is less strongly developed (n = 26, tau-b = +.402, p < .05). But neither of these general traits can account for the annual timing of rituals of conflict. However, in terms of establishing fertile conditions for their celebration one cannot discount the possibility of interaction between these political variables and hunger.[4]

I take these holocultural patterns as representing but the tip of an iceberg. With respect to the Black Saturnalia specifically, close study reveals not only far-reaching community decision-making specifically embodied in the plantation's highly regimented order and powerful sanctions enforced by the government of the cowskin as essential to explanation. We also see a confluence of numerous other factors—geographical, agricultural, industrial, and economic—coming together to create the precise conditions necessary for the annual cycle of sugar plantations to engender a relief induced agonism. It was a stress historically determined; relief induced agonism was in the fullest sense a product of a cultural ecology.

Even as such, it would account for little beyond origin. At most, relief induced agonism is an unusual turbulence in the stream of human emotion. To get from there to a maelstrom of bloody insurrection and intense, glittering displays of conflict requires traversing a complex cultural and historical landscape. It becomes in the process increasingly clear that, what with the life-threatening economy governing slave subsistence and the fierce competitive ethos that resulted, it probably required no more than a slight turbulence to produce great reverberations. How these came to assume the form they did is a matter of ethnohistorical study. Such study reveals the story of the Black Saturnalia proper. Relief induced agonism was no more than a tiny seed, a small thing that perhaps explains little about the particulars of the great institution the Black Saturnalia eventually became but without which there never would have been an institution like it to explain.

NOTES

1 I have had opportunity to conduct an ethological study of John Canoe among the Garifuna (Black Carib) of Belize who, judging from early nineteenth-century accounts of the dance, have preserved this rite with almost incredible fidelity (see Dirks, 1977; 1979a; 1979b; Dirks and Kerns, 1975).
2 For a list of dates, places, and references, see *The Black Saturnalia* (Dirks, 1987; 207–208; also 1978: 180).
3 For a more detailed discussion of ritualization see my forthcoming "Annual Rituals of Conflict" (Dirks, in press).
4 The political codes are borrowed from Ross (1983). The relationship between both of them and seasonal hunger is positive (decision-making: $n = 26$, tau-b $= +.313$, $p = .03$; sanctioning: $n = 26$, tau-b $= +.344$, $p = .02$). However, the small number of coded cases corresponding to Probability Sample societies precludes the control tests that might document an interaction effect on annual rituals of conflict.

APPENDIX

This section recounts in brief some of the definitions, scales, coding rules, and quality assurances used testing the holocultural theories described in this paper. A fuller discussion can be found in my forthcoming article, "Annual Rituals of Conflict" (Dirks, in press).

Part 1: Annual Rituals of Conflict

Annual rituals of conflict were defined as noncontingent, yearly events or periods marked by regular, stereotypic, and expected aggressions or contention. Such acts, playfully or otherwise, might be verbal (including threats, insults, and ridicule) or nonverbal (including theft, property damage, contestive sports, and fights). A preliminary review of the literature established that activities of these sorts quite often were to be found nested within larger, multifaceted ceremonies and extended celebrations, parts of which contained no discernible element of conflict whatsoever. In such cases only a portion of or episode within the whole might appear agonistic. This was not allowed to confound identification. Each episode, every event within a larger complex, was evaluated separately.

Evaluation for each society in the sample involved examining Human Relations Area File (H.R.A.F.) sources with specific attention to Outline of Cultural Materials (O.C.M.) categories 527, 541, 786, and 796. Notes relevant to the assignment of codes were taken. Assessments were made according to the following informational requirements:

Rank Information Required

0   When sources contain no description of festivals, celebrations, ceremonies, or other ritual events.

1   When sources report festivals, periods of celebration, ceremonies, or other ritual events but contain no descriptions of conflict associated with such events.

2   When sources describe an annual ritual of conflict.

Coding was carried out by the author and a second rater. Their first assessments showed a fair measure of consistency (tau-b = +.790). Inconsistencies were resolved by discussion and restudy of sources.

Part 2: Seasonal Hunger

The definition of seasonal hunger and the evidence accepted as documenting it are set forth in the main body of this paper. Research was conducted using H.R.A.F. sources contained in O.C.M.

categories 146, 262, and 264. Categories 221, 241, and 805 were studied if the above failed to yield substantial information. The coders consulted unprocessed sources as a last resort. Values were assigned to each case according to the following rules:

Rank   Information Required
0   When sources report no data regarding food supply or diet.
1   When report states that food is never in short supply.
2   When report describes food supply or diet as either steady or seasonally changing and no regular shortages or periods of poor nutrition are mentioned.
3   When report associates food shortage or hunger with a particular time of year; occasionally (but not every year) at least some people actually experience want (owing to weather conditions, a short crop, or some other seasonal event).
4   When report indicates that a hunger season (lean months, difficult period, etc.) manifests itself annually.

Coder agreement in evaluating annual food supply was good (tau-b = +.900). Disagreements were handled as previously described.

Part 3: Agonistic Expression in Annual Rituals of Conflict

Amplitude of agonistic—that is, aggressive or contentious—expression was coded according to the following informational requirements:

Rank   Information Required
1   Coder notes annual ritual of conflict involving teasing or other verbal expression of hostility among adults or agonistic activity on the part of children.
2   Coder notes annual rituals of conflict involving agonistic activity other than verbal on the part of adults.
3   Coder notes annual ritual of conflict accompanied by actual quarreling or fighting.

Determinations for the level of agonistic expression in each case were made by the author using notes that both he and his assistant had recorded while coding for the presence of annual rituals of conflict. In those instances where coders' notes disclosed multiple events—say, an interlude of lewd jokes, a tug of war between sets of villagers, and playful assaults upon men by women—the highest-ranking event in the cluster determined the overall score. In cases where coders' notes contained discrepancies—for example, if one failed to record the occurrence of actual fighting—data sources were rechecked and the highest value consistent with the activities noted was assigned.

REFERENCES

Beckwith, M. (1929) Black Roadways. Chapel Hill: University of North Carolina Press.

Bettelheim, J. (1979) "Jamaica Jonkonnu and related Caribbean festivals," in M. Crahan and F. Knight (eds.) Africa and the Caribbean. Baltimore: Johns Hopkins University Press.

Chapple, E. (1970) Culture and Biological Man. New York: Holt, Rinehart, and Winston.

Craton, M. (1982) Testing the Chains. Ithaca: Cornell University Press.

Dirks, R. (1975) "The Slaves' holiday." Natural History 84(10): 82–91.

——— (1976) "Socio-behavioral responses to famine (review and synthesis)," a paper presented at the Seventy-fifth Annual Meeting of the American Anthropological Association. Washington, D.C.

——— (1977) "Ritualized threat and total institution," in R. Gordon and B. Williams (eds.) Exploring Total Institutions. Champaign: Stipes.

——— (1978) "Resource fluctations and competitive transformations in West Indian slave societies," in C. Laughlin and I. Brady (eds.) Extinction and Survival in Human Populations. New York: Columbia University Press.

——— (1979a) "John Canoe: ethnohistorical and comparative analysis of a Carib dance." *Actes du XLII Congres International des Americanistes* 6: 487–501.

——— (1979b) "The Evolution of a Playful Ritual: The Garifuna's John Canoe in Comparative Perspective," in E. Norbeck and C. Farrer (eds.), Forms of Play of Native North Americans. 1977 Proceedings of the American Ethnological Society. St. Paul: West.

——— (1979c) "Relief Induced Agonism." Disasters 3(2): 195–198.

——— (1980) "Social Responses during Severe Food Shortages and Famine." Current Anthropology 21(1): 21–44.

——— (1987) The Black Saturnalia. Gainesville: University Presses of Florida.

——— (in press) "Annual rituals of conflict." American Anthropologist.

Dirks, R. and V. Kerns (1975) "John Canoe." National Studies 3(6): 1–15.

Frazer, J. (1911–1915) The Golden Bough. 3d ed. London: Macmillan.

Gluckman, M. (1954) Rituals of Rebellion in South-East Africa. Manchester: University of Manchester Press.

Keys, A., et al. (1950) The Biology of Human Starvation. 2 vols. Minneapolis: University of Minnesota Press.

Laughlin, C. and I. Brady (1978) Extinction and Survival in Human Populations. New York: Columbia University Press.

Long, E. (1774) The History of Jamaica. 2 vols. London: Lowndes.

Murdock, G. and C. Provost (1973) "Measurement of Cultural Complexity." Ethnology 12: 379–392.

Naroll, R., G. Michik and F. Naroll (1976) Worldwide Theory Testing. New Haven: Human Relations Area Files.

Norbeck, E. (1963) "African rituals of conflict." American Anthropologist 65(6): 1254–1279.

Robson, J. (1972) Malnutrition. 2 vols. New York: Gordon and Breach.

Ross, M. (1983) "Political Decision Making and Conflict: Additional Cross-Cultural Codes and Scales." Ethnology 22(2): 169–192.

Welch, B. (1965) "Psychophysiological Response to the Mean Level of Environmental Stimulation," in Symposium on Medical Aspects of Stress in a Military Climate. Sponsored by Walter Reed Army Institute of Research. Washington, D.C.: United States Government Printing Office.

A Dreadful Childhood: The Excess Mortality of American Slaves

RICHARD H. STECKEL

MORTALITY RATES IN early childhood are widely regarded as a sensitive index of the health and living standards of a population (United Nations, 1973: 138–139; Williamson, 1981; Haines, 1985). The debate over the health and treatment of American slaves has led scholars to investigate various data and methods to construct these measures. Early work based on plantation records placed the infant mortality rate (the proportion of live births that die within one year of birth) at 152.6 per thousand (Postell, 1951: 158). Using census data and indirect techniques, estimates of the infant mortality rate climbed from 182.7 per thousand by Evans (1962: 212) to 274 to 302 per thousand by Farley (1970: 33) and 246 to 275 per thousand by Eblen (1972; 1974). Recent work based on height data and indirect techniques places the infant mortality rate in the neighborhood of 350 per thousand and total losses before the end of the first year (stillbirths plus infant deaths) at nearly 50% (Steckel, 1986a). Thus, measurements

Richard H. Steckel is associate professor of economics at Ohio State University, Columbus, OH 43210 and a research associate in the National Bureau of Economic Research.

The author has benefitted from comments by or discussions with John Campbell, Catherine Clinton, Stanley Engerman, Robert Fogel, Ken Kiple, John Komlos, Robert Margo, John Olson, Jeffrey Williamson, the editors, and workshop participants at Chicago and Harvard.

Social Science History 10:4 (Winter 1986). Copyright © 1986 by the Social Science History Association. CCC 0145-5532/86/$1.50.

Table 1   Mortality rates per thousand for
slaves and the antebellum population

Age	Slaves	Entire United States
0	350	179
1–4	201	93
5–9	54	28
10–14	37	19
15–19	35	28
20–24	40	39

Sources: Age 0, slaves, see Notes 5 and 17; slaves aged 1 and above, Steckel
(1979b: 92); United States, Haines and Avery (1980: 88), average of Model
West and logit tables.

over the past four decades have gravitated toward the judgment of
southern planter Thomas Affleck (1851: 435) who wrote, "Of
those born, one half die under one year."[1]

The magnitudes of the most recent estimates suggest the need
for a reexamination of the determinants of health in early childhood. Recognizing that decisions were made in an environment
of poor medical knowledge and that many deaths would have occurred despite the best intentions and despite the best care that
was available, this paper seeks to explain the excess mortality of
young slave children.[2] Figures in Table 1 show that most of the
excess losses were concentrated before age 5.[3] Notably, the infant mortality rate for slaves was about 17 percentage points above
the rate for the entire antebellum population in the United States.

Maternal carelessness and neglect, perhaps caused by exhaus-
tion and exacerbated by ignorance, have been recurrent themes in
the literature on determinants of health. Slaveowners blamed care-
less mothers for smothering infants by rolling on them while sleeping. Some observers have attributed these deaths to infanticide,
but many people now think that instances of "smothering" were
examples of Sudden Infant Death Syndrome (Fogel and Engerman, 1974; Sutch, 1975; Savitt, 1978; Johnson, 1981), which
occurs frequently from 1 to 6 months after birth and which
often has causes stemming from deprivation during the fetal period (Naeye, 1980; Valdés-Dapena, 1980). Fogel and Engerman

(1974: 122) argued that slaves had good prenatal care, but Campbell (1984) linked higher infant mortality rates to work before birth. Steckel (1979a) sought explanations in terms of maternal variables such as age and parity and environmental variables such as plantation size, main crop, region, and time period. Kiple and Kiple (1977), Kiple and King (1981), and Kiple (1984) argued that poor health of slave children was heavily influenced by a diet and climate ill-suited to persons of African descent.

This paper reexamines data on individual slaves from plantation records in a search for underlying determinants of excess infant mortality. The analysis departs from earlier work in this vein by using recent estimates of neonatal (birth to one month) mortality to adjust explicitly for underreporting of early infant deaths in the plantation records.[4] The separation of infant mortality into neonatal and postneonatal (second month to one year) components helps to address issues of pre- versus postnatal care.[5] Circumstances during pregnancy primarily determined stillbirths and other losses soon after birth whereas later infant deaths often had diverse causes associated with breastfeeding practices, diet, and other aspects of infant care.[6] Taking a cue from research on human height data, the approach of this paper exploits the concept of net nutrition (or nutritional status). Research using heights has made clear that diet, disease, and work cannot be evaluated in isolation. Instead, these factors are components of the same package that interact to determine the level of health or deprivation.

The paper concentrates on prenatal conditions because most of the excess infant losses occurred before the end of the first month. It is argued that patterns of disease and diet, and especially work, expressed by season of the year and by main crop were important influences on newborn health. Attenuated breastfeeding practices and a poor diet aggravated the health of older infants. Adverse conditions of the 1820s and the 1830s and early childbearing also contributed to excess mortality. Fundamentally, the system of forced labor under slavery raised women's productivity in the fields and placed high value on their time. Combined with planter ignorance and other factors, it led to pre- and postnatal practices detrimental to health.

THE DATA AND GENERAL CONDITIONS

Lists of slave births and deaths maintained by slaveowners were a type of business record that also included planting and harvesting accounts, financial ledgers, inventories of slaves and equipment, and food and clothing allotments to slaves. An extensive search of southern archives identified over 30 birth lists for which the deaths were frequently recorded. On these, 11 large plantations have substantially complete death lists as characterized by regular chronological entries and the absence of "X" or "dead" notations. The infant mortality rates on these units are plausible and range from 176 to 392 per thousand live births. However, the shares of neonatal deaths among all infant deaths were implausibly low on some plantations, which suggests that some early deaths and the corresponding births were not recorded. The plantations ranged in size from 65 to 230 slaves, collectively grew cotton, rice and sugar, and operated in South Carolina, Georgia, Alabama, and Louisiana from the 1780s to the early 1860s.[7]

Although data on the heights of children are not the direct object of study in the paper, this source is mentioned because diet, disease, child care, and growth were components of the health complex. Children and other slaves were measured in compliance with the bill for the abolition of the slave trade, which was passed by Congress in 1807. The law abolished the African slave trade but permitted the coastwise trade to continue as a monitored activity. Ship captains recorded heights, ages, and other characteristics on manifests as part of an identification scheme designed to prove that slaves entering American ports were not smuggled from Africa.

The picture of poor health suggested by the height data is consistent with the high mortality rates observed in the plantation records.[8] At age 3, for example, slave children attained about centile 0.2 of modern height standards, which places them among the poorest populations ever studied by auxologists. Comparative heights suggest that children from the slums of Lagos, Nigeria, and from urban areas of Bangladesh had an environment for growth superior to that of American slave children.

MORTALITY WITHIN THE FIRST MONTH

There is a high correlation between birth weights and heights in early childhood among poor populations in developing countries. This evidence and information on the health and prenatal condition of slave women suggest that the very low birth weights were a major cause of high mortality rates of slaves in early infancy. Specifically, the majority of slave newborns probably weighed less than 2500 grams or 5.5 pounds and neonatal mortality rates were at least 150, and possibly as high as 250 per thousand.[9] Moreover, the share of stillbirths among all births may have been in the range of 10 to 15%.

Studies of fetal development and birth weights in developed and developing countries show that the following factors are systematically associated with stillbirths and neonatal deaths.[10] (1) general malnutrition of the mother; (2) specific dietary deficiencies of the mother; (3) maternal and fetal infections; (4) work during pregnancy, especially effort that requires standing; (5) ingestion of toxic substances, such as alcohol and tobacco; (6) small stature of the mother; and (7) possibly genetic factors. This section analyzes these risk factors for slaves using a regression model of neonatal mortality. Although data are lacking to incorporate maternal height and genetic factors into an analysis of variance framework, a tentative appraisal of relative importance suggests that the first four factors on the list, and especially work, disease, and diet, were important contributors (Steckel, 1986a).

Determinants of early mortality are investigated using a logit regression model (Maddala, 1977: 162–171). The dependent variable is dichotomous and takes on the value of 1 if death occurred within one month of birth and is 0 otherwise.[11] The plausible determinants of early death that are available from the plantation records are listed below and include mother's age, plantation size as measured by the average number of slaves, year of birth, and month of birth. Sex of the child, region, and main crop of the plantation may have been relevant, but unfortunately data are lacking for a complete analysis of these factors; experiments involving gender and crop are reported at the end of this section.[12]

Mother's age may operate primarily through birth order. Birth weight increases roughly 0.2 pounds from the first to the second child and there is possibly a smaller rise to the third child (Hytten and Leitch, 1971: 301–304). The effect of higher birth order is ambiguous: Some studies show a small trend toward larger size, but with weight falling (for a particular parity) with age of the mother, and others show little or no further change. Increased capacity of the circulatory system to nourish the fetus may explain the rise of birth weight with birth order. Mother's age rather than parity is used in the regression because these variables are highly correlated and because mother's age is known reliably for more observations.

Plantation size may have influenced early mortality through the work routine, the incidence of diseases, the availability of medical care and child care, and supplementation practices. The labor demands on slaves were probably greater on larger units (Fogel and Engerman, 1974: 203–206). The fact that owners of small units ordinarily worked along with the slaves may have contributed to an easier pace. Overseers and drivers achieved an intensive work routine through the gang system that characterized large farms. Thus, claims on the diet may have been greater on large plantations, but interviews with ex-slaves suggest that diets were about the same on small and large plantations (Crawford, 1980: 123). The greater numbers and higher density of people on large units probably promoted the spread of communicable diseases among children and pregnant women. Infections in pregnant women diminished nutrition available to the fetus. Slaves on large plantations may have had greater access to hospitals and medical care, but many early nineteenth-century medical practices no doubt increased the probability of death. If slave women were relatively more productive in field work on large units (Fogel and Engerman, 1974, 192–194), this would have raised the costs of breastfeeding and encouraged supplementation at an earlier age. Greater numbers on large plantations facilitated specialization and division of labor in many areas including child care, and ordinarily older women and perhaps young girls were assigned to this task. Ironically the health of infants could have deteriorated for this reason because it allowed supplementation to replace breastfeeding. In other words, some small units lacked older women and young girls, which left no alternative to breastfeeding. On the other hand, group child care may have had positive aspects, such as systematic monitoring of infant needs that improved health. Judgements about the net effects of work, disease, care, and feeding on infant health must be cautious given the lack of information on practices by plantation size. Yet infant feeding practices were central to health during this era and supplementation was probably uncommon during the neonatal period. Moreover, factors that reduced birth weight increased mortality in both the neonatal and the postneonatal periods. Consequently, the effects of plantation size on mortality rates were likely to have been greater during the postneonatal period than during the neonatal period.

The probable effect of year of birth on early mortality is uncertain because many, possibly opposing, changes that are not in the regression could have occurred over time. The disease environment, for example, may have been adversely influenced by increased transmission of communicable disease by migration, and migration rates were relatively high during the 1830s and 1850s (Fogel and Engerman, 1974: 46).[13] Similarly, changes in diet or in the intensity of work may have occurred over time. One can speculate about possible influences that were correlated with time, but it would be difficult to identify the specific sources of change given that little is known about the details of operation on these particular plantations.

Seasonal variations in diet, disease, and work are plausible determinants of fetal and infant health. Neonatal mortality is particularly sensitive to birth weight, and losses increase rapidly as newborn weight declines below 2500 grams or 5.5 pounds (Hytten and Leitch, 1971: 324). The demand for labor was greatest during the preparation and planting season of late winter and early spring, and during the harvest season of late summer and autumn. Fresh foods were in greatest supply beginning with the maturation of vegetables in midsummer and continuing through the slaughter season of early winter. Fevers were prevalent during the "sickly season" of late summer. Seasonal patterns of health generated by rhythms of weather, work, and diet have been documented for agricultural populations in developing countries (Hytten and Leitch, 1971: 452–54).

Although there are 11 plantations for which seasonal data could be studied (details about the units are given in Steckel, 1979b: 90), as an aid to the measurement and interpretation of seasonal factors, it is desirable to investigate as a unit farms for which seasonal patterns of diet, work, and disease were approximately the same. The cotton plantations (five in number) are the only group with enough observations on these grounds.[14] The recording practices on some of these plantations are suspect because the reported share of neonatal deaths among infant deaths was as low as 15%.[15] Selecting only those plantations that had plausibly high shares, say above 30% (three plantations), is one approach to the problem.[16] It is possible, however, that some shares were simply low and removing these plantations from the sample may bias the results, and for this reason a second group consisting of all five plantations is also studied. The dependent variable includes stillbirths because deprivation near conception causes stillbirths and neonatal deaths. Moreover, misreporting neonatal deaths as stillbirths was probably more likely than misreporting stillbirths as neonatal deaths. The technique of choice-based sampling was used to adjust for underreporting of stillbirths and neonatal deaths.[17]

Table 2 shows the regression results. The first equation pertains to cotton plantations for which the recorded share of infant deaths that occurred within 28 days of birth was at least 30%. As a way to adjust for probable underreporting, the second regression (all cotton plantations) also includes the reported share of infant deaths that occurred with 28 days as an independent variable. The statistics $-2 \log \lambda$ has a chi-square distribution with as many degrees of freedom as there are regressors (except the constant), and the values reported at the bottom of the table show that the regressions are significant at less than 0.005.

As expected, losses were high among young mothers. If other independent variables are evaluated at their sample means, the probability of loss in the first equation was about 32.9% for women under age 20 and about 15.3% for women aged 25–29. The corresponding probabilities in the second equation were 35.5% and 24.4%. The implied probabilities are generally consistent with expectations given that the effects of high birth order on birth weight are unclear.

Plantation size had no systematic influence on early death in either equation. In assessing this result it is important to remember that all plantations in the sample were large by standards of the American South. The smallest unit in the sample, for example, had about 65 slaves. Within the range of observation size may have had no effect, but it is worth noting that regressions on heights from Civil War military records show that the stature of

Table 2 Regression of death within one calendar month on mother's age, plantation size, the recorded proportion who died within 28 days, year of birth, and month of birth

Variable	Rate > .30		All plantations	
	Coefficient	t-value	Coefficient	t-value
Mother aged 20–24	−0.7636	−1.78	−0.4621	−1.50
Mother aged 25–29	−1.002	−2.13	−0.6469	−1.98
Mother aged 30–34	−0.3749	−0.79	−0.4195	−1.25
Mother aged 35+	0.2500	0.49	−0.7268	−2.03
Plantation size	0.007301	1.03	−0.001889	−1.04
Prop. who died within 28 days			2.165	2.23
Year Birth 1	−5.553	−1.15	0.04617	0.014
Year Birth 2	1.186	1.35	0.1455	0.27
Year Birth 3	−0.07114	−1.44	−0.01522	−0.53
February	0.7725	0.75	1.247	2.08
March	2.845	3.31	1.487	2.76
April	1.347	1.68	0.9638	1.87
May and June	0.6324	0.80	0.2395	0.49
July and August	−0.8377	−0.87	−0.1877	−0.37
September	1.890	2.23	0.6779	1.28
October	1.379	1.61	0.2532	0.44
November	1.544	1.93	0.8605	1.68
December	1.013	1.23	0.3712	0.60
Constant	3.219	0.41	−3.152	−0.48
	N = 288		N = 574	
	$-2 \log \lambda = 61.58$		$-2 \log \lambda = 81.40$	

Source: Cotton plantation birth and death lists.
Definition of variables: Dependent variable = 1 if child died (including still-birth) within one calendar month of birth, 0 otherwise; Year Birth i = ((year of birth−1770)/10)^i. The definitions of other variables are clear from the table. The omitted variables are Mother Aged Less than 20, and January.

blacks declined as the median size of holding in the county of residence increased (Margo and Steckel, 1982).

The data for the first equation are not well-suited to examine the influence of time because there are no observations for the late 1820s or the early 1830s. While keeping this feature of the data in mind, likelihood ratio tests were conducted and the time coefficients were statistically significant at 0.01 in the second equation but insignificant (in excess of 0.25) in the first equation. In the second equation the estimated probability of loss more than doubled during the early 1800s, reaching a peak of 35% during the mid 1830s and then declined to about 15% by the late 1850s. This general profile appears if dummy variables by decade replace the polynomial in time. Possible causes of this profile are discussed in the section on postneonatal mortality.

As a group the month-of-birth coefficients are statistically significant at 0.005 in each equation. The lack of deaths required that births be combined in May and June and in July and August. The pattern of the coefficients establishes a peak in late winter and early spring centered in March and a second, smaller concentration of early deaths for births from September through November. Table 3 converts these coefficients into probabilities by evaluating other independent variables at their sample means. Although noticeable differences existed in particular months such as February, the overall seasonal patterns were similar and striking in both equations. In the first equation the average probability per month in February–April and in September–November was 40.6% compared with 10.5% in other months. In the second equation the figures were 36.9% and 13.1%. Depending on month of birth, slaves had diverse prospects for health and survival.

Table 3   The probability of death within one calendar month of birth by month of birth and data source[a]

Month of birth	Rate > .30	All plantations
January	0.116	0.179
February	0.221	0.471
March	0.692	0.488
April	0.335	0.375
May and June	0.197	0.222
July and August	0.054	0.154
September	0.464	0.310
October	0.342	0.220
November	0.380	0.351
December	0.265	0.230

Source: Calculated from Table 2.
[a] Probability per month of 30.4 days.

Possible causes of these prospects are examined in the next section.

Although cotton was the dominant cash crop in southern agriculture during the late antebellum period, other crops were important in certain localities. From the colonial era rice was a major crop along the coastal areas of South Carolina and Georgia, and by the 1830s sugar predominated in southern Louisiana. It was explained earlier that observations are lacking for a regression analysis of seasonal patterns in crops other than cotton. However, if the data base is expanded to all plantations and if main crops other than cotton are added to the list of explanatory variables used for the regression involving all cotton plantations, then rice emerges as a high mortality crop. If other independent variables are evaluated at their sample means, the expected loss was 23.3% in cotton but 47.2% in rice (t = 3.66). The expected loss was 35.0% on sugar farms (this result is marginally significant; t = 1.78). Malaria and other diseases prevalent in coastal counties may have contributed to illness during pregnancy and therefore to high rates of loss in rice and sugar compared with cotton (none of the cotton plantations in the sample was located in a coastal county). Yet rice and sugar were produced in similar, swampy localities, and losses in rice exceeded those in sugar. Work routines may explain the difference. Unlike sugar and cotton that had episodes of heavy labor demands followed by lay-by periods, rice cultivation was characterized by a seasonal sequence of labor activities that were moderate and capable of being performed by women.[18] Therefore the typical woman on a rice farm may have exerted more effort during pregnancy and fewer newborns may have escaped the adverse consequences of this work. The next section discusses the relationship of work to the outcome of pregnancy in more detail.

One could argue that gender should be included in the regressions on the grounds that early infant mortality rates tend to be higher among males for biological reasons. In contrast, some societies invest more in the health of male children, and for this reason the chances of survival could be higher for males. Unfortunately the sex was not recorded for a large share of newborns that died soon after birth. If female gender is included in a regression involving all observations for which sex is known, the coefficient is negative but statistically insignificant (t = −0.73).

ANALYSIS OF SEASONAL PATTERNS

The regression analysis establishes that seasonal patterns of early mortality deserve further study. The seasonal fluctuations are statistically significant, and the wide swings in the estimated probabilities establish their practical importance.[19] The average probability per month in February–April and September–November was 280% to 390% higher (depending on the equation) than the average probability in other months. The methodology behind these figures does not justify their use as a measure of the excess mortality of young slave infants, in part because data are lacking (at least for this paper) on the seasonal pattern of losses among whites. However, the average monthly probability in December–January and May–August (10.5% in the first and 13.1% in the second equation) was only slightly above the probability of neonatal death of about 0.090 suggested for whites in note 39.[20] It will be argued that the high probabilities of death during certain months were heavily influenced by the slave work routine. Thus, patterns of work endured by slaves but not by whites could explain much of the excess infant mortality among slaves.

Modern studies of the process of human growth provide clues about influences on the health of slave children. Human growth occurs in two ways (Tanner, 1978; Hurley, 1980). One is an increase in the number of cells and the other is an increase in the size of cells. Initially organisms grow through proliferation of cells, then during a second phase cell proliferation slows down and cell size increases rapidly. In the third phase, there is almost no cell proliferation and cell size increases rapidly. If conditions are poor during the phase of rapid cell proliferation, the number of cells is restricted and cannot be increased even by supplementary feeding at a later time. However, reversal of small cell size may be possible by later feeding.

Although various organs of the body have different time sequences for the various phases of growth, cell multiplication as opposed to the growth in cell size is largely responsible for the high growth rate of the fetus compared with the child. It is thought that few, if any, nerve cells and only a small proportion of new muscle cells, for example, appear more than 28 weeks after fertilization has occurred (Tanner, 1978: 39). The process of growth indicates that conditions during the fetal period, and especially during the initial phase, are critical to later development. Studies of fetal growth under poor or unfavorable conditions show that the outcome of pregnancy depends upon the extent, timing, and duration of deprivation (National Research Council, 1970: 21). Wartime conditions created a type of laboratory for investigation of these issues. Studies of the Dutch famine during the winter of 1944–1945 show that the outcome of pregnancy is particularly sensitive to conditions in the first and last trimesters. The rates of neonatal mortality, and particularly stillbirths, were highest among pregnancies conceived in famine or exposed to famine during the first trimester only. On the other hand, undernutrition during the last trimester alone did not elevate stillbirths, but reduced birthweight by about 300 grams and increased neonatal mortality (Stein, et al., 1975: Ch. 10 and 12; and especially Moore, 1983: 247–251). Because high rates of stillbirth signify deprivation at or near conception, comparisons of neonatal and stillbirth losses by month or season may clarify the seasonal timing, and therefore the causes, of insults during pregnancy. The correlation between the mother's weight gain during pregnancy and newborn weight is higher (in absolute terms) among women who were underweight before pregnancy (Lechtig, et al., 1975). Thus chronic or extended malnutrition compounds the effects of a given environmental insult during pregnancy.

The discussion of possible causes of the monthly variations in neonatal mortality rates begins with the seasonal work routine.[21] The requirements of cotton and food crops, the weather, and the characteristics of the labor force in relation to these factors combined to create seasonal patterns in the demand for labor expressed in terms of the duration and intensity of the work day and the number of days worked per month. Although some work may have been done, ordinarily the period from Christmas through New Year's Day was a holiday or slack season. The hours of daylight were near the minimum at this time of year, which considerably shortened the length of the work day. January was a relatively light month for work. The cotton harvest was virtually complete, there were relatively few hours of daylight, and inclement weather may have discouraged or prevented field work. Removal of brush and the remnants of the previous crop began by late January or early February, followed by plowing and preparation for the planting season of March and April. The months of February through April were particularly strenuous for adults because the tasks were physically demanding and little help could be obtained from the old and the young. Owners pressed work at an intense pace to secure degrees of freedom to cope with planting deadlines beyond which yields deteriorated, unscheduled interruptions for rain, and needs to replant parts of the crop. Cool weather meant that breaks for breakfast, lunch, and rest could be short. Examination of the work records on four plantations shows that the number of days actually worked in the fields as a share of the total days was highest in March, followed by April and February.[22] A brief lay-by period followed planting, and the hoeing season, in which the cotton was thinned and weeded, continued through June or early July. The next lay-by period extended from the remainder of July until the harvest began in mid- or late August. During the height of the season owners may have required work from first light until dark, weighing the cotton after dark. Although the total number of hours devoted to the harvest was substantial compared with other seasons, the work was physically less demanding and the pace easier than preparation and planting, and the effort was distributed over more workers. Young teenage girls, for example, who were incapable of hard labor, may have been very productive at picking cotton.

How important may seasonal variations in work effort have been to the health of newborns? Plantation manuals, daily work

Table 4   Daily cotton picking rates before and after birth

Time period	Rate (lbs.)[a]	Percent
9–12 weeks before	73.2	83.4
5–8 weeks before	69.2	78.8
1–4 weeks before	67.0	76.3
Week of birth and week after	31.3	35.6
2–3 weeks after	8.6	9.8
4–7 weeks after	58.9	67.1
8–11 weeks after	80.6	91.8
Other weeks	87.8	100.0

Source: Calculated from Metzer (1974: 27–28).
[a] Assumes the woman was 25 years old.

records, and other sources show that women's work was arduous and that pregnant women had little or no reduction in work loads before the fifth month (Campbell, 1984; Jones, 1985: 16–17). Table 4 shows that women continued to work in some capacity almost until delivery, at least during seasonal peaks in the demand for labor. Productivity in cotton picking by pregnant women was down by less than one-quarter in the period one to four weeks before delivery, and output exceeded one-third of normal levels during the week before delivery.[23]

Modern studies of women's work and birth outcomes help to interpret the consequences of slave work routines. Ethiopian mothers who engaged in "hard" physical labor had newborns weighing 210 grams below those of less physically active mothers (Tafari, Naeye, and Gobezie, 1980).[24] Black women in the United States who worked while standing (as retail sales workers, private household workers, service workers, and laborers) through the 38th week of gestation had births that were about 130 grams below those who never worked (Naeye and Peters, 1982). However, the work efforts of Ethiopian and especially American women must have been modest by standards of slaves, particularly during seasonal peaks in the demand for slave labor.[25] Low birth weights attributable to demanding work are a familiar problem in many developing countries, and many antenatal programs now stress the benefits of less work for pregnant women (Ashworth, 1982: 20).

The relationship of pre- and postnatal care to women's work and infant health became political issues within industrialized countries in the early twentieth century, and laws regulating or forbidding work before and after delivery were passed in many countries (West, 1914). Legislation was motivated in part by studies showing the sensitivity of birth weight or neonatal death to work during the last trimester, and especially to work that continued nearly until delivery. Birth weights in Britain were about 350 grams lower among women who worked up to the day of confinement compared with mothers who spent more than 10 days in a pre-maternity home (Ashby, 1915: 62).[26] Neonatal mortality rates in the United States were nearly twice as high (113.1/1000 vs. 65.7/1000) among black women who continued working beyond two weeks before confinement compared with those who ceased two weeks before delivery (Rochester, 1923: 119).[27]

Table 5   Mortality and discharge for fevers
in New Orleans by month in 1850

Month	Mortality[a] (Percent)	Discharges[b] (Percent)
January	6.3	9.4
February	4.0	3.8
March	4.7	0.9
April	3.0	2.1
May	3.4	3.4
June	4.3	3.8
July	8.4	6.8
August	29.6	14.5
September	19.1	17.1
October	7.2	18.4
November	4.7	13.7
December	5.2	6.0
Total	99.9	99.9
N	920	234

Source: Editor (1851: 81) and McKelvey (1851: 292).
[a] New Orleans Charity Hospital.
[b] United States Marine Hospital.

Infections lower nutritional status by reducing appetite and by reducing nutrient absorption and utilization (Martorell, 1980). Fetal infections are common and important causes of intrauterine malnutrition in developing countries (Urrutia, et al., 1975). Maternal illnesses such as respiratory and gastrointestinal infections and malaria retard intrauterine growth. African women infected with *Plasmodium falciparum* malaria, for example, had newborn weights that were 263 grams below those born to non-infected mothers (Jelliffe, 1968). Synergy between malnutrition and infection exacerbates the effects of these factors on health (Scrimshaw, 1975).

Monthly patterns of illness and mortality suggest that infections were prevalent during the summer and early autumn. Mortality rates for slave adults were highest during June, July, and August, and these months accounted for 34.2% of all deaths for the age group 15–49 (Steckel, 1979b: 108). The "sickly season" of late summer and early autumn is clearly revealed in Table 5. Nearly 30% of the deaths from fevers occurred during August and about

19% occurred during September.[28] The discharge dates incorporate a period of recovery and show that attack rates were highest during the late summer and early autumn.

Although seasonal fluctuations in diet probably contributed to seasonal patterns of stillbirths and neonatal mortality, the available evidence suggests that fluctuations in other factors were much more important for health. Nominally the diet was probably best from mid-summer through early winter. By July fresh vegetables were available, and the slaughter of livestock ordinarily occurred from late December to January. If fluctuations in diet were primarily responsible for the seasonal patterns, then losses would have been greatest during the spring and approximately 6 to 8 months thereafter. Thus the low rates of loss in December and January and during May and June create difficulties for an approach that emphasizes the diet.

Table 6 presents evidence on stillbirths and early neonatal deaths by month of birth and day after birth.[29] What is the most reasonable scenario of actors among work, disease, and diet, given that deprivation near the time of conception causes high rates of stillbirth whereas neonatal deaths are caused largely by depriva-

Table 6 Mortality rates per thousand
by month of birth and day after birth

		Days from birth to death				
Month of birth	Still-births	0–1	2–6	7–29	0–29[a]	Number of stillbirths plus births
January, May, June, July	0	8	21	24	52	387
February, March, April	18	36	19	43	95	224
August, September, October	3	10	23	36	67	314
November, December	31	21	16	11	48	194
All months	10	17	21	30	64	1,119

Source: Five cotton plantations, observations for which month, day, and year of birth and death were reported. Three of these plantations regularly reported stillbirths and one occasionally reported stillbirths. Evidence discussed in Steckel (1986a) suggests that early infant deaths, and especially stillbirths, were substantially underreported.
[a] The rows do not sum to the figure in this column because the number at risk changed from one age-group to the next. For example, those who survived day 1 formed the group at risk in days 2–6.

tion near conception or near delivery?[30] The highest rate of still-birth loss occurred in November and December, which is consistent with hard work and net nutritional deprivation during the preparation and planting season.[31] The adverse effects of work during the harvest and diseases of the "sickly season" may have more than offset any improvements in the diet because stillbirth rates were also elevated during the late winter and early spring. The lack of stillbirths in September and October, combined with the high neonatal mortality rates during these months, points to deprivation shortly before delivery at this time of year as an important, adverse ingredient in newborn health. Hard work shortly before delivery probably contributed to the high ratio of neonatal losses to stillbirths from February through April. The relative incidence of neonatal deaths and stillbirths and the finding that stillbirths were highest near the end of autumn suggest that the preparation and planting season was the time of greatest deprivation. However, this conclusion is advanced cautiously in view of the small sample sizes for stillbirths.

POSTNEONATAL MORTALITY

Although low birth weight increases the risk of mortality beyond the neonatal period, the chances of survival for the remainder of the first year depend heavily on diet, disease, and care. The approach taken for the analysis of postneonatal mortality is similar to that employed earlier. The plausible explanatory variables that are available for the logit regression model are sex, plantation size (number of slaves), main crop, year of birth, and month of birth. However, the motivation of the variables emphasizes diet, disease, and care as opposed to low birth weight and abnormalities that arose during pregnancy. Differences in interpretation are highlighted in the discussion below of the results in Table 7.

The effect of gender on postneonatal mortality is ambiguous. Some societies emphasize male children and devote relatively more resources to their survival, but whether this was encouraged or permitted and whether it was effective if practiced among slaves is unknown. As early as midway through the fetal period girls are more developed than boys, and at birth the difference corresponds to 4 to 6 weeks of maturation (Tanner, 1978: 58). The advantage

Table 7 Regressions of mortality from the second month through
the eleventh month on sex, mother's age, plantation size, main crop,
year of birth, and month of birth.

Variable	Coefficient	t-value
Female	0.02266	0.11
Mother aged 20–24	−0.6245	−2.00
Mother aged 25–29	−0.7980	−2.33
Mother aged 30–34	−1.030	−2.71
Mother aged 35+	−1.046	−2.70
Plantation size	0.00450	3.33
Mixed farming	0.1422	0.34
Rice	0.00206	0.01
Sugar	−0.9019	−2.22
Year Birth 1	−3.7260	−0.37
Year Birth 2	−1.4390	−0.44
Year Birth 3	0.79051	1.34
Year Birth 4	−0.10884	−1.91
Year Birth 5	0.0047377	2.20
February	0.2012	0.34
March	0.8418	1.62
April	0.0363	0.07
May	0.1761	0.35
June	−0.4530	−0.84
July	0.0893	0.17
August	−0.0915	−0.18
September	0.0585	0.12
October	0.2267	0.42
November	−0.3202	−0.55
December	0.2891	0.59
Constant	5.928	0.44

$$N = 743, \; -2 \log \lambda \; -46.062$$

Source: Plantation records.
Note: The dependent variable equals 1 if a child who survived to the second
calendar month following birth died before or within the eleventh calendar
month and is 0 otherwise. Other variables, if not self-explanatory, are defined in the notes to Table 2. The omitted variables are Mother Aged Less
than 20, Cotton, and January.

of earlier maturation may have reduced mortality rates among females after the first month of life. Since the relative advantage of females tends to diminish as the mortality level rises (United Nations, 1973: 115–118), it is perhaps not surprising that the co-efficient of the gender variable is small and positive but statistically insignificant.

Many studies have noted that perinatal mortality (stillbirths plus early neonatal deaths) rates rise with advancing age of the mother, particularly after age 30 (United Nations, 1973: 127). One might suppose that some of the disadvantages which mother's age conveyed to losses before the first month would carry over to later periods of infancy, and on these grounds the sharp decline in postneonatal mortality rates with mother's age may seem surprising. If other independent variables are evaluated at their sample means, the probability of postneonatal death was 24.0% for mothers under age 20 but only 10.1% for mothers aged 30 or more. If the first month was so harsh that it eliminated marginal children who would ordinarily have perished in the postneonatal period, then postneonatal mortality rates should have been high for mothers' ages at which rates of early mortality were low. Yet rates were high in both periods for young mothers. The value of womens' time by age cannot explain this pattern because annual net earnings of slave women from field work peaked for those in their mid 30s (Fogel and Engerman, 1974: 82). Thus it is doubtful that owners would have encouraged older women to breastfeed more frequently during the day or for a longer period of time after birth. Postneonatal mortality may have declined with the mother's age simply because experience was important in improving child care.

Losses systematically increased with plantation size as measured by the number of slaves. The expected probability of postneonatal death was about 8.4% at size 75 but 13.8% at size 200. Postneonatal mortality rates may have risen with size because greater numbers and higher density promoted the spread of disease. This effect alone should have increased disease among pregnant women, which would have reduced birth weights and elevated early infant losses, but no systematic, positive association was found between size and early infant mortality. Extensive specialization and division of labor made field labor relatively more productive, and therefore breastfeeding and other time spent on child care were relatively more expensive to owners of working mothers on large units. Unfortunately the data available do not permit separate measures of the importance of care versus the disease environment for children. The adverse effect of size on survival agrees with Higman's (1984) finding for Jamaican slaves.

The finding that postneonatal mortality rates were lower on sugar plantations suggests that the poor reputations of the crop and the areas in which it was grown may be undeserved, at least for this age group. The expected mortality rate was 14.9% on cotton plantations but only 6.6% if sugar was the main crop. The probabilities of death in rice and mixed farming were not systematically different from that on cotton farms. High losses before the end of the first month in rice agriculture may have eliminated many of those who would have been vulnerable to illness and mortality in the postneonatal period. The work routine in sugar often required heavy labor for ditching and plowing, which may have freed womens' time for postnatal care (Gray, 1933: v. 2: 749–751). Breastfeeding may have been abbreviated during the sugar harvest, but labor demands for women could have been relatively even and low during the rest of the year such that breastfeeding was encouraged.

Although the dates of seasonal work patterns differed by the main crop under cultivation, ordinarily crops were planted in the spring and harvested in the fall. The common seasonal fluctuations might have generated systematic seasonal patterns of postneonatal mortality that operated through the age at which infants received food supplements and through seasonal patterns in the quality of the diet or the severity of the disease environment. However, no systematic pattern appears in the month of birth coefficients. These coefficients are jointly significant at greater than 0.25, and this result holds if the test is performed on data for cotton plantations only.

The profile of postneonatal mortality over time was statistically significant at 0.05. If other independent variables are evaluated at their sample means, the probability of death was lowest (under 100 per thousand) before 1825. By the late 1830s the expected rate climbed to approximately 250 per thousand, and then fell by the late 1850s to roughly 120 per thousand. The steep climb and the fall cannot be explained by changes in the completeness of enumeration of deaths, at least as measured by the recorded share of infant deaths occurring within 28 days of birth. This share was lowest (19%) during the 1830s and above average (30%) after 1850 (Steckel, 1979b: 98). The time profile for losses before the end of the first month and for the age group one to three years was similar to that for postneonatal infants. Moreover, the heights of children declined during the 1830s and began to recover during the 1840s, reinforcing the credibility of the mortality pattern observed in plantation records (Steckel, 1979a). Increasing rates of migration that spread communicable disease may have contributed to the pattern. However, migration rates were also high during the 1850s, and this simple explanation cannot account for the decline in mortality rates unless the disease environment eventually became more homogeneous as a result of previous migration. Cotton prices were low near the peak in the mortality rates (Gray, 1933: v. 2: 1027), and owners may have invested less in slave health during these years. Cholera was prevalent in the South during the 1830s and 1840s (Rosenberg, 1962). These and other possible explanations for the time pattern of mortality will be explored in detail elsewhere using a very large sample of height data.[32] Whatever the causes that may be found for this phenomenon, the focus of Vinovskis (1972), Meeker (1972; 1976), Easterlin (1977) and others on identification and explanation of long-term trends has missed the aspect of cycles or fluctuations in health.

Although month of birth did not systematically influence the chances of postneonatal death, there was a seasonal pattern of postneonatal mortality. Table 8 shows that the probability of death was moderately elevated during the summer.[33] The specific causes of these deaths are unknown, but gastrointestinal diseases have been widely observed as a major source of illness and mortality among infants. Warm temperatures promote the growth of Salmonella, Shigella, and E. coli bacteria in food, water, and milk. The incidence of gastrointestinal infections depends upon resistance relative to doses of bacteria. It is likely that warm weather helped to create pathogenic doses of bacteria in foods and liquids given to infants. A summer peak in infant mortality was observed among urban residents during the late nineteenth century (Cheney, 1984; Lentzner and Condran, 1985).

The duration of breastfeeding and the timing of food supplements are final points relevant to infant mortality. The scanty evidence available on breastfeeding patterns suggests that whites fre-

Table 8   The mortality rate at age two months
to eleven months, by month

Month	Rate per thousand	Number at risk
January	13.6	1,614
February	15.9	1,636
March	16.7	1,681
April	18.8	1,699
May	19.4	1,653
June	20.9	1,629
July	29.6	1,620
August	25.4	1,534
September	32.0	1,500
October	19.2	1,566
November	15.5	1,616
December	20.3	1,627

Source: Plantation records.

quently continued for more than one year while slaves may have nursed for less than one year.[34] The nature and timing of food supplements were important to health because breast milk is clean, nutritionally ideal, and provides some immunity (Knodel and Kinter, 1977; Wray, 1978). But supplements, such as pap and gruel that were common during the nineteenth century, were nutritionally poor, especially in protein.[35] Moreover, the supplements were frequently contaminated or fed to slaves in contaminated utensils. Under these conditions, attenuated breastfeeding increased the risk of illness and mortality. Evidence from plantation work records and instructions to overseers suggests that supplements may have begun within 2 to 3 months following birth.[36] The pattern of high mortality rates from 3 to 7 months following birth, shown in Table 9, is consistent with early supplementation.[37]

CONCLUDING REMARKS

The evidence at hand is approximately consistent with Thomas Affleck's observation (1851: 435) that "the mortality of negro children is as two to one when compared with the whites."[38] Contemporaries cited the adverse location of the slave quarters on the plantation and poor care for the high rates of loss. According to

Table 9   Slave mortality rates in early childhood

Month after birth	Number of deaths within two months per 1000 survivors to the beginning of the interval	Number of survivors to the beginning of the interval
1	54.4	2,002
3	44.9	1,893
5	28.2	1,808
7	38.7	1,757
9	26.1	1,689
11	21.9	1,645
13	22.4	1,609
15	26.1	1,573
17	16.3	1,532
19	14.6	1,507
21	16.2	1,485
23	12.3	1,461
25	10.4	1,443
27	9.1	1,428
29	9.9	1,415
31	7.1	1,401
33	6.5	1,391
35	7.2	1,382

Source: Plantation records.
Note: As used here month refers to calendar months after birth. For example, July is the first month after birth for a child born in June. This approach is taken because owners sometimes failed to record day of birth or day of death.

Affleck (1851: 435) the "quarters are often badly located; children allowed to be filthy; are suckled hurriedly, whilst the mother is overheated; are laid on their backs when mere infants on a hard mattress, or a blanket only, and rocked and bumped in badly-made cradles; not a few are overlaid by the wearied mother." Poor care was important to health, but primarily for reasons other than the ones cited by contemporaries. The adverse consequences of the "wearied mother" for infant health began at conception. Seasonal extremes in nutritional status and a high general level of work effort were substantially responsible for high rates of stillbirth and for neonatal mortality that may have been approximately 2.5 times that for whites.[39] The effects of fetal deprivation continued into the postneonatal period through sudden infant deaths, and low-birth-weight infants were at greater risk to insults from poor nutrition and disease. Early supplementation of infants and a short duration for breastfeeding aggravated health in the postneonatal period. Low birth weight and a poor diet may have contributed to high mortality rates for several years beyond infancy.

Early childhood mortality rates peaked during the 1830s and were roughly twice as high during the 1830s as they were before 1825 and after 1850. Mortality data for Massachusetts (Vinovskis, 1972) and indirect evidence for whites in the country as a whole (McClelland and Zeckhauser, 1982) suggest that conditions may have been approximately constant before 1860. On the other hand, the average heights of white soldiers who fought during the Civil War declined by an inch between birth cohorts of 1820 and 1860 (Margo and Steckel, 1983) and genealogies show a downward drift of five years in life expectation of whites at age 10 during the same time period (Fogel, 1986: 41). However, for the country as a whole infant and child mortality rates during the late antebellum period were considerably below those for slaves. This package of evidence on levels and trends suggests that slave children were relatively worse off earlier in the period, and therefore circumstances adverse to slaves during the 1820s and the 1830s contributed to excess mortality.

Early childbearing contributed a small but relevant amount to the excess mortality of slave infants. The average age at first birth was 22.7 years among antebellum southern whites and about two years less among slaves recorded in probate records (Steckel, 1985: 103). How much lower would infant mortality have been if slaves had the same fertility rates as whites below age 20? The actual birth rates are unknown, but the percent of women listed with a surviving child was about three times higher among slaves compared to whites in the age group 15–19 (Steckel, 1985: 116). If the percent with surviving children is used as an index of relative birth rates, then the reduction in losses can be estimated by changing the weights applied to the regression coefficients in Table 2 and Table 8. If the sample weight is diminished by two-thirds for the under 20 age group and the sample weights are increased accordingly for the older ages, then the expected loss rate before the end of the first year declines by 4.7% (using equation two of Table 2) to 5.8% (using equation one of Table 2).

Given present knowledge, one must be cautious in discussing the possible effects of plantation size on excess mortality. Higher mortality that accompanied larger plantations may have operated in part through work requirements and breastfeeding patterns. To the extent that aggregation of people promoted the spread of communicable disease, one must compare residential living arrangements. Slaves lived overwhelmingly in rural areas, but on units that had several times the population of the typical free household.[40] On the other hand, a substantially higher percentage of the white population resided in cities and towns, where the mortality rates were high.[41] The disease environment was probably more hostile in the South compared with the North, and within the South, slaves were concentrated in coastal and river-bottom areas where they were more vulnerable to insect-borne diseases.[42] Measurement of these assorted influences on health would be an important contribution to knowledge.

Slaves lost roughly 54% or more of their pregnancies to stillbirths, infant mortality, and early childhood mortality.[43] These high rates may seem implausible given the known high rate of natural increase of American slaves.[44] The apparent contradiction arises in part from conventions distilled from the behavioral patterns of western European and free North American populations. The geographical proximity of slaves and North American whites and similar high rates of natural increase suggest parallels in behavior. However, women were highly productive in the fields under slavery, the rigors of their work created substantial stress on reproduction, and the high value of their time encouraged early supplementation of infants. Seasonal episodes of deprivation, from which workers could recover, left permanent marks on fetal development. Children who survived early infancy faced a regimen of disease and a poor diet. On balance, members of the labor force had good nutrition and mortality rates were relatively low. Thus, Model West life tables, which have low rates of infant and child mortality compared with older ages, are poorly suited to the slave experience.[45] The apparent contradiction between rapid population growth and high mortality at young ages can be explained by high fertility rates and by mortality rates for workers that were below those implied by Model West tables chosen to accommodate a high crude death rate. High fertility was achieved in part because losses from stillbirths and neonatal mortality were rapidly replaced by new pregnancies.[46] Moreover, attenuated breastfeeding increased the chances of conception among women whose newborns survived beyond early infancy.[47] As a result, previous estimates of slave fertility are too low because the interval between births was shorter than previously thought.

The evidence on early supplementation of slave infants is relevant to the debate over forces shaping slave culture. African origins have generally been recognized as relevant to the experience in the Western Hemisphere, and discussion has focused on the extent, sources, and goals of cultural evolution. Unlike the United States, a high volume of imports to the Caribbean constantly renewed African customs and, consistent with those customs, breastfeeding in the sugar colonies continued in some form for about two years after birth (Klein and Engerman, 1978; Handler and Corruccini, 1986). The available evidence shows that the duration was much shorter in the United States and was abbreviated compared with upper class southern whites. Thus the goals were not to imbue black slaves with southern ideals, and clearly slaves were not the source of change. Instead, the example of breastfeeding indicates that planters reckoned with the high value of women's time in formulating rules and regulations that shaped cultural practices.[48] This line of thought in no way suggests that slaves were (or would have become had the institution lasted longer) merely creatures of profit and loss, devoid of their own identities. One would expect that slaveowners had to contend with firmly established cultural traditions, but ultimately slaves did relinquish or modify those customs that were costly to their owners. The slaves maintained or manipulated those of little or no cost, while owners had an incentive to discourage or forbid changes of African customs that actually promoted capitalist objectives. The extent to which slaves were able to impose costs and deny profits by successfully resisting changes desired by owners or by successfully initiating changes unwanted by owners is a measure of the autonomy of slave culture. In this regard it would be interesting to know the extent to which long intervals of breastfeeding in the sugar colonies were driven by an accommodation to prior beliefs or by a low value of women's time in sugar cultivation.

NOTES

1   Contemporary reports also suggest that stillbirths were numerous. Ten out of 48 births from 1809–1861 were listed as stillbirths by a Georgia physician (cited by Postell, 1951: 116). The precise definition of a "stillbirth" used in this record is unknown and may have differed from modern usage.

2   The confusion in medical knowledge is illustrated by neonatal tetanus. This disease, which may have claimed 5 to 10% of slave newborns (Kiple, 1984: 122), baffled observers but is now known to have been caused by poor antiseptic procedures involving the umbilical stump. By the late antebellum period some observers such as Affleck (1851: 435) recognized that neonatal tetanus followed poor treatment of the navel, but it is doubtful that these observations had much impact on neonatal health during this era.

3   Haines and Avery (1980) recommend the Meech, Brass logit, and the Model West life tables for study of mortality during the antebellum period. They suggest the Brass logit and the Model West tables for study of infant and child mortality. The comparison in Table 1 understates excess mortality because the figures for the United States include slaves. However, slaves comprised only 12.6% of the population in 1860.

Little work has been done on possible undercounting of white mortality. Fogel (1986: note 21) observes that practices of treating infant deaths during the first several days after birth as stillbirths would impart a downward bias to measured estimates of infant mortality. Possible sources of downward bias in the infant mortality rate reported for slaves in Table 1 are noted elsewhere in this paper and in Steckel (1986a).

Relative levels of health may be measured by life expectation at birth. Unfortunately the length of the chronological record on most plantations for which mortality data are available limits calculation of mortality rates beyond the age group 20–24. However, life expectation at birth can be estimated by appending rates at older ages. This approach is justified in part because mortality rates in early childhood ordinarily are the most important element in estimates of life expectation at birth. Moreover, the data available on heights (see Steckel, 1986b) and the mortality data from plantation records indicate that the age pattern of mortality for American slaves was unusual; specifically, mortality rates in early childhood were high whereas the rates as teenagers and adults were low compared with other life tables (for comparisons see the Model West tables in Coale and Demeny, 1966). Calculations of life expectation at birth are robust to reasonable choices; the figure is 22.0 years using Model West level 8 rates beyond ages 20–24, but is 21.3 using Model West level 6 and is 22.8 using Model West level 10. Previous estimates range from 27.8 years (Farley, 1970: 67) to 38.1 years (Evans, 1962: 212).

Life expectation at birth may have declined with increasing plantation size (see the discussion in the latter part of the paper), but unfortunately the mortality data from plantation records necessary to make an adjustment for small sizes are lacking. The estimates of life expectation at birth (average for males and females) in the tables recommended by Haines and Avery (1980: 88) range from 40.9 to 43.2 years. Therefore, a reasonable, and perhaps conservative, conjecture on the difference in life expectations at birth between slaves and whites is 15 years.

4 Recording of these deaths may have been poor in part because owners felt that control or influence, and therefore monitoring, was hopeless.

5 Usage varies and the time interval of the neonatal mortality rate may be defined as birth to four weeks. The base for the postneonatal mortality rate in this paper is the number who survive to the beginning of the postneonatal period.

Discussion in note 17 suggests that 227 per thousand is a reasonable conjecture for the slave neonatal mortality rate. This rate combined with a postneonatal mortality rate of 162 per thousand calculated from plantation records used in this paper, imply an infant mortality rate noted in Table 1 of 350 per thousand.

6 The division of infant mortality into "exogenous" and "endogenous" components that correspond to the neonatal and postneonatal periods is partly arbitrary but reflects the fact that endogenous factors (postnatal practices) become increasingly important to survival with time elapsed after birth (see Shryock and Siegel, v. 2, 1973: 405). However, fetal stress increases the risk of mortality in the postneonatal period and beyond (Fitzhardinge and Steven, 1972; Christenson, et al., 1981; McCormick, 1985).

7 See Steckel (1979b) for additional discussion of these records.

8 For discussion and analysis of these records see Steckel (1979a; 1986a; 1986b) and Margo and Steckel (1982).

9 The methodology and evidence assembled in support of this conclusion are discussed in Steckel (1986a).

10 General references in this area include Hytten and Leitch (1971), Tanner (1978), Hurley (1980), Hytten and Chamberlain (1980), and Naeye and Tafari (1983).

11 Month of birth and death were used to calculate the dependent variable. The measure includes deaths that could have occurred at the end of the month after the calendar month of birth.

12 Heights and probably health improved with movement away from Gulf coast and lower Atlantic states and toward upper and especially interior states of the South (Margo and Steckel, 1982: 526). Unfortunately all the plantations in the mortality sample were located in the first region.

13 Curtin (1968) discusses migration and disease in the context of the African slave trade. Affleck (1851: 434) suggests that acclimation of slaves transported from upper to lower states of the South required about two years.

14 The data available for regression analysis includes 574 recorded births

for all cotton farms (288 for cotton farms that had a reported share of neonatal deaths among infant deaths in excess of 30%), 71 births for mixed farming, 75 for rice, 135 for sugar, and zero for tobacco.

15 Based on observations for which the month, day and year of birth and death are known (see Steckel, 1979b).

16 The share of neonatal deaths among infant deaths is generally 35 to 70% in countries that have infant mortality rates of 10% or more Bouvier and van der Tak, 1976; Matta, 1978: 38, Ashworth, 1982).

17 Choice-based sampling was developed to cope with the situation in which one or more alternatives were rarely chosen (see Cosslett, 1981). The method was designed to improve the precision of estimates from a given sample size by oversampling infrequently chosen outcomes and reweighting the observations. The technique can be applied to the problem at hand, assuming that underreporting of losses occurred at random and that a reliable estimate of the extent of underreporting is available. Though it cannot be verified, the assumption of randomness seems reasonable because reporting probably improved with time lived after birth and late neonatal death often have causes, such as low birth weight, that produce early neonatal deaths. In other words, the causes of the reported neonatal losses were probably the same or approximately the same as the causes of the unreported losses.

An estimate of the actual loss rate before the end of the first month is available by combining estimates of neonatal mortality and stillbirths. A neonatal mortality rate of 152 per thousand was calculated from estimated birth weights and a schedule of neonatal mortality by birth weight (Steckel, 1986a). The mortality schedule by birth weight employed by the procedure incorporates technology available to southern midwives in 1950, which probably included antiseptic treatment of the umbilical stump. If the mortality rate from neonatal tetanus was 75 per thousand during the antebellum period (the average of the 5 to 10% range suggested by Kiple (1984: 122)), then the neonatal mortality rate adjusted for tetanus was $151 + 75 = 227$ per thousand. The figure of 227 may be conservative (low) because other sources of downward bias may remain in the estimated neonatal mortality rate. A schedule of stillbirths by birth weight and the estimated birth-weight distribution implies that losses from stillbirths were at least 114 per thousand (Steckel, 1986a). At these rates, losses before the end of the first month were $1 - (1 - 0.114)(1 - 0.227) = 0.315$ or 315 per thousand. The reported rate of loss for stillbirths and neonatal deaths was 125 per thousand (17% of losses were stillbirths) in the first equation (cotton plantations with shares of neonatal deaths among infant deaths in excess of 0.30) and 87.1 per thousand (16% of losses were stilbirths) in the second equation (all cotton plantations). The appropriate weight for the observations in which loss was reported is the ratio of the actual to the reported loss rate, or $0.315/0.125 = 2.52$ in the first equation. The weight for the observations in which loss was not reported is the ratio of one minus the actual to one minus the reported loss rate or, $(1 - 0.315)/(1 - 0.125) = 0.78$.

18 The comparative advantage of women in rice agriculture is clear from data on sex ratios. For the age group 15 and above in 1860 the ratio of men to women was 0.861 in the five largest rice-producing counties, but 1.288 in the five largest cane sugar-producing counties, and 1.001 for the slave population as a whole.

19 In the absence of information on the habits and motives of these slaveowners, it is difficult to appraise the assumption that underreporting was a random process (in other words, deaths unreported in a particular month were proportional to those actually reported). It could be argued, for example, that absences from the plantation, which may have occurred during the summer and the winter, contributed to a lapse in recordkeeping. Although it is clear that owners traveled, their diaries of plantation operations suggest that absences for half the year on a regular basis (or lack of attention to recordkeeping for this duration) would have been unusual. In addition, management of the cotton fields during May and June was important to the success of the crop, and the recorded probabilities of neonatal death were low during these months. Furthermore, reductions in work loads that often occurred around the fifth month of pregnancy imply that births were anticipated, i.e. that owners had information on what should have occurred during their absence, and this would have prompted an update of the birth and death list after returning. Moreover, the reported postneonatal deaths were relatively abundant during the summer (see Table 8).

One may object to the seasonal patterns of Table 3 on the grounds that the months of high probabilities did not have poor reputations for newborn survival, as the "sickly season" of August and September had a notorious reputation for fevers. However, in a given year there were ordinarily no more than two to six births on a typical southern plantation, and it would have been difficult to detect a seasonal pattern of stillbirths and neonatal mortality without aggregating data over many years. The chronological form in which the birth and death lists were usually maintained did not enhance the detection of seasonal patterns. Late summer fevers were noticeable because the attack rate was reasonably high and the group at risk in a particular year included much of the population.

20 The figures of 10.3% and 13.1% include stillbirths, which on average comprised about one-third of losses before the end of the first month. If reduced by one-third, the average of the figures ($11.8 = (10.5 + 13.1)/2$) is slightly less than the figure of 9% suggested for whites.

21 Information on the timing, duration, and intensity of activities for growing cotton are available in Covert (1912), Gray (1933), and diaries maintained by planters. Summary results from diaries are presented in Olson (forthcoming). Discussions and examples of diaries include Riley (1909), Davis (1943), and Stephenson (1936). See also Sydnor (1933), Davis (1939), Sellers (1950), and Taylor (1963). Southern agricultural journals noted in Gray (1933: v. 2: 1008–9) discussed the work routine and other aspects of plantation operations.

22 Based on calculations by John Olson for the Bermuda-Prudhomme,

Monette, LeBlanc, and Kollock plantations. See Olson (forthcoming) for discussion of the data.

23   The results are based upon weekly picking records of 15 female slaves on the Leak plantation who gave birth a total of 28 times between 1841 and 1860.

24   Women engaged in "hard" physical labor in this study lacked domestic help, and many therefore spent 16 minutes per day carrying heavy jars of water and from one to three hours grinding grain and hops.

25   Skeletal evidence sheds light on the diet, disease, and work of slaves. Bone development, for example, shows that rigorous physical labor was a common feature of slave life (Rathbun, 1986). The typical slave work week was about 54 hours (Olson, forthcoming). Moreover, most of the time was spent standing or stooped, and according to Fogel and Engerman (1974: 192) slaves produced nearly 30% more output than their southern, free labor counterparts. Physical labor, especially effort that requires standing, may retard fetal growth by diverting blood flow away from the placenta (see Briend, 1979; 1980).

26   Ashby reports the sample sizes (500 in each case), but not the standard deviations. Modern studies (see World Health Organization, 1980) suggest that 700 grams is a reasonable upper bound for the standard deviation of a birth weight distribution. If this figure is used, the averages are significantly different at less than 0.001.

The figures cited may overstate the "pure" effect of a given level of work effort on birth weight because mothers who worked longer may have come from lower-income households. On the other hand, it is noted in the text that the level of work effort was probably much higher for slaves.

27   Stillbirth rates were only slightly higher (96.8/1000 versus 91.7/1000) among those who worked beyond two weeks before delivery. The neonatal mortality rates were significantly different at 0.07 ($z = 1.82$). The stillbirth rates were not significantly different ($z = 0.20$).

28   Diagnosis of the causes of the fevers is difficult from the terminology employed to describe them. Malaria was no doubt heavily involved. "Intermittent" fevers accounted for 52% of the discharges. The deaths were concentrated among "congestive" (14%), "typhoid" (11%), "typhus" (21%), and "yellow" (12%) fevers. The editor of *Southern Medical Reports* (1851: v. 2: 84) pinpoints the "true sickly season" from August 1 through October 1.

29   The sample size in Table 6 exceeds that in Table 2 because mother's age was required information for the regressions.

30   An estimate of the birth weight distribution and a schedule of stillbirths by birth weight suggest that the stillbirth rate exceeded 11% (Steckel, 1986a). This result indicates that the stillbirths reported in Table 6 for the five plantations as a whole were underenumerated by a factor of 11 or more.

31   Stillbirths and neonatal deaths tend to be pre-term, and may have an average gestation period of roughly 7 to 8 months. The process of counting months to pinpoint times of deprivation is at best approximate given

possible variations in gestation and the small sample sizes for stillbirths and neonatal deaths. Taken at face value, the results suggest that the rigors of the preparation and planting season (in relation to the diet) produced a state of considerable net nutritional deprivation by March and April from which it may have taken a short time to recover.

Based on a chi-square test the pattern of stillbirths is significantly different from a random (flat) pattern at 0.005 ($\chi^2 = 15.44$, d.f. $= 3$). The finding of statistical significance is not simply an artifact of the way in which the data are arranged by groups of months. However, November and December were isolated in an attempt to identify the sources of deprivation. If the data are arranged by groups of three months beginning with November, December, and January, the pattern is significantly different from a random pattern at 0.025 ($\chi^2 = 9.36$, d.f. $= 3$). The stillbirth and neonatal mortality distributions are significantly different at 0.01 ($\chi^2 = 11.37$, d.f. $= 3$), which suggests that deprivation shortly before delivery was important to neonatal health.

Throughout the discussion deprivation refers to net nutritional deprivation, which is determined by the actual diet minus claims on the diet made by maintenance, work, and disease.

32   Work is in progress to code all the available data from manifests lodged in Record Group 36 at the National Archives. These data may exceed 500,000 observations, permitting detailed assessments of health by region and perhaps by year of birth.

33   The pattern is significantly different from a random pattern at 0.005 ($\chi^2 = 27.24$, d.f. $= 11$).

34   McMillen (1985: 344) finds a range of 6 to 22 and an average of 13.5 months based upon the journals and correspondence of southern white women (N $= 16$). She notes that women avoided the summer months for weaning. Recommendations for slaves were 9 months (Affleck, 1851: 435) to one year (Hammond, 1844).

35   Wickes (1953) discusses weaning practices during the nineteenth century. McMillen (1985: 349) notes that a mixture of bread, cow's milk, water, and brown sugar was the most common breast-milk substitute in the antebellum South. Kiple and Kiple (1977: 288–89) discuss the diet of young slave children.

36   Rates of cotton picking, shown in Table 4, exceeded two-thirds of normal in weeks 4 to 7 after delivery and were nearly 92% of normal in weeks 8 to 11 after delivery. The achievement of near-normal levels by 8 to 11 weeks and of normal levels thereafter suggests that little work time was lost for breastfeeding after the second month following delivery. James Hammond rated "sucklers" as half hands for one month after going out and as three-quarter hands thereafter (Tucker, 1958: 363).

37   The adverse effects of very short breastfeeding practices on health were observed in parts of nineteenth-century Finland, where mortality rates of 124 to 201 per thousand were sustained for the interval 1 to 6 months following birth (Lithell, 1981: 185). The corresponding rate calculated from Table 9 was 122 per thousand, but this rate may have been elevated in part by very low birth weights.

38 Specifically, the estimated mortality rate was about 96% higher for slave infants (350 versus 179) and about 116% higher for slaves at ages 1 to 4 (201 versus 93).

39 The share of neonatal deaths among infant deaths ranges from 35 to 70% across countries that have high infant mortality rates. The actual share for antebellum whites is unknown, but 50% is a reasonable conjecture. The average of the infant mortality rates (male and female) for the Brass logit and the Model West life tables in Haines and Avery (1980: 95) is 179.1. If x is the neonatal and y the postneonatal mortality rate per thousand, then $x + (1 - (x/1000))y = 179.1$ and $x/(x + (1 - (x/1000))y) = 0.5$. By solution, $x = 89.55$ and $y = 98.36$. The value of x is approximately 39% of the value of 227 suggested for the slave neonatal mortality rate in Note 17. The estimated postneonatal mortality rate for whites is about 60% of the rate of 162 per thousand calculated for slaves. At these rates about 70% of the excess infant mortality of slaves is attributable to the neonatal period.

40 In 1850 about 96% of all slaves lived in rural areas (Goldin, 1976: 12), and about 51% resided on units with 20 or more slaves (Gray, 1933: v. 1: 530). The average size of the free household was 5.55 persons in 1850 (U.S. Bureau of the Census, 1975: 41).

41 In 1850 about 17.1% of the nonslave population lived in urban areas calculated from data in Goldin (1976) and U.S. Bureau of the Census (1975: 12, 14). Kunitz (1984: 565–569) discusses mortality rates in urban and rural areas.

42 Warm temperatures and high humidity in river-bottom and coastal areas promoted the growth of insects, such as mosquitoes, that spread malaria and yellow fever, and of bacteria that caused gastrointestinal diseases. Slaves may have been less susceptible than whites to malaria and yellow fever, but other aspects of diet and climate in the United States may have worked to the disadvantage of blacks (Kiple, 1984).

43 The stillbirth rate was probably no less than 114 per thousand (Steckel, 1986a). An infant mortality rate of 350 per thousand was conjectured earlier in the paper, and the mortality rate for children aged 1–4 was 201 per thousand in plantation records. At these rates about $0.46 = (1 - .114) \times (1 - .35) \times (1 - .201)$ who survived to the 28th week of gestation survived to age 5. These calculations exclude pregnancies ending in abortion or miscarriage.

44 From 1800–1810 to 1850–1860 the average of the rates of natural increase was about 2.55 for whites, and about 2.22 for slaves (McClelland and Zeckhauser, 1982: 72, 81). These figures embody estimates of net migration, and in the case of slaves, of manumission and smuggling. Western hemisphere slave populations outside the United States generally had negative rates of natural increase (Curtin, 1969).

45 The Model West tables were constructed using data primarily from Australia, Canada, Denmark, England and Wales, France, Ireland, the Netherlands, New Zealand, Scotland, and the United States. See Coale and Demeny (1966) for discussion of these and other tables.

46 Steckel (1982; 1985) discusses slave fertility.

47 The sucking stimulus of breastfeeding increases the production of the hormone prolactin and is the major determinant of prolonged anovulation accompanying lactation (Habicht, et al., 1985). Birth intervals are therefore a function of the frequency and duration of breastfeeding episodes during the day. Movement from a regimen of regular and exclusive breastfeeding to one of partial breastfeeding and supplements may have an important influence on fertility.

48 Preliminary calculations of expected gain and loss show that it was profitable for women to work rather than breastfeed during the day. A woman's time was worth about 70 cents per hour during the harvest, based on a cotton price of about 10 cents per pound during the 1850s and a picking rate (from Table 4) of about 7 pounds per hour. An infant was worth about $50 (Fogel and Engerman, 1974: 76). Suppose that actual practice eliminated two feedings per day, that each feeding required 1 hour, and that these feedings (from months 4 through 12 after birth) could have reduced the observed postneonatal mortality rate to zero (from 16%). Then the expected gain would have been 0.16 × $50 = $8 and the expected cost would have been the number of work days (240) times $1.40, or $336. Of course, costs could have been reduced further by planting less cotton, and the woman's time was worth less in slack seasons of the year. However, even if expected costs were lower by 95% (a plausible upper bound) it would have been profitable to eliminate the daytime feedings.

REFERENCES

Affleck, T. (1851) "On the hygiene of cotton plantations and the management of Negro slaves." Southern Medical Reports 2: 429–436. ‧

Ashby, H. T. (1915) Infant Mortality. Cambridge: Cambridge University Press.

Ashworth, A. (1982) "International differences in infant mortality and the impact of malnutrition: a review." Human Nutrition: Clinical Nutrition 36c: 7–23.

Bouvier, L. F. and J. van der Tak (1976) "Infant mortality: progress and problems." Population Bulletin 31: No. 1.

Briend, A. (1979) "Fetal malnutrition—the price of upright posture?" British Medical Journal 2: 317–319.

——— (1980) "Maternal physical activity, birth weight and perinatal mortality." Medical Hypotheses 6: 1157–1170.

Campbell, J. (1984) "Work, pregnancy, and infant mortality among southern slaves." Journal of Interdisciplinary History 14: 793–812.

Cheney, R. A. (1984) "Seasonal aspects of infant and childhood mortality: Philadelphia, 1865–1920." Journal of Interdisciplinary History 14: 561–585. ‧

Christanson, R. E., B. J. Van den Berg, L. Milkovich, and F. W. Oechsli (1981) "Incidence of congenital anomalies among white and black births with long-term follow-up." American Journal of Public Health 71: 1333–1341. ‧

Coale, A. J. and P. Demeny (1966) Regional Model Life Tables and Stable Populations. Princeton: Princeton University Press.

Cosslett, S. R. (1981) "Maximum likelihood estimator for choice–based samples." Econometrica 49: 1289–1316.

Crawford, S. C. (1980) "Quantified Memory: A Study of the WPA and Fisk University Slave Narrative Collections," Ph.D. Dissertation, University of Chicago.

Covert, J. R. (1912) Seedtime and Harvest: Cereals, Flax, Cotton, and Tobacco. USDA Bureau of Statistics Bulletin 85. Washington, D.C.: U.S. Government Printing Office.

Curtin, P. D. (1968) "Epidemiology and the Slave Trade." Political Science Quarterly 83: 190–216. •

——— (1969) The Atlantic Slave Trade: A Census. Madison: University of Wisconsin Press.

Davis, C. S. (1939) The Cotton Kingdom in Alabama. Montgomery: Alabama State Department of Archives and History.

Davis, E. A. (1943) Plantation Life in the Florida Parishes of Louisiana, 1836–1846, as Reflected in the Diary of Bennet H. Barrow. New York: Columbia University Press.

Easterlin, R. A. (1977) "Population issues in American economic history: a survey and critique." Research in Economic History, Supplement 1: 131–158.

Eblen, J. E. (1972) "Growth of the black population in antebellum America, 1820–1860." Population Studies 26: 273–289. •

——— (1974) "New estimates of the vital rates of the United States black population during the nineteenth century." Demography 11: 301–319. •

Editor (1851) "Special report on the fevers of New Orleans in the year 1850." Southern Medical Reports 2: 79–99.

Evans, R., Jr. (1962) "The economics of American Negro slavery," in Universities–National Bureau of Economic Research, Aspects of Labor Economics. Princeton: Princeton University Press: 185–243.

Farley, R. (1970) Growth of the Black Population. Chicago: Markham Publishing.

Fitzhardinge, P. M. and E. M. Steven (1972) "The small-for-date infant, I. later growth patterns." Pediatrics 49: 671–681.

Fogel, R. W. (1986) "Nutrition and the decline in mortality since 1700: some additional preliminary findings." NBER Working Paper No. 1802. Cambridge, MA: National Bureau of Economic Research.

——— and S. L. Engerman (1974) Time on the Cross: The Economics of American Negro Slavery. Boston: Little, Brown.

Goldin, C. D. (1976) Urban Slavery in the American South, 1820–1860. Chicago: University of Chicago Press. •

Gray, L. C. (1933) History of Agriculture in the Southern United States to 1860. 2 vols. Washington, D.C.: Carnegie Institution.

Habicht, J.-P., J. Davanzo, W. P. Butz, and L. Meyers (1985) "The contraceptive role of breastfeeding." Population Studies 39: 231–232.

Haines, M. R. (1985) "Inequality and childhood mortality: a comparison of

England and Wales, 1911, and the United States, 1900." Journal of Economic History 55: 885–912.

——— and R. C. Avery (1980) "The American life table of 1830-1860: an evaluation." Journal of Interdisciplinary History 11: 73–95.

Hammond, J. H. (1844) "Plantation manual." Manuscript of the South Carolina Library, University of South Carolina, Columbia.

Handler, J. S. and R. S. Corruccini (1986) "Weaning among West Indian slaves: historical and bioanthropological evidence from Barbados." William and Mary Quarterly 48: 111–117.

Higman, B. W. (1984) Slave Populations of the British Caribbean, 1807–1834. Baltimore: Johns Hopkins.

Hurley, L. S. (1980) Developmental Nutrition. Englewood Cliffs: Prentice-Hall.

Hytten, F. E. and I. Leitch (1971) The Physiology of Human Pregnancy. Oxford: Blackwell.

Hytten, F. and G. Chamberlain [eds.] (1980) Clinical Physiology in Obstetrics. London: Blackwell.

Jelliffe, E. F. P. (1968) "Low birth-weight and malarial infection of the placenta." Bulletin of the World Health Organization 33: 69–78.

Johnson, M. P. (1981) "Smothered slave infants: were slave mothers at fault?" Journal of Southern History 47: 493–520.

Jones, J. (1985) Labor of Love, Labor of Sorrow: Black Women, Work, and the Family from Slavery to the Present. New York: Basic Books.

Kiple, K. F. (1984) The Caribbean Slave: A Biological History. Cambridge: Cambridge University Press.

Kiple, K. F. and V. H. King (1981) Another Dimension to the Black Diaspora: Diet, Disease, and Racism. Cambridge: Cambridge University.

——— and V. H. Kiple (1977) "Slave child mortality: some nutritional answers to a perennial puzzle." Journal of Social History 10: 284–309.

Klein, H. S. and S. L. Engerman (1978) "Fertility differentials between slaves in the United States and the British West Indies: a note on lactation practices and their possible implications." William and Mary Quarterly 35: 357–374.

Knodel, J. and H. Kinter (1977) "The impact of breast feeding pattern on the biometric analysis of infant mortality." Demography 14: 391–409.

Kunitz, S. J. (1984) "Mortality change in America, 1620–1920." Human Biology 56: 559–582.

Lechtig, A., J. Habicht, H. Delgado, R. E. Klein, C. Yarbrough, and R. Martorell (1975) "Effect of food supplementation during pregnancy on birthweight." Pediatrics 56: 508–520.

Lentzner, H. and G. Condran (1985) "Seasonal patterns of infant and childhood mortality in New York, Chicago and New Orleans: 1870–1920." Paper given at the Population Association of America meetings, Boston.

Lithell, U-B. (1981) "Breast-feeding habits and their relation to infant mortality and marital fertility." Journal of Family History 6: 182–194.

Maddala, G. S. (1977) Econometrics. New York: McGraw–Hill.

Margo, R. A. and R. H. Steckel (1982) "The heights of American slaves:

new evidence on slave nutrition and health." Social Science History 6: 516–538.

——— (1983) "Heights of native-born whites during the antebellum period." Journal of Economic History 43: 167–174.

Martorell, R. (1980) "Interrelationships between diet, infectious disease, and nutritional status," in L. S. Green and F. E. Johnston (eds.), Social and Biological Predictors of Nutritional Status, Physical Growth, and Neurological Development. New York: Academic Press: 81–106.

Mata, L. J. (1978) The Children of Santa Maria Cauqué: A Prospective Field Study of Health and Growth. Cambridge, MA: MIT Press.

———, J. J. Urrutia, and A. Lechtig (1971) "Infection and nutrition of children of a low socieconomic rural community." American Journal of Clinical Nutrition 24: 245–259.

McClelland, P. D. and R. J. Zeckhauser (1982) Demographic Dimensions of the New Republic: American Interregional Migration, Vital Statistics, and Manumissions, 1800–1860. Cambridge University Press.

McCormick, M. C. (1985) "The contribution of low birth weight to infant mortality and childhood morbidity." New England Journal of Medicine 312: 82–90.

McKelvey, P. B. (1851) "United States marine hospital." Southern Medical Reports 2: 290–293.

McMillen, S. (1985) "Mother's sacred duty: breast-feeding patterns among middle- and upper-class women in the antebellum South." Journal of Southern History 51: 333–356.

Meeker, E. (1972) "The improving health of the United States, 1850–1915." Explorations in Economic History 9: 353–374.

——— (1976) "Mortality trends of southern blacks, 1850–1910: some preliminary findings." Explorations in Economic History 13: 13–42.

Metzer, J. (1974) "Efficient operation and economies of scale in the antebellum southern plantation." (Unpublished).

Moore, W. M. O. (1983) "Prenatal factors influencing intrauterine growth: clinical implications," in R. Boyd and F. C. Battaglia (eds.), Perinatal Medicine. London: Butterworths: 245–263.

Naeye, R. L. (1980) "Sudden infant death." Scientific American 242 (April): 56–62.

——— and E. C. Peters (1982) "Working during pregnancy: effects on the fetus." Pediatrics 69: 724–727.

Naeye, R. L. and N. Tafari (1983) Risk Factors in Pregnancy and Diseases of the Fetus and Newborn. Baltimore: Williams and Wilkins.

National Research Council, Committee on Maternal Nutrition/Food and Nutrition Board (1970) Maternal Nutrition and the Course of Pregnancy. Washington, D.C.: National Academy of Sciences.

Olson, J. F. (forthcoming) "Clock-time vs. real-time: a comparison of the lengths of the northern and the southern agricultural work years," in R. W. Fogel and S. L. Engerman (eds.) Without Consent or Contract: Technical Papers on Slavery.

Owens, L. H. (1976) This Species of Property: Slave Life and Culture in the Old South. New York: Oxford University Press.

Postell, W. D. (1951) The Health of Slaves on Southern Plantations. Baton Rouge: Louisiana State University Press.

Rathbun, T. A. (1987) "Health and disease at a South Carolina plantation: 1840–1870." American Journal of Physical Anthropology.

Riley, F. L. (1909) "Diary of a Mississippi planter, January 1, 1840 to April, 1863." Publications of the Mississippi Historical Society 10: 305–481.

Rochester, A. (1923) Infant Mortality: Results of a Field Study in Baltimore, Md. Based on Births in One Year. Children's Bureau Publication No. 119. Washington, D.C.: U.S. Government Printing Office.

Rosenberg, C. E. (1962) The Cholera Years. Chicago: University of Chicago Press.

Savitt, J. L. (1978) Medicine and Slavery: The Diseases and Health Care of Blacks in Antebellum Virginia. Champaign: University of Illinois Press.

Scrimshaw, N. S. (1975) "Interactions of malnutrition and infection: advances in understanding," in R. E. Olson (ed.) Protein-Calorie Malnutrition. New York: Academic Press: 353–367.

Sellers, J. B. (1950) Slavery in Alabama. University, AL: University of Alabama Press.

Shryock, H. S. and Siegel, J. S. (1973) The Methods and Materials of Demography, 2 vols. Washington, D.C.: U.S. Government Printing Office.

Steckel, R. H. (1979a) "Slave height profiles from coastwise manifests." Explorations in Economic History 16: 363–380. •

——— (1979b) "Slave mortality: analysis of evidence from plantation records." Social Science History 3: 86–114. •

——— (1982) "The fertility of American slaves." Research in Economic History 7: 239–286. •

——— (1985) The Economics of U.S. Slave and Southern White Fertility. New York: Garland Press. •

——— (1968a) "Birth weights and infant mortality among American slaves." Explorations in Economic History 23: 173–198. •

——— (1986b) "A peculiar population: the nutrition, health and mortality of American slaves from childhood to maturity," Journal of Economic History 46: 721–741. •

Stein, Z., M. Susser, G. Saenger, and F. Marolla (1975) Famine and Human Development: The Dutch Hunger Winter of 1944–1945. New York: Oxford.

Stephenson, W. H. (1936) "A quarter-century of a Mississippi plantation: Eli J. Capell of 'Pleasant Hill'." Mississippi Valley Historical Review 23: 355–374. •

Sutch, R. (1975) "The treatment received by American slaves: a critical review of the evidence presented in 'Time on the Cross'." Explorations in Economic History 12: 335–438.

——— (1976) "The care and feeding of slaves," in P. A. David, H. G. Gutman, R. Sutch, P. Temin, and G. Wright (eds.) Reckoning with Slavery. New York: Oxford University Press: 231–301.

Swados, F. (1941) "Negro health on the antebellum plantations." Bulletin of the History of Medicine 10: 460–472. •

Sydnor, C. S. (1933) Slavery in Mississippi. New York: D. Appleton-Century.

Tafari, N., R. L. Naeye, and A. Gobezie (1980) "Effects of maternal undernutrition and heavy physical work during pregnancy on birth weight." British Journal of Obstetrics and Gynecology 87: 222–226. •

Tanner, J. M. (1978) Fetus Into Man: Physical Growth from Conception to Maturity. London: Open Books.

Taylor, J. G. (1963) Negro Slavery in Louisiana. Baton Rouge: Louisiana Historical Association.

Tucker, R. C. (1958) "James Henry Hammond: South Carolinian," Ph.D. dissertation, University of North Carolina.

United Nations (1973) The Determinants and Consequences of Population Trends, Vol. 1. Department of Economic and Social Affairs, Population Studies, No. 50. New York: United Nations.

Urrutia, J. J., L. J. Mata, F. Trent, J. R. Cruz, E. Villatoro, and R. E. Alexander (1975) "Infection and low birth weight in a developing country: a study in an Indian village of Guatemala." American Journal of Diseases in Childhood 129: 558–561.

U.S. Bureau of the Census (1975) Historical Statistics of the United States, Colonial Times to 1970, Bicentennial Edition. Washington, D.C.: U.S. Government Printing Office.

Valdés-Dapena, M. A. (1980) "Sudden infant death syndrome: a review of the medical literature, 1974–1979." Pediatrics 66: 597–614. ✦

Vinovskis, M. A. (1972) "Mortality rates and trends in Massachusetts before 1860." Journal of Economic History 32: 184–213.

West, M. (1914) "The development of prenatal care in the United States." Transactions of the American Association for the Study and Prevention of Infant Mortality 5: 69–108.

World Health Organization (1980) "The incidence of low birth weight: a critical review of available information." World Health Statistics Quarterly 33: 197–224.

Wickes, I. G. (1953) "A history of infant feeding, parts I–V." Archives of Disease in Childhood 28: 151–158, 232–240, 332–340, 416–422, 495–502.

Williamson, J. G. (1981) "Urban disamenities, dark satanic mills, and the British standard of living debate." Journal of Economic History 51: 75–83.

Wray, J. D. (1978) "Maternal nutrition, breast-feeding and infant survival," in W. H. Mosley (ed.) Nutrition and Human Reproduction. New York: Plenum Press: 197–229.

The New "Black Death": Cholera in Brazil, 1855–1856

DONALD B. COOPER

ON REPEATED OCCASIONS in the nineteenth century, Asian cholera erupted from its traditional center in the great river basins of India and spread in pandemic waves throughout parts of Europe, North Africa, and North America. In Spain alone 600,000 deaths resulted from cholera during four great invasions (Cárdenas, 1971: 224). The United States experienced terrifying outbreaks beginning in 1832, 1849, and 1866 (Rosenberg, 1962) which also touched parts of Mexico, Central America, and the Caribbean. Initially South America escaped the onslaught. Some Brazilians speculated that the intense heat of the equator, or the vast expanse of the Atlantic ocean, somehow offered an effective buffer to the southward spread of cholera (Rego, 1872: 84). But this "sweet illusion" was shattered in 1855. Indeed the first city in Brazil struck by Asian cholera was Belém, capital of the vast northern

Donald B. Cooper is a professor in the department of history, Ohio State University, Columbus, OH 43210.

This publication was supported in part by NIH Grant LM 04342 from the National Library of Medicine, and also by the College of Humanities of the Ohio State University. Of the numerous persons who assisted me I wish to acknowledge Janice Karlak, Pedro Haegler, Dr. Eduardo Augusto de Caldas Brito, Filho, Dr. Reginaldo Fernándes, Dr. Dahas Zarur, and Maria Madelena dos Santos.

Social Science History 10:4 (Winter 1986). Copyright © 1986 by the Social Science History Association. CCC 0145-5532/86/$1.50.

province of Pará located astride the equator at the mouth of the Amazon river.

Thus began what José Pereira Rego (1873: 79) called "the blackest page in the medical history of Brazil," for it has been estimated that by the time the first great epidemic of Asian cholera in Brazil had run its course in 1856, more than 200,000 Brazilians had lost their lives (A. Peixoto, 1917: 556).

Yet it may have been a black page in more than one sense of the word. For as studies of cholera elsewhere in the Americas have shown, blacks suffered far more than whites from the disease (Kiple and King 1981, Kiple 1984, 1985). This study thus is an attempt to analyze the contours of cholera's course in Brazil and the means adopted to try to stem that course, and to determine if the disease sought out more black victims than whites as it did elsewhere in the hemisphere.

BACKGROUND

Numerous governmental and medical institutions played their parts in seeking to fend off or diminish the disease, but Brazil's main line of defense was her doctors. Licensed physicians were rarely found in the poor and remote northern provinces where the cholera first struck; one, in fact, Rio Grande do Norte, had none at all in 1855. The country's two medical schools, in Rio de Janeiro and Bahia, together graduated fewer than one hundred physicians per year in a country of eight million people. Some Brazilians had trained at European medical schools, and a few foreign practitioners were present. There was only one professional association of physicians—The Imperial Academy of Medicine in Rio de Janeiro—and this body published the *Annaes Brasilienses de Medicina,* the sole medical journal of the 1850s which lasted for more than two years. The few libraries contained little on medicine that was printed in Portuguese, the language of Brazil. Thus keeping current in scientific matters was no small challenge for the Brazilian doctor of the 1850s. Even so, some of them struggled against great odds to upgrade medical practice in a tropical country better known for sugar, coffee, and slaves than science and learning. But the fight against cholera bitterly divided the medical community and pushed it to its professional limits.

Doctors received scant help from the Imperial Government of

Brazil. Not until 1851 was the Central Board of Public Health (Junta Central de Higiene Pública) created at Rio de Janeiro, but it had little influence outside of the capital city (Brazil. Directoria geral, Barbosa and Rezende 1909: 1: 66). Some, but not all, of the provinces established their own Boards of Health. Routine aspects of public health and sanitation were relegated to meagerly funded municipal offices. The network of hospitals scattered throughout the country, mostly founded by the church in the colonial period (but increasingly under state control by the 1850s) comprised another major division of the medical support system. The best known was the venerable Santa Casa da Misericordia of Rio de Janeiro founded in 1562 (Zarur, 1985). In the popular view, the hospital was seen more as a place to die than as a center for treatment, although even in times of epidemics a majority of patients survived. All major cities had their own Santa Casa da Misericordia, and some foreign groups, such as the English and the Portuguese, had their own hospitals and cemeteries. Most Brazilians went through life never having been admitted to a hospital, or even having been treated by a licensed doctor or pharmacist. The medical irregulars, such as homeopaths, herbalists, spiritualists, and assorted other quacks and healers, more often than not served the sick poor and the slaves. Not a few of these self-taught practitioners became "instant experts" on cholera in 1855 as quickly as they had for yellow fever in 1849–1850.

These two deadly epidemics—cholera and yellow fever—both assaulted Brazil in rapid succession about the middle of the nineteenth century. Yellow fever, known in epidemic form in Pernambuco in the late seventeenth century, attacked Bahia in 1849 and Rio de Janeiro in early 1850 (Franco, 1969: 5–44). Within five years all sizable cities of the littoral had been stricken, and it seems likely that before the end of the century some 100,000 persons had died (Cooper, 1975: 692, n.4). These twin disasters of yellow fever and cholera undermined much of the optimism with which Emperor Pedro II (1840–1889) and most Brazilian leaders had viewed the state of the country just before mid-century. Although sugar prices were down, coffee exports and profits were booming. The last of several regional revolts (which had threatened the stability of the country ever since independence from Portugal in 1822) had been crushed in 1848. Pedro II felt so secure that by 1850 he dared to incur the wrath of the great rural landlords (*fazendeiros*) by halting the slave trade. The passage of the *Queiroz* law in that year effectively stopped the international traffic, although domestic slavery continued until 1888. It was hoped that Europeans could be enticed to settle in Brazil in large numbers as replacements for the once-imported Africans. A major incentive was to have been that Brazil be known as one of the most healthful tropical countries in the world. But in just half a decade between 1850 and 1855 this argument was demolished. First yellow fever attacked whites (especially newcomers) in the cities of the seaboard, and next cholera decimated blacks in both urban and rural areas, including many thousands of slaves. Although immigrants soon began to pour into Brazil, and the coffee crops were always harvested, nonetheless these two diseases generated shock waves in immigration and agriculture that were felt for years to come (Cooper, 1975).

Cholera in particular is one of the most terrifying diseases known to man. It passes from person to person through communal water and food and strikes quickly and massively, attacking entire families, villages, cities, and provinces. Typical symptoms include a feeling of fullness in the stomach and loss of appetite. The victim's extremities become cold and clammy. He may vomit and pass great quantities of "rice water" stool that is characteristic of acute cholera. Excruciating cramps are followed by deep shock. Death, essentially the result of extreme dehydration, may come within hours (Hirschhorn and Greenough, 1971: 15–16). Little was known anywhere at this time of the etiology, mode of transmission, or treatment of this baffling disease. Another generation would pass before the researches of Louis Pasteur and Robert Koch, who discovered the causative agent of cholera in 1883 (*vibrio cholerae*), would be available to and generally accepted by physicians.

Cholera reached Brazil in the bowels of sailors and ship passengers in 1855 and entered the country at three primary locations—all port cities—from which it fanned out to engulf parts of thirteen provinces. The first entry point, as mentioned, was the northern city of Belém. The second was Bahia, today known as Salvador, until 1763 the capital of Brazil, and after that year still the capital of a wealthy but declining sugar province with the same name of Bahia. The third was Brazil's capital and largest city, Rio de Janeiro, from which the national effort against the epidemic was coordinated by the Central Board of Public Health, the Congress, and Pedro II, the emperor. Each entry point will now be considered in turn.

CHOLERA IN PARÁ AND AMAZONAS

Dr. Americo Marques de Santa Rosa was the first physician to encounter a case of cholera on Brazilian soil. On May 26, 1855, Dr. Santa Rosa examined two young soldiers in Pará whose symptoms of pallid skin, sunken eyes, weak pulse, severe diarrhea, frequent vomiting, and stomach pains, seemed classic symptoms of the dreaded Asian cholera. Dr. Santa Rosa, although new both to the medical profession and to the city of Belém, having graduated from the faculty of medicine of Bahia as recently as 1853, wrote "I found myself in the midst of a horror greater than I had ever seen" (Rocha, 1952: 1). Ominously he pronounced the young soldiers, both of whom died within hours, victims of Asian cholera. He further declared that the disease had been imported, probably by means of the ship *Defensor* which had just arrived from Portugal after having lost to a strange malady some 37 of its 288 passengers. If the disease was imported then immediate protective measures such as quarantines and sanitary cordons might well be recommended, but only at great cost to the trade and commerce of the province. Sensing the opposition his diagnosis would provoke, Dr. Santa Rosa said "May God permit that I be a false prophet" (Rocha, 1952: 2–6).

Immediately the acting governor of Pará, Angelo Custodio Correa, named a commission of physicians who interviewed passengers, crew members, the captain, and the ship doctor from the *Defensor*. It quickly concluded that Dr. Santa Rosa's diagnosis was wrong. Evidence was obtained which suggested that the dried codfish fed to the passengers had been nearly putrid, the galley filthy, the copper cooking pots tarnished, and the ship doctor (who claimed to have lost the only copy of his medical license to pirates off the coast of Africa in 1824) but an ignorant, self-taught country surgeon with no formal medical training. Thus the deficient shipboard hygiene, compounded by the greed of the captain and the ignorance of the doctor (all conditions peculiar to a single ship) had given rise to the unknown illness. The medical commission righteously concluded that Dr. Santa Rosa was not so much a false prophet as a rash and inexperienced newcomer. His hasty cry of cholera regrettably had provoked a panic throughout the city and the province (Rocha, 1952: 3–6).

Thus broke out in the Amazon, as it had in so many other places, the bitter and generally sterile debate between "contagionists," who usually argued that a disease had been imported from elsewhere and hence was likely to be transmittable from object to object or person to person, and the "anti-contagionists," who spoke for local causes and limited, if any, transmission by personal or other means. The majority of the medical commission was composed of anti-contagionists who judged the sickness to be of local origin, not cholera, and not imported. Therefore it gave the *Defensor* a clean bill of health to continue her fateful journey to the southern ports of Brazil. In rejecting quarantine as a harmful and useless measure (a logical conclusion in view of its premise) the commission might well have cited numerous eminent authorities of the day in support of its opinion. For example, the Royal College of Physicians of London stated in 1852 that "cholera appears to have been very rarely communicated by personal intercourse, and all attempts to stay its progress by cordons or quarantines have failed" (Gr. Brit. General Board of Health, 1852: 3). But when the epidemic soon spread from the vicinity of the ship to the town of Belém, thence to many other places in the province, and beyond, anti-contagionists were hard put to explain how local atmospheric and climatic conditions that were not really any different in 1855 from those of so many previous years could suddenly cause cholera to spread like a prairie fire. As the epidemic widened Dr. José Pereira Rego of the Central Board of Public Health wrote, "It seems that reason is on the side of the advocates of importation" (1873: 86).

The British consul in Belém, Samuel Vines, reported that by the middle of June all parts of the city had been attacked. The terror was so great that many of the sick were abandoned, and the dead went unburied. Vines wrote that about 4% of the population died, but that "the malady has been chiefly confined to the negro, the mixed races, and the indians. Among the last named especially it committed great havoc, carrying off the entire crews of canoes coming to town with produce, and almost depopulating small villages in the interior" (Gt. Brit. Foreign Office, FO13/332, 1855: 482). This was confirmed by Arthur Vianna (1975: 169), who reported 1,052 deaths from cholera in the city of Belém, of whom 18% were whites and 82% blacks, Indians, and Mestizos.

From the city of Belém the cholera followed the Amazon river upstream into the interior of Pará and westward into the province of Amazonas. Fortunately it diminished in virulence as it moved upstream, and only 23 lives were lost in Amazonas. In Pará the city most afflicted was not Belém but nearby Cametá, where 1,415 deaths were recorded. At the height of the epidemic the acting governor of Pará, Angelo Custodio Correa, arrived in Cametá by steamer to bring in relief supplies and to evacuate many of the survivors. When he departed he took with him "close to two hundred persons emigrating in the saddest possible circumstances, families decimated, . . . children isolated by the death of all members of their family; orphaned infants being delivered to public charity" (Rocha, 1952: 21). Sadly Governor Correa himself took sick with cholera early in the morning of departure, and he died that same afternoon. His body was presented briefly for public viewing in the governor's palace before burial that same day at sundown. Pedro II immediately approved a pension for his widow (Brazil, Ministro do Imperio, 1856: 78). Such instances of persons who were healthy in the morning and buried by evening were not rare, and naturally terrified one and all. But fortunately, according to Vines (Gt. Brit. Foreign Office, FO13/332, 1855: 482) the governor was the only person "of the better class" who died of cholera in Pará. Yet in time this province came to be regarded as such an unhealthful bastion of tropical and other diseases that J. Orton Kerbey (1911: 142), an American consul in Belém in the early twentieth century, wrote "To no place on earth, perhaps, can be more truthfully applied than to Pará the scriptural quotation, 'in the midst of life we are in death'."

CHOLERA IN BAHIA AND THE NORTHEAST OF BRAZIL

Seven weeks after the first cases were reported at Pará, the cholera broke out on July 21 at Bahia, a city some 800 miles distant by sea. All intervening points between the two ports were spared for the time being. The United States consul in Bahia, John Gillmer, informed Secretary of State William Marcy on September 13, 1855 that the cholera is devastating the towns, in, and around this Bay, and in this City, the number of deaths is alarming. . . . The distressing accounts from many sugar estates, leads to the conclusion, that the new crop will suffer to a very great extent for want of hands to get it in, owing to the mortality amongst the negroes on them [U.S. Consular Despatches, Bahia, T331, Roll 1, 1855: 2].

Within six months the cholera had doubled back northward into the neighboring provinces of Sergipe, Alagoas, Rio Grande do Norte, Paraíba, and Pernambuco; all of these provinces were attacked at about the same time in January, 1856. No region of Brazil suffered greater devastation from cholera than the northeast; only Ceará was spared in 1856. According to Dr. Domingos Rodrigues Seixas (1860: chart following 294), 35,981 persons likely died from cholera in the province of Bahia alone while the city of Bahia lost 9,849. The governor of Bahia, however, gave lower figures—26,414 deaths for the province, and 4,870 for the city of Bahia (U.S. Consular Despatches, Bahia, T331, Roll 1, 1856: Table 5).

The two districts (*municípios*) of the province of Bahia that suffered the worst, indeed legendary, devastations from cholera were Cachoeira and Santo Amaro. Dr. Estevão Cavalcanti de Albuquerque (1856: 27) wrote in his thesis that in Cachoeira, "The most sacred ideals were violated, the city was left without physicians, the authorities abandoned their posts, relatives and friends abandoned the unfortunate patients who died unattended, hundreds of cadavers rotted unburied inside their houses, . . . all was confusion, all was horror." The provincial government dispatched relief supplies, as well as several physicians, 17 medical students, and several Sisters of Charity who were nurses. One of the physicians, Dr. J. A. d'Oliveira Botelho, reported that as he entered the emergency infirmary at Cachoeira he found suffering beyond belief. In the men's ward the dead and the near dead were lying abandoned on the floor, patients were covered with sheets filthy from the vomiting of the deceased, and survivors reported that no doctor or medical student had been seen in five days. Conditions in the women's ward were similar except that it was more crowded (Seixas, 1860: 43–44). Drinking water was so scarce that the Sisters of Charity carried barrels of water on their shoulders to the sick. The doctors' first need was to see to the burial of the dead, no small task since the gravediggers had fled the city with most of the rest of the panic-stricken residents. Before the epidemic ran its course, 7,580 deaths were confirmed from cholera in Cachoeira, and another 713 persons were considered likely victims (Seixas, 1860: chart following 294).

In the city of Santo Amaro it was more of the same. The local judge, physicians, and police had all fled the city. The medical relief commission of two doctors and twelve students arrived to find more than 300 unburied bodies. These were immediately incinerated (Rego, 1873: 99). All together more than 5,000 persons died from cholera within the city of Santo Amaro, and another 3,500 died in the outlying areas of the district (Rego, 1873: 105).

Throughout the entire country there was by this time a fatal mood of despair. Dr. Seixas (1860: 3) doubted that Brazil could stop cholera since Europeans, especially the English, had failed to do so despite greater resources and longer experience with the disease. Henry Cowper, British Consul at Pernambuco (Gt. Brit. Foreign Office, FO 13/333, 1855: 152), reported to Lord Clarendon on July 17, 1855, that "it almost amounts to a certainty, that the fatal epidemic will overrun the whole empire, decimating its population and injuring its prosperity." Furthermore, Cowper concluded that whether viewed in a social, political, or sanitary light the impact of chlorea would be far worse in Brazil than in Europe. As he explained,

> The destroyer will find in Brazil a field rich in victims, the great bulk of the population, particularly the rural whether slave or free, being ill fed, ill clothed, ill sheltered and overworked, their food consisting of fruit and roots, with a small proportion of salt fish or dried beef and the lower classes of the urban population are in no better condition; for though less worked, and somewhat better sheltered and clothed, and perhaps fed, it is only in a degree, and is quite counterbalanced by those disadvantages of air and ventillation, from which the former are exempt; and when I add that neither sewers or drainage exist in the cities, a water closet in any garden not inhabited by the English, your Lordship may conceive the devastation which the cholera in its first irrup-

tion is likely to cause amongst a people so circumstanced [Gt. Brit. Foreign Office, FO 13/333, 1855: 152].

The course of the epidemic throughout the rest of the Northeast furnished ample testimony to the consul's fears. One who saw with his own eyes much of the devastation in several northeastern provinces was Antonio Canavarro, a sixth-year medical student at Rio de Janeiro, and native of Amazonas, who left his classes to volunteer for emergency duty. After serving for several weeks in Pará and Amazonas, he stopped in Alagoas on his way back to Rio de Janeiro. Canavarro reported that a "black shroud" of cholera covered the entire province—the smallest in Brazil at the time—and that 17,000 persons had died from cholera in Alagoas. The need was so great and the resources so scarce that Canavarro in frustration (1857: 14–20) felt compelled "to curse his own existence, to curse the books he had studied, and the lessons he had learned from his teachers." Nothing in his previous experience had prepared him for the horrors he saw in Alagoas. In the village of Assemblea 334 persons out of 700 died within two weeks. The governor of Alagoas sent a detachment of six soldiers to the village to aid the stricken town, but all six died within days (Canavarro, 1857: 17). The village of Santo Antão was totally abandoned, and there the army burned it to the ground to destroy the uninterred bodies (Gt. Brit. Foreign Office, FO13/342, 1856: 203).

Not only disease but hunger stalked Alagoas and most other provinces of the country. The laboring class, especially slaves, were the usual victims; for the time being crops went unplanted and many fields were unharvested. Another sort of plague denounced by Canavarro (1857: 21) was the abundance of charlatans and quacks which he claimed to encounter "everywhere." Many of these were homeopaths; others were herbalists or nondescript healers. It did not seem right, said the young medical student, that "scientific men, who had consecrated their lives to study . . . in order to earn a privileged position" should see their future threatened by unlicensed practitioners. Many persons, however, clearly preferred the gentle herbal teas of the homeopaths to the harsh regimen of purges, bleedings, calomel, and leeches still prescribed by many of the licensed doctors. One "problem" with the quacks was that they so often helped their patients.

Canavarro's next stop was the "unfortunate and forgotten" province of Rio Grande do Norte which he said "lives like a bastard beside her sisters, virtually abandoned and struggling with all the misfortunes of poverty" (1857: 21). Not only that but the governor of the province, Antonio Bernardo de Passos, was denounced as an "assassin of humanity" who did nothing to aid the sick, and who treated the volunteer physicians who risked their careers and lives as "the last mercenaries of society." For Canavarro (1857: 22–23), Rio Grande do Norte was a worse experience than Alagoas. He estimated that 12,000 persons died of cholera there including some who "preferred to die rather than accept treatment from an Italian charlatan."

The greatest mortality of any northeastern province of Brazil was in Pernambuco. According to the governor of the province, 37,586 persons died of cholera between January 17, 1856, when the first death was reported, and June 1856 when the epidemic ceased (Rego, 1873: 153). Dr. José Pereira Rego (1873: 141) reported that so many gravediggers had died that often no one could be found to bury the dead. In one village the police forced the oldest resident to dig the graves until he himself died of cholera. There was wholesale dumping of cadavers at cemeteries or in rivers, and others were abandoned in their homes as survivors fled. As was reported frequently, black persons, especially slaves, were the most common victims. Consul Cowper (Gt. Brit. Foreign Office, FO13/342, 1856: 236v) wrote: "For a colored man to be attacked, is almost certain death; many estates have stopped working owing to the mortality amongst the slaves; and produce and provisions having in a great measure ceased to be sent into the city [of Recife], famine is the result." Indeed, he wrote, the price of meat increased twenty-fourfold in just three months.

The situation in the city of Recife was one of the utmost terror and chaos. Cowper reported,

> The town has had all the appearance of a city of the plague, business is at a standstill, the streets deserted, tar barrels burning in them by day, and penitential processions by night, which carried the mind back to the middle ages, men and women with torches, covered with sheets and barefooted, groaning, weeping, praying, chanting, and scourging; and the dead carts galloping to and fro with six or eight bodies,

by day and by night [Gt. Brit. Foreign Office, FO13/342, 1856: 286v].

Dr. Cosme de Sá Pereira (1885), president of the Commission for Public Health in Recife, wrote a thoughtful appraisal of the ways in which the cholera epidemic modified some of his basic medical tenets. He said that until the cholera epidemic anti-contagionists had held sway in Brazil; indeed he himself had been one before 1855. But after six months of personal observation of the epidemic he concluded that cholera moved in a chain of contagion. "Cholera follows the man as the shadow follows the body." Furthermore, he had come to believe that cholera had a *specific* cause, one "that is born, lives, and dies." He felt the evidence was inescapable that the way to mitigate the epidemic was not to lament "unseasonable atmospheric conditions" but to impose a rigorous program of public and private cleanliness. He also recommended (1885: 44–48) quarantines, strict isolation of all infected persons, and disinfection of all ships, rooms, and other objects that had been in contact with the victims, including cadavers. Such measures had been employed only erratically in places, such as Pará, where the anti-contagionists had been dominant.

CHOLERA IN RIO DE JANEIRO AND THE SOUTH

The third major entry point of cholera into Brazil was the city of Rio de Janeiro, the capital of the country and at 266,000 persons the largest city of the nation. The first case in Rio was observed on July 15, 1855. Initially there was great reluctance to admit that the disease, already known to be present in Pará, had invaded the southern half of the country. As late as August 9 the British *Charge d'Affaires* in Rio de Janeiro, William S. G. Jerningham, denounced the "unfounded alarms" of a cholera epidemic. He assured Lord Clarendon (Gt. Brit. Foreign Office, FO13/330, 1855: 182v) that an autopsy on one of the presumed victims, a young orphan girl, revealed she had eaten to excess of *feijoada,* that "extraordinarily coarse food of this country—salt beef and black beans." This, he felt, was a more likely explanation than cholera for the girl's severe indigestion and death.

Just two days before the first case was reported in the city, Dr. A. F. Peixoto of Rio de Janeiro published (1855) his *Instructions*

Against the Cholera Epidemic, which was intended as a practical guide for public authorities, physicians, and citizens. He states (1855: 7) that cholera "prefers dirty and unhealthful places, and individuals debilitated, poorly fed, badly dressed and of irregular life." Since persons so situated abounded in Rio de Janeiro, Dr. Peixoto asked (1855: 3) his readers to "pray to heaven that our weak voice will find an echo in the hearts of those responsible for improving the shameful, lamentable, and nauseous state of this filthy capital." Dr. Peixoto believed that the role of the government should be to provide current, official, and accurate information, organize and finance neighborhood commissions to provide food, shelter, and medications to all in need, and establish infirmaries where the sick could be isolated and cared for. The city government should provide health inspectors who would inspect public buildings, such as jails, barracks, hospitals, markets, schools, and also private residences, especially *cortiços,* or tenements. A specific suggestion for the Health Inspector was to advise residents that what Peixoto politely called "butter barrels" (*barril de mantiega*) should not be stored too close to the kitchen, must be disinfected after each deposit of human waste, and emptied at least every other day (Peixoto, 1855: 28–32). Physicians were advised to read the best works on cholera, including the *Encyclopædia Brittanica.* Among numerous suggestions (Peixoto, 1855: 34–42), citizens were advised to maintain regular habits in eating and sleeping and to avoid sweating, humidity, excessive exercise and strong emotions, unripe fruit, cold drinks, and young wine.

By early August most physicians realized that it was Asian cholera that had attacked Rio de Janeiro. The head of the Central Board of Public Health, Dr. Francisco de Paula Candido, imposed a quarantine of forty days on ships coming from infected ports, including Bahia, Pará, and some European ports including Liverpool. The lazareto for seamen at Jurujubá (Santa Isabel), across the harbor from Rio de Janeiro at Niteroi, was reopened. The government provided a launch to visit twice a day ships quarantined in the harbor so that the sick could be removed to the lazareto and the quarantined passengers and crew supplied with necessities. But by September the quarantine was imperfectly enforced, perhaps because of damage to the "extensive commercial intercourse" between Brazil and England, or more likely

because Dr. Paula Candido—who doubted that cholera was contagious—had little confidence in its efficacy.

On shore in the city of Rio, the Central Board of Public Health
organized parish committees of physicians to aid the sick poor.
The lazareto of Maricá, constructed in 1854, was made ready as
an isolation hospital for residents of the city. The Santa Casa da
Misericordia, the city's largest hospital, opened free infirmaries at
various points in the city. Most of these were staffed in part by
students from the Faculty of Medicine of Rio de Janeiro; indeed
so many students were excused in 1855 that although no courses
were cancelled, few students were present to hear the lectures,
and only five new students enrolled that year (Lobo, 1969: 55).
Nursing care was provided in part by the French Sisters of Charity.
The public infirmaries and even many private pharmacies offered
free medications, a not entirely altruistic action since when persons
came forward for the free medications authorities could then determine who had the disease and who might require confinement in
one of the infirmaries (Cabral, 1942: 176). Dr. Dahas Zarur
writes (1985: 69) that a special dock had to be constructed to
facilitate a rapid transfer of cadavers by sea to the cemeteries.[1]

By early November Rio de Janeiro was confronted with a full-
blown crisis, and before the month had ended 2,700 persons had
died of cholera. Nothing this devastating in such a short time had
happened during the dreadful yellow fever epidemic of 1850 when
4,160 persons died in Rio de Janeiro (Franco, 1969: 43). Among
those who died from cholera in 1855 were "a great many Africans,
slaves, and emancipated; as also creole black, and amongst the
whites and halfcasts, attached or who have died, are to be chiefly
numbered persons of the humbler walks of life." (Gt. Brit. Foreign
office, FO 13/331, 1855: 198v). A similar view was expressed by
Dr. Paula Candido in his official report to the Minister of Empire
on the epidemic. In his view 95% of the victims of the disease
were "slaves and the poorest class who paid the least attention to
personal hygiene" (Braz. Ministerio do Imperio, 1856: 22). Most
victims of cholera were widely believed to have "predisposed"
themselves to the disease through overindulgence in food, drink,
or even sex. Thought guilty of all three of these indiscretions were
the many Irish railworkers who died of cholera as they labored to
build Brazil's first railway, the Pedro II line to Petrópolis. Dr.
G. Lee, an English physician with 26 years' residence in Rio,

reported that only two of his patients died of cholera, and these were both "old black drunkards" (Gr. Brit. Ministry of Health, MH 98/25, 1856: 7). Yet even the more advantaged classes had no guarantee of immunity. The beautiful Tijuca hills, a locality favored by the well-to-do and regarded as the most healthful district in the city, reported some cases, including the young daughter of the prominent merchant and author, Thomas Ewbank.[2] By the time the epidemic finally ended in Rio de Janeiro in April, 1856, 4,843 persons had died, including 2,513 slaves (Gt. Brit. Ministry of Health, MH 98/25, 1856: 29). Clearly the poor, the black, and the social outcasts suffered the most from this terrible epidemic in Rio de Janeiro.

Perhaps the most frequently asked question in Rio de Janeiro at this time was what explained the sudden onslaught of yellow fever in 1850 and cholera in 1855. In just half a decade, more than 10,000 lives were lost in Rio de Janeiro from just these two diseases. The cholera epidemic tended to undermine the confidence and influence of those who explained the origin of disease in terms of "local causes," such as atmospheric conditions of temperature, rainfall, or humidity; or telluric conditions, such as miasmatic exhalations from swamps or decaying organic matter. Dr. G. Lee was among those who shifted his ground in this argument. He conceded that "poverty with its attendant miseries, bad food, bad clothing, filthy habitations, unwholesome occupations, drunkenness and dissolute habits" could predispose a person to contracting a disease, but in terms of the ultimate cause of the epidemics he wrote (Gt. Brit. Ministry of Health, MH 98/25, 1856: 21–22), "I feel myself forced to look beyond the local condition of the city for the origin of yellow fever and cholera. . . . I cannot help concluding that these epidemics make their appearance independently of filth and uncleanliness." In his view (which differed from that of Dr. A. F. Peixoto, previously mentioned) the city of Rio within the last four years—or since the yellow fever epidemic of 1850—had very much improved in matters of cleanliness and attention to public hygiene. According to Dr. Lee the principal streets of Rio were well paved and some enjoyed gas lighting; residents were "compelled to rid their houses of human ordure and other impurities daily," and the city was abundantly supplied with good water. He felt it was clear the epidemics had flourished at the very time when public hygiene was better than ever, but beyond that he could not go. It is better "to acknowledge our ignorance" than rush to judgment of a question "which as yet it is not permitted to us to solve" (Gt. Brit., Ministry of Health, MH 98/24, 1856: 423–424).

Although the city of Rio de Janeiro suffered the worst outbreak of cholera in the south of Brazil, various other places were also attacked, notably the provinces of Rio de Janeiro and Rio Grande do Sul. Brazil's most populous province in 1855, landlocked Minas Gerais, however, totally escaped the disease, and the province of São Paulo, except for the port of Santos, was only slightly affected. In the province of Rio de Janeiro one of the worst afflicted places was Campos, a major sugar growing area with a large slave population. Out of a population of 10,000 persons 1,200 had died from cholera by mid-November including 107 buried in a single day; most of these were slaves (Gt. Brit., Foreign office, FO13/331, 1855: 269v). José Pereira Rego (1873: 119) thought the mortality among slaves was probably higher than actually reported since frequently slaves were buried on the *fazendas* in private cemeteries without authorities ever being notified. The governor of the province estimated that undocumented mortality among slaves reached one-half of the total which was known, but Dr. Rego thought 20% would be a more accurate percentage. All together he estimated (1873: 119) that 1% of the population of the province died from cholera during the epidemic of 1855–1856, and that most of these were blacks or slaves.

The epidemic reached Rio Grande do Sul, Brazil's most southern province, by November, 1855. Entry was blamed on arrival at Porto Alegre of the steamer *Imperatriz,* which had already introduced cholera into the province of Santa Catarina just to the north. The ship was ordered into quarantine, but some passengers jumped ship and eluded the authorities. The province was already reeling from epidemics of smallpox and scarlet fever, but by January 8, 1856 some 2,000 persons, "mainly colored," had died of cholera. The chief of police of Porto Alegre estimated the deaths in the capital alone at 1,742, or about 10% of the population of the city (Rego, 1873: 22–23).

CONCLUDING REMARKS

The cholera epidemic of 1855–1856 had moved all the way from the Amazon River to the Río de la Plata. Total mortality in Brazil has been variously estimated. The annual report of the head of the Central Board of Public Health, as cited by Dr. Estevão Albuquerque (1856: 37), listed 130,940 deaths, but some provinces, for example, Paraíba, were not included. According to Oscar Oliveira Castro (1945: 275), there were 30,000 deaths in Paraíba from cholera in 1956, or 10% of the population of the province. Statistics from remote rural areas were notoriously inaccurate or simply unavailable. A report prepared by the Faculty of Medicine of Rio de Janeiro (Brazil, 1884: 10) estimated that this epidemic claimed 160,000 lives in Brazil. Afranio Peixoto (1917: 556) has estimated that 200,000 persons died, but his figure includes additional deaths suffered in smaller outbreaks in the northeast in 1861–1863. Still more cholera deaths occurred among Brazilian troops involved in the Paraguayan War from 1865 to 1870 (Rego, 1873: 206–16), and there were minor outbreaks in São Paulo in 1893 and the province of Rio de Janeiro in 1894–1895 (Carvalho, 1897: 194). By the twentieth century, Brazil was free of the disease, but the effects of the country's "blackest page" in her medical history had significant consequences for many Brazilians during the second half of the nineteenth century.

José Pereira Rego, Brazil's most prolific medical historian of the nineteenth century, was chiefly interested in the lessons of the cholera epidemic for public health and medicine. Despite improvements in public hygiene in the larger cities of Brazil, such as the provincial capitals and Rio de Janeiro, Rego said (1873: 222) the cholera epidemic had proven that next to nothing had been done to safeguard the health of the "cities, villages and settlements of the interior, which have no less right to protection of their health and welfare than larger, more influential centers." Not only did the countryfolk generally live in ignorance, misery, and poor health, but except for the sugar and coffee regions (themselves usually located close to the littoral), residents of the interior generally contributed little to public welfare or income. In the cities of Brazil Rego also found much need for reform. He complained that many municipal governments during the epidemic had "maintained themselves in complete inaction, or abandoned their fellow citizens at the moment of crisis." Experience with the epidemic showed, according to Rego, the need for reform of the weak, ineffective municipal structure of the cities, and a need for a meaningful Imperial Department of Public Health. Only then could one effectively fight epidemics such as cholera and yellow fever, as well as attend to other public health problems such as smallpox, tuberculosis, syphilis, and leprosy (Rego, 1873: 222–225). Good suggestions, all of these, but most would not be considered seriously until well into the twentieth century. By then, of course, both administrators and physicians would be better armed to fight epidemics and other diseases owing to advances in microbiology, nutrition, pathology, and other sciences.

Some tentative changes in medical attitudes could already be discerned. Many Brazilian physicians became convinced as a result of the great epidemic that cholera was a *specific* disease which required some *specific* causative agent even though such an agent could not be identified. At the same time, increasingly, they argued that cholera was contagious and could be transmitted from place to place if not necessarily from person to person. Placed on the defensive by the cholera pandemic were followers of traditional Hippocratic principles, as modified in the seventeenth century by Thomas Sydenham, who had argued that "epidemics were primarily caused by an 'effluvium' in the air (miasma), arising from the unfavourable telluric and cosmic influences, and was not contagious" (Arvidsson, 1971: 296). Increasingly after the 1850s, Brazilian physicians took pen in hand to publicize their positions and opinions on such issues. The *Catalog da Exposição Medica Brasileira* compiled by Dr. Carlos Costa lists 72 works on cholera (1884: 282–288) published by Brazilians prior to 1885 plus 221 more (1884: 265–281) on yellow fever.

The loss of thousands of laborers to cholera was a terrible blow to Brazil particularly since importation of new slaves from Africa had legally terminated in 1850, and the recent and devastating yellow fever epidemics had complicated recruiting European replacements. In the first days of the epidemic, Consul Henry Cowper at Pernambuco wrote that,

> In its social view the crisis must be lamentable. The aggregate labor of a nation is its capital, but here [in Brazil] it is not only collectively the capital of the country, but individu-

ally that of every free citizen, for it unhappily almost entirely exists in the slave population, and as in all probability these will be the chief victim of the disease, a state of social suffering and disorganization must arise, hitherto unparalleled [Gt. Brit. Foreign Office, FO 13/333, 1855: 153–153v].

The baleful prediction of Consul Cowper was of course substantially borne out by events. The Minister of Empire, Luiz Pedreira do Coutto Ferraz, in a speech to the Brazilian Chamber of Deputies in September, 1856, reported that rural estates have been "suddenly deprived" of slave labor by the cholera. He referred to "the vacuum occasioned by the last epidemick [sic] which ravaged many of the plantations in the north and south of the empire." Furthermore, he warned that if this loss of workers were not restored promptly through colonization it could "cause the ruin of great establishments of agricultural products in the country" (Gt. Brit. Foreign Office, FO 13/340, 1856: 55v). It is no wonder that some feared efforts would be made to restore the African slave trade. In his Speech from the Throne on October 14, 1856, Pedro II underscored the conclusions of his Minister of Empire. He stated that "sugar and coffee are the only real sources of wealth and industry in Brazil" (Gt. Brit. Foreign Office, FO 13/340, 1856: 124v). Yet these two indispensable economic activities had suffered substantial losses because of the cholera epidemic. The solution, as Pedro II and so many other Brazilians saw it, was to promote the immigration to Brazil of thousands of European colonists.

There can be no doubt that it was the blacks of Brazil who were the people most cruelly decimated by cholera. Many statistical summaries of the epidemic offer breakdowns by "slave" and "free," but the latter category also included many black people. One that offered a "strict" racial breakdown was prepared by *Charge d'Affaires* Jerningham for the city of Rio on November 17, 1855, well before the epidemic had run its course. On a sample of 3,449 persons (excluding 23 whose race was unknown) 67% were described as "coloured" and 33% were said to be "white." The whites (until that point in time) had lost 1,131 persons out of a total population of 142,403, or .0079%, while the blacks had lost 2,368 out of a total estimated population of 124,063 (110,602 slaves; 13,461 "free colored"), or .0190% (Gt. Brit. Foreign

Office, FO13/331, 1855: 266v–268). In other words whites had died at the rate of almost eight per thousand, while blacks had died at a rate of nineteen per thousand. It would seem reasonable to conclude that in the countryside where the proportion of blacks to whites was greater than in the cities, especially the capital city, the blacks proportionally would have suffered still greater losses.

We have seen that the cholera epidemic of 1855–1856, which invaded thirteen provinces of Brazil from north to south and killed upwards of 200,000 persons, was the single worst medical crisis ever to confront Brazil. It had a deleterious effect on agriculture and commerce from the level of production to that of international maritime trade. The medical community, ineffective and divided, moved cautiously to challenge traditional notions without being able to substitute new dictums and certainties; that would be the task of the sons and grandsons of the generation of the 1850s. No class or race escaped the ravages of cholera completely, but black people paid by far the highest tribute to the disease. It seems certain that no less than two-thirds of the victims of cholera in Brazil were black. It was a nineteenth-century, South American holocaust, a new "black death" that ranks as Brazil's greatest and most dramatic demographic disaster.

NOTES

1   Dr. Zarur is the current Director of the Santa Casa da Misericordia of Rio de Janeiro. He has published extensively on the history of that hospital and other subjects. I wish to acknowledge his gracious permission to consult in 1983 the rich historical archive of the Santa Casa.
2   Thomas Ewbank. Life in Brazil; or the Land of the Cocoa and the Palm (New York: Harper & Brothers, 1856). Ewbank's daughter recovered.

REFERENCES

Albuquerque, E. C. (1856) Do cholera-morbus, sua sede, natureza e tratamento. Será contagioso? These apresentada á Faculdade de Medicina do Rio de Janeiro. Rio de Janeiro: Typographia Universal de Laemmert.
Arvidsson, S. O. (1971) "Epidemiological Theories during the Cholera Epidemics of the Nineteenth Century," in Nordisk Medicinhistorisk Årsbok. Stockholm, Sweden: Museum of Medical History: 296–297.
Brazil. Directoria geral de saúde publica (1909) Os serviços de saúde publica no Brasil especialmente na cidade do Rio de Janeiro de 1808 a

1907 (Esboço historico e legislação), Placido Barbosa and Cassio Barbosa de Rezende (comps.) Volume One. Rio de Janeiro: Imprensa Nacional.

—— Faculdade de Medicina do Rio de Janeiro (1884) Parecer sobre a prophylaxia, natureza e tratamento do cholera morbus. Rio de Janeiro: N.P.

—— Ministerio do Imperio (1856) Relatorio apresentado á assemblea geral legislativa na quarta sessão da nona legislatura pelo Ministro do Imperio, Luiz Pedreira do Coutto Ferraz. Rio de Janeiro: Typographia Nacional.

Cabral, O. R. (1942?) Medicina, médicos e charlatães de passado. Florianápolis?: Departamento Estadual de Estatística, Estado de Santa Catarina, Publicação N. 25.

Canavarro, A. D. V. (1857) Relatorio acerca do cholera-morbus reinante nas provincias de Amazonas, Pará, Alagoas e Rio Grande do Norte em 1855 a 1856. Pará [Belém]: Typographia Commercial.

Cárdenas, E. A. (1971) "Datos para la historia del cólera en España." Revista de sanidad e higiéne pública 45 (Marco): 223–245.

Carvalho, [J. E. S.?] Bulhoes (1897) Annuario [1895] de estatística demographo-sanitaria. Rio de Janeiro: Imprensa Nacional.

Castro, O. O. (1945) Medicina na Paraíba. Flagrantes de sua evolução. João Pessoa, Brazil: Imprensa Nacional.

Cooper, D. B. (1975) "Brazil's Long Fight Against Epidemic Disease, 1849–1917, with special emphasis on Yellow Fever," Bulletin of the New York Academy of Medicine 51 (May): 672–696.

Costa, C. (1884) Catalogo da exposição medica Brasileira realizada pela Bibliotheca da Faculdade de Medicina do Rio de Janeiro a 2 de dezembro de 1884. Rio de Janeiro: Typographia Nacional.

Franco, O. (1969) História da Febre-amarella no Brasil. Rio de Janeiro: Impressora Brasileira.

Great Britain. Foreign Office (1855) FO13/330, "On the subject of the epidemic at Pará and alarm circulated at Rio," August 9, 1855: 182–184; FO13/331, "Report on cholera in the capital and provinces," December 7: 262–270; FO13/331, "Report of the cholera," October 15: 198–200; FO13/332, "Health Report on cholera," October 25: 480–484v; FO13/333, "On the Outbreak of cholera in Brazil," July 17: 152–154.

—— (1856) FO13/342, "Yellow Fever at Pernambuco & Paraíba, & Cholera at Pernambuco & Maceio," February 19: 203–203v; FO13/342, "State of the effect of cholera morbus," March 20: 236–238; FO13/340, "Extracts from speech and printed report of the Minister of Empire," September 11: 50–72; FO13/340, "Emperor's speech on closing the chambers," October 14: 121–130v.

Great Britain. General Board of Health (1852) Second Report on Quarantine. Yellow Fever. London: W. Clowes & Sons.

Great Britain. Ministry of Health (1856) MH98/25 "Cholera. Various papers. Dr. G. Lee. Observations on the epidemic cholera as it appeared in Rio de Janeiro during 1855 and 1856," July 13: [29 pp.] Original document lacks pagination.

Hirschhorn, N. and W. B. Greenough III. (1971) "Cholera," Scientific American (August): 15–21.

Kerbey, J. O. (1911) An American Consul in Amazonia. New York: William Edwin Rudge.

Kiple, K. F. (1984) The Caribbean Slave: A Biological History. New York: Cambridge University Press.

——— (1985) "Cholera and Race in the Caribbean," Journal of Latin American Studies," 17: 157–177.

Kiple, K. F. and V. H. King (1981) Another Dimension to the Black Diaspora: Diet, Disease, and Racism. New York: Cambridge University Press.

Lobo, F. B. (1969) O ensino da medicina no Rio de Janeiro. Volume IV. Rio de Janeiro: N.P.

Peixoto, A. (1917) Higiene, 2ª edição. Rio de Janeiro: Francisco Alves.

Peixoto, A. F. (1855) Instrucçoes contra a cholera epidémica. Rio de Janeiro: Dous de Dezembro de Paula Brito.

Pereira, C. de S. (1885) Cholera-morbus. Medidas preventivas. Reminiscencia do cholera em Pernambuco nos annos de 1855 a 1856. Recife: Typographia de Manoel Figueiroa.

Rego, J. P. (1872) Esboço histórico das epidemias que tem grassado no cidade do Rio de Janeiro desde 1830 a 1870. Rio de Janeiro: Typographia Nacional.

——— (1873) Memoria histórica das epidemias da febre amarella e choleramorbo que tem reinado no Brasil. Rio de Janeiro: Typographia Nacional.

Rocha, A. (1952) "A cholera-morbus no Pará e o Dr. Americo Marques de Santa Rosa," Revista Brasileira de historia de medicina 3 (III Trimestre): 1–21.

Rosenberg, C. E. (1962) The Cholera Years. The United States in 1832, 1849, and 1866. Chicago and London: University of Chicago Press.

Seixas, D. R. (1860) De cholera-morbus epidemica de 1855 no provincia da Bahia. Bahia: Typographia de Antonio Olavo da França Guerra.

U.S. Consular Despatches (1855) Bahia, T331. Roll 1: 2.

——— (1856) Bahia, T331, Roll 1: Table 5.

Vianna, A. (1975) As epidemias no Pará 2ª edição. Belém: Universidade Federal do Pará.

Zarur, D. (1985) Uma velha e nova historia da Santa Casa. 2ª edição, revista e ampliada. Rio de Janeiro: Binus Artes Graficas.

Africa, Afro-Americans, and Hypertension: An Hypothesis

THOMAS W. WILSON

HYPERTENSION, OR high blood pressure, affects nearly twice as many black Americans as white Americans, and with disproportionately more devastating effects. Black hypertension victims suffer kidney disease at up to eighteen times the rate of white victims, and have three to four times the fatal stroke rates (USPHS, 1980). Although no clear cause has surfaced for the overwhelming majority of hypertensive cases (Lancet, 1980; Gillum, 1979), there is mounting evidence that hypertension among blacks is related to sodium (salt) metabolism.

It has long been believed that "excess" salt consumption elevates blood pressure (Kark and Oyama, 1980: 1007–1020; Ruskin, 1956: xiii). Today it is known that a high intake of salt can result in excess sodium retention, which can influence blood plasma volume, cardiac output, vascular resistance, and blood pressure (Williams and Hopkins, 1979). Blacks, however, apparently do not consume any more salt than whites (Luft et al., 1977). But, significantly, it would seem that blacks do have a tendency to retain much more sodium "on the same salt load" than whites (Luft et al., 1977). Moreover, the volume of blood plasma in blacks may be higher than in whites (Schacter and Kuller, 1984). Consequently, some researchers argue that many of

Thomas W. Wilson is a graduate student who teaches in the department of history, Bowling Green State University, Bowling Green, OH 43403.

Social Science History 10:4 (Winter 1986). Copyright © 1986 by the Social Science History Association. CCC 0145-5532/86/$1.50.

the hypertensive cases among blacks are the result of an excessively high intake of salt combined with an inherited inability to excrete the mineral efficiently (Grollman, 1978; Williams and Hopkins, 1979). Thus, while the estimated mean salt intake of all Americans today—10 to 15 grams per day (Abrams, 1983: 28)—is significantly above the amount—3 grams—recommended by the U.S. Senate subcommittee on nutrition (1977: 48–51), it would seem to be dangerously high for Afro-Americans. If true, then, this tendency of Afro-Americans to retain salt is very probably the result of the biological adaptation of their African ancestors to a low-salt, tropical ecology that increased the frequency of beneficial salt-retaining genes (Grollman, 1978; Gleiberman, 1973; Denton, 1982: 546–547, 616; Williams and Hopkins, 1979: 190; Hemler, 1967: 123; Luft, et al., 1977: 560). To assist in determining the validity of this thesis, this brief study will present a rough estimate of the amount of salt available to the West Africans and will attempt to demonstrate that the problem of hypertension is not confined to today's Afro-Americans; it has been a problem since they were first forcibly removed from Africa.

In most of yesterday's West Africa the only locally available "salt" was produced from vegetable matter (Mauny, 1961: 334; Sundström, 1965: 124–126; Buschman, 1909: 235, 259). Thus, as is the case with this type of "salt," it would have been very high in potassium and very low in sodium (Sundström, 1965: 125). However, in some parts of the region—along the coast and in the desert—others had access to salt deposits or marine salts that were high in sodium. In fact, salt existed in such great quantities in these "salt-rich" areas that it became an important item of trade with the people of the "salt-poor" interior.

Salt was mined in the Sahara desert (near Ijil and Taoudenni), beginning at least by the tenth or eleventh century (Bovill, 1958; Alexander, 1975; McIntosh and McIntosh, 1981) and around Lake Chad (in the ancient state of Borno) at least since the fifteenth century (Lovejoy, 1978; Gouletquer, 1975). This salt in turn was transported by camel caravans to the interior, where trading networks extended throughout the forest regions of West Africa. However, in some areas desert salt competed with marine salt supplied by coastal producers (Curtin, 1984: 17–18; Sutton, 1981; Lovejoy, 1978; Curtin, 1975: 224–228; Good, 1972: 544–545; Rodney, 1970: 18–20; Sundström, 1965; Buschman, 1909: 221, 257–285). Salt was produced all along the coast, but the most important sites were in Senegambia[1] (Curtin, 1975: 224–228) and near the mouth of the Volta River in present day Ghana (Sutton, 1981). In the most common method of salt extraction, ocean water was directed to artificial or man-made depressions in the earth where it would be evaporated by the sun, leaving a salt residue which would then be available for local consumption and trade with the interior (Curtin, 1975: 225–227; Sundström, 1965: 122; Buschman, 1909: 257–259).

Working from trading data generated at the end of the nineteenth century, Curtin (1975: 227) estimated that 75% of the salt that was transported to the "salt-starved" interior originated in the desert and about 25% came from Senegambia. However, he probably underestimated the impact of other salt traders in the region,[2] especially the Volta River area (Sutton, 1981) and producers in Borno (Lovejoy, 1978). Thus, to get a more accurate idea of the amount of salt produced and traded in West Africa, his estimate will be revised.

In the Sahara the estimate of the salt transported from Ijil and Taoudenni in the late nineteenth century falls between 3000 [metric] tons (Curtin, 1975: 227) and 4000 metric tons per year (Harris, 1908: 239), and the coastal trade from Senegambia exported about 500 to 1000 metric tons of salt per year (Curtin, 1975: 227). Working from records at Krachi between 1914 and 1921, Sutton (1981: 51) estimates the production from the Volta River sites at between 20,000 and 30,000 bags per year. Because these bags weighed 150 pounds (Sutton, 1981: 49), this equals 1,400 to 2,000 metric tons produced from the Volta River area annually in the early decades of the twentieth century. Lovejoy (1978: 639–640) estimated that each year (late nineteenth and early twentieth centuries) the Borno salt industry produced 6000 to 9500 metric tons. Thus, an estimated total of 10,900 to 16,500 metric tons of indigenous salt was potentially transportable to the interior each year in the late nineteenth to early twentieth century.[3]

The 3 grams of salt recommended per individual per diem breaks down into 1095 grams (38 oz. per year) or about 2.5 pounds per individual per year. Put another way, one metric ton of salt (about 2,200 lbs) would take care of the "needs" of approximately 900 individuals per year.[4] Therefore, Curtin's estimated trade from the Saharan and Senegambian regions (around

3500–5000 tons metric per year) would have supported between 3.1 and 4.5 million people per year according to today's recommended intake. Adding the estimates of Sutton (1981) on the Volta river trade (1400–2000 metric tons) for a total of 4,900–7,000 metric tons, the trade would have supported between 4.4 and 6.3 million. Adding in Lovejoy's (1978) computed figures on the Borno salt trade (6000–9000 metric tons) the total West African salt industry (10,900–16,500 metric tons) would have had the potential to supply salt to between 9.8 and 14.8 million people at today's recommended intake.

At the beginning of the twentieth century, Buschman (1909: 237, 262) estimated French West Africa's population alone at about 21 million people, and British West Africa's at about 26 million. This would indicate a combined population of 47 million people.[5] Thus, rough as Buschman's estimate might have been, it is nonetheless obvious that the West African salt trade could hardly have provided enough sodium to the interior during the beginning of the European colonization period to meet today's recommended levels.

Obviously, populations close to the source of sodium salts were better supplied than those far away. Senegambia is a good example. Curtin (1975: 227) wrote that contemporary observers of the late nineteenth century noted that one-half of the Senegambia salt produced locally was consumed locally, suggesting production for local needs at 500 to 1000 metric tons. Thus, at the 3 gram recommended dose per individual per day this salt could have supported between 450,000 and 900,000 individuals per year.

Gambia's population was estimated at 49,000 in 1850; by 1901 it had nearly doubled to 90,000; and by 1931 it had doubled again to 200,000 (Mitchell, 1982: 39). Although early figures for Senegal are not available, we can use the growth percentages of Gambia to estimate Senegal's turn-of-the-century population from the 1931 figure (1,638,000) (Mitchell, 1982: 40). Thus, a reasonable estimate for 1901 would be 800,000 (.50 × 1,600,000). This works out to a population of somewhere around 1,000,000 people for Senegambia in 1900. Thus, the mean intake of locally produced salt could have been almost 3.0 grams per day. Individuals from the Volta River sites and other "salt-rich" areas may have been similarly supplied.

Farther away from the source of coastal and desert producers, however, salt was in terribly short supply for a number of reasons. First of all (and perhaps most importantly), these salt production data are from the late nineteenth and early twentieth centuries, and one assumes that in previous times, with less developed trade routes, West Africans of the interior would have been even more "salt-starved." Second, much of the Lake Chad (Borno) salt (more than half of West Africa's production) was used for livestock and therefore was unavailable for human consumption (Lovejoy, 1978: 635). Third, although trade routes reached into most of West Africa, the price of salt rose rapidly as it was moved from its natural source (Sundström, 1981: 131–133; Good, 1972: 544–545; Buschman, 1909: 262; Curtin, 1975: 228): In 1850 salt was sold in the interior at ten times its coastal price (Alexander, 1975: 83) and at the turn of the century Borno salt which cost $1.00 in Bilma was sold in the Sudan for $30.00 (Harris, 1907: 240). Consequently, in areas of the interior, salt was frequently a luxury only for the well-to-do (Sundström, 1965: 124; Sutton, 1981: 46). Indeed the mineral was so valuable that Europeans noted its use as a currency in the eighteenth and nineteenth centuries (Alagoa, 1970: 326; Sundström, 1965: 127–131) and in their travel accounts of the interior they frequently mentioned an incredible lack of salt (Good, 1972: 544–545; Sundström, 1965: 125). Moreover, as salt was sometimes used to purchase slaves (Good, 1972: 545; Sundström, 1965: 129; Buschman, 1909: 234), the Moorish parable, "The price of a Negro is salt," (Bovill, 1958: 140) seems to have been a tragically accurate statement.

The point of all of this is that through most of West African history today's recommended levels of salt were potentially available only to those inhabitants who were near natural salt sources, while, to quote Sundström (1965: 259), "large parts of Negro Africa were perennially undersupplied with salt." The effect of this differential salt ecology on the biological evolution in West Africans is suggested by the fact that today with salt consumption widespread in Africa, tribes such as the Serer and the Mandinka in today's Senegal and the Gambia have significantly lower blood pressure levels than do the Yoruba of interior Nigeria. A logical conclusion flowing from this might be that those populations with the greatest amount of salt in their diets historically are best able to tolerate the mineral today (Wilson, 1986).

Those who do not tolerate the mineral in large amounts probably do not because of bodily mechanisms developed to conserve the mineral, which is crucial to life itself. The human body attempts to maintain a constant ratio between the levels of sodium and water, and if the supply of salt is diminished, progressively lower concentrations of salt are produced by the sweat glands and urinary sodium excretion falls off dramatically to maintain the constancy. On a completely saltless diet the body steadily loses small amounts of salt via the kidneys and sweat glands, and it attempts to adjust to these new lower levels by accelerating the secretion of water so the blood's salt concentration can be maintained at the vital equilibrium. Obviously, unless the situation is rectified, dehydration and ultimately death will result (Conn and Johnson, 1944).

That persons of African ancestry do seem to have an ability to retain salt has been established by experiments in North America. Although whites and blacks consume about the same amount of salt in these experiments, the perspiration of blacks is substantially lower in sodium than that of whites (Savitt, 1978: 41) and their urine contains less sodium as well (Luft et al., 1977). Certainly, this suggests that some sort of "natural selection" process occurred among Afro-Americans as far as sodium conservation is concerned.

The precise geographical origins of American slaves are not known; however, more than 70% came from West Africa, and as the slave trade moved from the sixteenth through the nineteenth century, progressively more slaves could trace their origins to the "salt-poor" interior of that region (Curtin, 1969: 102, 203, 252).[6]

Thus, this genetic proclivity of many blacks to retain salt was a characteristic arriving with the slaves, who settled into areas of the northern hemisphere that were as rich in salt as Africa was poor (Lefond, 1969: 1–103; Multhalf, 1978: 35–38). Indeed the diet of Americans—in North America and the West Indies—contained an incredible amount of the mineral. Salted pork and fish—staples in the slave diets—were so common on the tables of all Americans that one European traveler noted with surprise that even poor Americans ate salted meat for breakfast (Root and Rochemont, 1976: 122).

Certainly the diet of slaves was incredibly rich in salt. In his book on southern food, Hilliard (1972: 61) says that "salt was the only seasoning the slave saw regularly; other condiments were

unknown." And in Syckle's (1945: 511) history of American dietary habits she stated that "the weekly allowance for each slave
of three pounds of pork, a peck of corn, a pint of salt, and molasses became standard for thousands of plantations." In the Caribbean Africans reportedly received one to two pounds of salted fish
and between a quarter to a half pint of salt per week (Handler and
Lange, 1978: 88; Higman, 1984: 205, 208).

A quarter pint to a full pint of salt per week represents 16 to 64
grams per day, and the one to three pound allotments of salt pork
(Abrams, 1983: 147) or of salted fish (Shewan, 1961: 526)
would contain another 1 to 3 grams per day. Apparently the
slaves' total daily intake of salt was between 17 and 67 grams—6 to
22 times the amount recommended today. Compared with the consumption in West Africa, even in "salt-rich" Senegambia (perhaps
as high as 3 grams per day per individual in the late nineteenth
century), this is obviously far more salt than Africans were accus-
tomed to in their diet.

Moreover, since these slaves had fewer "Caucasian genes" than
today's Afro-American population (Reed, 1969), the proclivity to
retain salt in those Africans from "salt poor" regions must have
been even greater than today. Furthermore, with this level of consumption, what has been termed "salt induced genetic hypertension" (Williams and Hopkins, 1979: 189) must have been epidemic
in slave communities.

Unfortunately for the scholar looking for evidence of hypertension among slaves, the disease is often symptomless, and consequently the only way to detect hypertension with any certainty is
with a blood pressure cuff (sphygmomanometer) which was not
yet invented (Booth, 1977). However, severe cases of high blood
pressure are sometimes associated with edema (excess fluid retention), once called "dropsy," and "dropsy" was a major cause of
death in slaves.[7] Although some cases were identified as beriberi
(Kiple and King, 1981: 122; Kiple, 1985: 96–103) evidence presented here suggests that many others may have been cases of high
blood pressure.

In addition, the phenomenon called "dirt-eating" (pica or geophagy), which was notoriously present among the slaves of both
North America and the Caribbean, may have lessened the symptoms associated with hypertension. Hunter and DeKleine (1984)
pointed out that the "dirt" consumed by black Caribs is high in

Table 1   Deaths from dropsy among blacks

Location	Year	Percentage
Virginia, slave	1850	6.0
Virginia, slave	1853–1860	6.8
Virginia, free black	1853–1869	6.8
Virginia, free black	1850	7.5
Barbados	1796–1801, 1811–1825	8.2
Dominica	1829–1832	10.7
Berbice	1819–1822	11.4
Grenada	1817–1818	11.6
Tobago	1819–1821	12.1
Demerara-Essequldo	1829–1832	13.9
Grenada	1817	16.0

Source: Savitt (1978: 143–144), Higman (1984: 340), Koplan (1983: 313), and Handler and Lange (1978: 99).

calcium (26%), and Langford and Watson (1973) reported that black women today exhibiting lower blood pressure readings consumed more dietary calcium than did those with higher blood pressures. Moreover, other recent studies have revealed a correlation between high calcium intake and lower blood pressure (Parrott-Garcia and McCarron, 1984), while Forbes (1969: 29) has written that high levels of serum calcium accelerate the urinary excretion of sodium.

To conclude, then, the hypothesis that blacks are more prone to sodium retention and "salt induced genetic hypertension" than other Americans has been bolstered by this discussion of the low availability of salt in West African history. Moreover, because salt consumption increased dramatically for West Africans as they became Afro-Americans, an increase in blood pressure levels was a likely occurrence. It is highly likely, therefore, that hypertension must have been a very common disease in slave societies in the New World, just as it is in the black communities of today.

NOTES

1   The countries of Senegal and Gambia comprise the area known in historic times as "Senegambia."
2   Other coastal sites were probably not major exporters. See Alagoa (1970)

and Northrup (1972: 220) for information on salt production in the Niger River Delta region and Rodney (1970: 18–19, 224–26) for a short discussion of salt works in Sierra Leone.

3 The actual amount that reached the interior was probably much less than indicated because the estimates from the Borno area and the Volta River sites are production rather than transport figures.

Europeans, of course, were also importing salt to the continent throughout the nineteenth century (Newbury, 1971). These quantities have not been included, however, since the purpose of this study is to reveal how "salt-starved" most Africans would have been for the eons before the Europeans arrived.

4 This "need" includes the physiological requirement (about 500 to 1000 mg per day) for salt as well as an intangible "desire" or "taste" for the mineral. The 3 grams per diem (1095 grams or 1.095 kg per capita), which I have borrowed for my calculations from the original recommendation of the U.S. Select Committee on Nutrition (1977) is close to minimum acceptable levels for humans' taste for salt.

5 Mitchell's (1982: 37–47) 1931 population estimates for specific countries in West Africa are similar to Buschman's turn-of-the-century figures for the whole region. Thus, because the population was probably about one-half as large in 1900 as in 1931 (Mitchell, 1982: 37–47) Buschman's figures may be overestimated.

6 Most white Americans, on the other hand, trace their origins to Europe, where salt was found in such great amounts (Lefond, 1969: 173–257; Multhalf, 1978: 20–31, 39–61) that genetic adaptation of this sort (sodium conservation) was, no doubt, unnecessary. In fact, opposite "natural selection" (i.e. genetic-controlled sodium excretion) may have occurred because sodium consumption in Europe due to the meat and fish preservation process "exceeded maximum 'safe' levels" (Fogel 1986: 130).

7 Between 1583 and 1821 dropsy was responsible for about 3% of deaths in England and America (Estes, 1973: 407). Among eighteenth-century blacks, however, mortality was consistently higher than 3% (see Table 1).

REFERENCES

Abrams, L. H. Jr. (1983) "Salt and Sodium: An Anthropological 'Cross-Cultural Perspective in Health and Disease." Journal of Applied Nutrition 35: 127–158. •

Alagoa, E. J. (1970) "Long-Distance Trade and States in the Niger Delta." Journal of African History 11: 319–329.

Alexander, J. A. (1975) "The Salt Industries of Africa: Their Significance for European Prehistory," in K. W. deBrisay and K. A. Evans (eds.) Salt: The Study of an Ancient Industry. Colchester: 81–83.

Booth, J. (1977) "A Short History of Blood Pressure Measurement." Proceedings of the Royal Society of Medicine 70: 793–799.

Bovill, E. W. (1958) The Golden Trade of the Moors. London: Oxford University Press.

Buschman, J. O. F. Von (1909) Das Salz: Dessen Vorkommen Und Verwertung in Sämtlichen Staaten Der Erde. Leipzig: Verlag von Wilhelm Englemann.

Conn, J. and M. W. Johnson (1944) "The Function of Sweat Glands in the Economy of NaCl Under Conditions of Hard Work in a Tropical Climate." American Society for Clinical Investigation 23: 933.

Curtin, P. D. (1969) The Atlantic Slave Trade: A Census. Madison, Wisconsin: University of Wisconsin Press. •

——— (1975) Economic Change in Precolonial Africa: Senegambia in the Era of the Slave Trade. Madison, Wisconsin: University of Wisconsin Press.

——— (1984) Cross-Cultural Trade in World History. Cambridge, England: Cambridge University Press.

Denton, D. (1982) The Hunger for Salt: An Anthropological, Physiological, and Medical Analysis. Berlin: Springer-Verlag. •

Estes, J. W. (1983) "An Account of the Fox Glove in America." Bulletin of the History of Medicine 47: 394–407.

Fogel, R. W. (1986) Nutrition and the Decline in Mortality Since 1700: Some Additional Preliminary Findings. Cambridge, Massachusetts: National Bureau of Economic Research, Working Paper No. 1802.

Forbes, G. B. (1969) "Sodium," in C. L. Comar and F. Bronner (eds.) Mineral Metabolism: An Advanced Treatise. Vol. IIIB. New York: Academic Press: 2–72.

Gillum, R. F. (1979) "Pathophysiology of Hypertension in Blacks and Whites: A Review of the Basis of Racial Blood Pressure Differences." Hypertension 1: 468–75. •

Gleiberman, L. (1973) "Blood Pressure and Dietary Salt in Human Populations." Ecology of Food and Nutrition 2: 143–156. •

Good, C. M. (1972) "Salt, Trade, and Disease: Aspects of Development in Africa's Northern Great Lakes Region." The International Journal of African Studies 4: 543–586. •

Gouletquer, P. L. (1975) "Niger, Country of Salt," in K. W. deBrisay and K. A. Evans (eds.) Salt: The Study of an Ancient Industry. Colchester: 47–51. •

Grollman, A. (1978) "A Conjecture About the Prevalence of Essential Hypertension and Its High Incidence in the Black." Texas Reports on Biology and Medicine 36: 25–32. •

Handler, J. S. and F. W. Lange (1978) Plantation Slavery in Barbados: An Archeological and Historical Investigation. Cambridge, Massachusetts: Harvard University Press.

Harris, G. D. (1908) "Rock Salt, Its Origin, Geological Occurrences and Economic Importance in the State of Louisiana, Together with Brief Notes and References to All Known Salt Deposits and Industries of the World." Bulletin of the Louisiana Geological Survey 7: 1–259.

Hemler, O. M. (1967) "Hormonal and Biochemical Factors Controlling

Afro-Americans and Hypertension 267

Blood Pressure," in Les Concepts de Claude Bernard sur le milieu interieur. Paris: Libraries de l'Academe de Medicine: 115–128.

Higman, B. A. (1984) Slave Populations of the British Caribbean, 1807–1834. Baltimore: Johns Hopkins Press.

Hilliard, S. B. (1972) Hog Meat and Hoecake: Food Supply in the Old South, 1840–1860. Carbondale, Illinois: Southern Illinois University Press.

Hunter, J. M. and R. DeKleine (1984) "Geophagy in Central America." The Geographical Review 74: 158–169.

Kark, R. M. and J. H. Oyama (1980) "Nutrition, Hypertension, and Kidney Disease," in R. S. Goodhart and M. E. Shils (eds.) Modern Nutrition in Health and Disease. 6th ed. Philadelphia: Lea and Febiger: 998–1043.

Kiple, K. F. (1985) The Caribbean Slave: A Biological History. Cambridge, England: Cambridge University Press.

——— and V. H. King (1981) Another Dimension to the Black Diaspora: Diet, Disease, Racism. Cambridge, England: Cambridge University Press.

Koplan, J. P. (1983) "Slave Mortality in Nineteenth-Century Grenada." Social Science History 7: 311–320.

Lancet (1980) "Hypertension in Blacks and Whites." ii: 73–74.

Langford, H. G. and R. L. Watson (1973) "Electrolyte, Environment, and Blood Pressure." Clinical Science and Molecular Medicine 45: 111s–113s.

Lefond, S. J. (1969) Handbook of World Salt Resources. New York: Plenum Press.

Lovejoy, P. E. (1978) "The Borno Salt Industry." The International Journal of African Historical Studies 11: 629–668.

Luft, F. C., C. E. Grim, J. T. Higgens Jr. and M. H. Weinberger (1977) "Differences in Response to Sodium Administration in Normotensive White and Black Subjects." Journal of Laboratory and Clinical Medicine 90: 555–559.

McIntosh, S. K. and R. J. McIntosh (1981) "West African PreHistory." American Scientist 69: 602–613.

Mauny, R. (1961) Tableau géographique de L'Ouest African au Moyen Age: d'apres les sources écrites, la tradition et l'archéologie. Amsterdam: Swets and Zeitlinger, 1961.

Mitchell, B. R. (1982) International Historical Statistics: Africa and Asia. New York: New York University Press.

Multhalf, R. T. (1978) Neptune's Gift: A History of Common Salt. Baltimore: Johns Hopkins University Press.

Newbury, C. W. (1971) "Prices and Profitability in Early Nineteenth Century West African Trade," in C. Meillassoux (ed.) The Development of Indigenous Trade and Markets in West Africa. London: Oxford University Press: 91–106.

Northrup, D. (1972) "The Growth of Trade Among the Igbo Before 1800." Journal of African History 13: 217–236.

Parrott-Garcia, M. and D. A. McCarron (1984) "Calcium and Hypertension." Nutrition Review 42: 205–213.

Reed, T. E. (1969) "Caucasian Genes in American Negroes." Science 165: 762–767.

Rodney, W. (1970) A History of the Upper Guinea Coast, 1545–1800. Oxford: Clarendon Press.

Root, W. and R. de Rochemont (1976) Eating in America: A History. New York: William Morrow.

Ruskin, A. [ed.] (1956) Classics in Arterial Hypertension. Springfield, Illinois: Thomas.

Savitt, T. (1978) Medicine and Slavery: The Diseases and Health Care of Blacks. Urbana, Illinois: University of Illinois Press.

Schacter, J. and L. H. Kuller (1984) "Blood Volume Expansion Among Blacks: An Hypothesis." Medical Hypotheses 14: 1–19.

Shewan, J. M. (1961) "The Microbiology of Seawater," in G. Borgstrom (ed.) Fish as Food, New York: Academic Press: 487–560.

Sundström, L. (1965) The Trade of Guinea. Upsalla.

Sutton, I. B. (1981) "The Volta River Trade: The Survival of an Indigenous Industry." Journal of African History 22: 43–61.

Syckle, C. Van (1945) "Some Pictures of Food Consumption in the United States: Part I. 1630 to 1860." Journal of the American Dietetic Association 21: 508–512.

U.S. Select Committee on Nutrition and Human Needs, U.S. Senate (1977) Dietary Goals for the United States. Washington, D.C.: Government Printing Office.

U.S. Department of Health and Human Services, Public Health Service [cited as USPHS] (1980) Final Report of the National Black Health Providers Task Force on High Blood Pressure Education and Control. Bethesda, Maryland: National Institutes of Health; National Heart, Lung, and Blood Institute. NIH Publication No. 80–1474.

Williams, R. R. and P. N. Hopkins (1979) "Salt, Hypertension, and Genetic-Environmental Interactions." Progress in Clinical Biology 32: 183–194.

Wilson, T. W. (1986) "History of Salt Supplies in West Africa and Blood Pressures Today." Lancet i: 784–786.

Future Studies of the Biological
Past of the Black

KENNETH F. KIPLE

THE FIRST ARTICLE in this volume sketched out what has been done in the recent past on various biological aspects of the history of the black in Africa and in the Americas. The articles that followed revealed in splendid fashion the quality and sophistication of studies under way today. In concluding this volume I could not resist the temptation to discuss briefly what sorts of themes and issues I hope will be pursued tomorrow.

Central to future bio-studies of the black will be the growing realization that after stripping away those husks of scholarly posturing and platitudes that in the past have pronounced Afro-Americans and Africans a "biological elite," the kernel of truth remaining is that they were indeed such an elite, but not necessarily for the reasons offered. Those reasons generally have focused on the shock of capture, the long and deadly march to the sea, the squalor of the barracoons on the coast, the horrors of the middle passage, and the numbing, debilitating "seasoning" procedures on the plantations of the Americas. While there is no question that the whole of this represents a selection process of sorts, it

Kenneth F. Kiple is professor in the department of history at Bowling Green State University, Bowling Green, OH 43403.

The author wishes to express his gratitude to the American Council of Learned Societies for a grant-in-aid in 1985 and to the Faculty Research Committee of Bowling Green State University for the Major Research Grant awarded for the years 1985 and 1986 that made research for this and other projects possible.

was much too random to create an instant elite, as a bomb dropped on a city does not make an elite of the survivors.

What has been missed to this point is that those Africans who were put into the slave trade (just as those Africans who put them there) were already an elite, and probably much better able to withstand the ensuing stresses of nutritional deprivation and exposure to new epidemiological conditions than were any other people in the world at that time. For what had actually made them a biological elite was eons of a rigorous selection process in the hostile disease environment of West Africa, which offered little in the way of what today would be regarded as adequate nutritional fortification to withstand that environment.

This is not to say that we should ignore the slave trade "selection" process. On the contrary, each stage of that process requires very careful study from a biological perspective in order to discover, among other things, precisely what kinds of special genetic and biochemical survival equipment were selected for by African ecological circumstances with all of their complex climatic, nutritional, and parasitic variables. For astounding as it seems, after undergoing all of the debilitating trials of the slave trade "selection" process, the newly arrived African was nonetheless, as Richard Dunn (1984) has recently discovered, sturdier and longer-lived than a Creole-born black who had experienced none of the slave trade gauntlets. Moreover, mulattoes were even more fragile than island-born blacks, despite the lighter tasks they were generally assigned and a higher status that presumably also meant preferred treatment in diet.

At first glance the problem might be viewed as one of a decrease in immunities developed in Africa particularly in light of evidence that American-born blacks who returned to Africa were harshly treated by the disease environment there (Shick, 1971). Yet against this is the biological fact that genetically selected blood anomalies for malarial protection do not simply disappear in a generation or two, and blacks apparently never before exposed to yellow fever have proved resistant to it. On the other hand, the black returnees to Africa did not for the most part return to their ancestral regions, and we are beginning to discover that the place of origin in Africa may have had much to do with slave durability. Those who embarked from the Gold Coast, for example, were generally believed to be among the healthiest and sturdiest of the West Africans, and those from the Bight of Biafra the most fragile, save for the Bantu of Angola who were reportedly the weakest of all. To be sure, planter preferences and allegations of one African group's endowments and another's physical shortcomings were often capricious and fanciful. But we also know that many African groups lived in relative isolation for long centuries at a time, and certainly the kinds of foods consumed and immunities developed during these periods of isolation would have created differing human products.

Clearly, we need more of the kind of morbidity and mortality data with which Curtin in his article has provided us for Africans on both sides of the Atlantic. But just as clearly, we also need data of this sort within Africa for the various regions of that continent that supplied America's slaves. In addition, we need to know what the peoples of these regions ate, and what they did not eat, and finally we need to concentrate on other disease immunities that blacks acquired in Africa that, while not useful in the New World, would have been sorely missed by those American blacks returning to Africa. Resistance to sleeping sickness (which was never transferred to the Americas) comes to mind as an immediate example, but there are surely many more such concrete examples as well as possible candidates.

One clue to the relative healthiness of the diet of various African groups may lie in the height data that we already have. Does height, for example, seem to vary depending on the port of slave embarkation? Certainly, too, while on the subject of heights, we need many more comparative studies of heights within the hemisphere so we may know more about the nutritional and laboring conditions of various slave societies. We hope, in this latter connection, some enterprising scholar will turn up height data for the mostly Bantu slaves of Brazil so that we can compare the Bantu with West Africans in one case, and Brazilian slaves with slaves elsewhere in the hemisphere in another.

Without question it is going to require comparative studies of some sophistication and magnitude to resolve many questions associated with the biological history of the black in both Africa and the Americas. Richard Dunn's ongoing effort[1] comparing the demographic experience of slaves in Virginia and Jamaica represents the sort of ideal that we hope will be repeated by other scholars for other regions. Of enormous use would be a work that treats not only the heights but the whole of the biological experience of Brazilian blacks and compares this with that of slaves to the north. Such a study would throw light on both hemispheric slavery and the African biological background.

Much more needs to be done on the problem of slave infant and child mortality within a comparative framework. The study by Steckel has shown us that these mortality rates were probably much higher for North America than was previously believed by most. If this is true, then what must the rates have been in other slave societies where the slaves were considerably less well off in a material sense, and what ideas must be revised in view of Steckel's findings?

The kinds of diseases that killed the infants and children, as well as the nutritional status of their mothers, promises to be another fruitful area for comparisons, with Brazil presenting an outstanding opportunity for a very illuminating study within that country alone. This is because diets varied considerably in Brazil, with slaves of the northeast consuming a diet that appears to have been very West African in content, while slaves in the coffee regions to the south consumed foods in many ways quite similar to those on the tables of slaves in the United States. What differences in fertility as well as infant and child mortality patterns might such an effort yield?

An extremely interesting and important phenomenon that requires explanation has to do with another question of relative durability—that of the durability of the African female when contrasted with the male. Indeed, this greater durability begins in the womb with the male fetus much more likely than the female to be aborted and continues throughout a lifetime. Surely this phenomenon, which meant a population with females in a considerable majority, must have had something to do with the organization of the family in Africa, as well as with attitudes toward male as opposed to female offspring, and perhaps even with the appointment of women as the agriculturalists. Surely, too, it must have had many, as yet unexamined, influences on the mechanism of supply and demand in the slave trade.

We know that this greater male fragility had tremendous demographic repercussions in the Caribbean where, with the end of a slave trade that had reversed the African situation by rendering the population top-heavy with males, the sex ratios began to plunge in startling fashion until the women again, as in Africa, significantly outnumbered the males.

The cessation of the slave trade with the United States, however, produced no such abrupt demographic reversal, and while it is true that North American black males have never been as durable as females, the situation has always been comparatively much worse in the West Indies. One vivid documented difference between the slave populations of the two regions is the difference in diet, which brings up the question of whether or not it is nutritional stress that the black female is better able to withstand from the womb forward. And if so, what can we make of this in light of evidence that Africans in their homeland have generally accorded the male priority in access to the best portions in the cooking pot?

It goes without saying that slave fertility questions will require comparative airing. It has generally been held that Caribbean slave fertility was quite low. Perhaps it was, but the very high infant and child mortality levels reported for the slaves of the region suggest caution lest the equation wind up revealing more infant and child deaths than births. Poor nutrition has also come under suspicion as an impediment to slave fertility in the West Indies, but again caution seems wise, for as we are all too painfully aware, today the world's highest fertility rates are managed by the world's poorest-nourished peoples.

Moving to the period after slavery, we know that for reasons yet to be explained blacks throughout the hemisphere found themselves the target of near-epidemic tuberculosis and syphilis. Was the plantation such an effective quarantining device? Or was the upsurge in these diseases the result of epidemiological and immunological factors?

Interestingly and happily, although black people were reeling from these and other illnesses during the latter part of the nineteenth century and early years of this century, they too began to experience a mortality decline much like that which Northern Europeans and North American whites had already experienced, and (as Curtin has shown in this volume) one that blacks in the British Army had also witnessed. We would hope that mortality decline studies in the future would concentrate on this phenomenon among American blacks as well as whites.

Until very recently research stopped short at the border between the physical and the social sciences with the result that the lines of communication between such disciplines as anthropology, biochemistry, genetics, nutrition, geography, medicine, and history seldom traversed that border. It has been bio-historians of the black who, more than anyone else, have obliterated that border and forced open the communication lines. With that accomplished, the heavy agenda of work yet to be done in the field represents a challenge in interdisciplinary and cross-disciplinary research totally without precedent in the annals of historical inquiry. What a marvelously exciting time to be a historian, and what a marvelously exciting investigation to be a part of.

NOTES

1   Richard Dunn recently gave a preliminary report (1984) on his project of comparing the experience of some two thousand slaves in Virginia and Jamaica for which he has laboriously unearthed records. The publication of his findings promises to be a very momentous event indeed.

REFERENCES

Dunn, R. S. (1984) "History from Below: Reconstructing the Careers of Two Thousand Slaves from Jamaica and Virginia, 1760–1860," a paper presented to the Southern Historical Association Annual Meeting, Louisville.
Shick, T. W. (1971) "A Quantitative Analysis of Liberian Colonization from 1820 to 1843 with Special Reference to Mortality." Journal of African History 12: 45–59.

Index

Adamo, S., 21
Affleck, T., 196, 217–218
Africa: British perceptions of, 9;
disease environment, 2–3, 9, 10,
11, 19, 20, 22, 35–93 passim,
111–138 passim, 270–271; disease
and the slave trade, 2–3, 9–11,
35–93 passim; and European
colonization, 9–10, 22; famine
in, 2–3, 19–20, 35–93 passim;
and salt, 5–6, 258–260; smallpox
in, 35–95 passim
Africans: genetics, 19, 23, 115,
257–265 passim, 270–274;
hardiness, 7, 8, 269–274; heights,
23 (*see also* Slaves: Caribbean;
general and comparative; North
American); hypertension (*see*
Hypertension); nutritional status,
22–23. *See also* West India
Regiments
Alden, D., 2, 22
Allison, A. C., 9
Anemia: iron deficiency, 14; sickle
cell, 15
Angel, J., 13, 14
Angola, 20, 35–93 passim
Antigua, 18
Araujo, C. de S., 66
Ashburn, P. M., 35

Ashcroft, M. T., 18
Aufderheide, A., 3

Barbados, 14, 16, 18, 140–161
passim
Beckwith, Martha, 188
Bell, J. U., 148
Bennett, H., 16
Beriberi, 18, 263
Betendorf, J. F., 48, 49, 50
Black Caribs, 19
Black Saturnalia in Jamaica: and
Actor-Boy, 170–171; and African
rituals, 172–173, 174, 179, 180;
comparative models and mechanisms, 175–187 passim; diet
during, 4, 169, 176; drinking
during, 170; festivities during,
169–171, 187–188; and John
Canoe (Junkunno), 170, 187,
188; modern day, 168–169, 188;
in other West Indian islands, 171;
and planter attitudes toward, 175;
as relief induced agonism, 189–
190; seasonality, 4, 169, 174, 176;
and slave nutrition, 4, 173–174,
175, 188; and slave uprisings, 4,
172. *See also* Jamaica
Black troops, 11, 19. *See also* West
India Regiments